Measuring Gender Equality

OTHER TITLES IN THE ADePT SERIES

ADePT

Key Labor Market Indicators—Analysis with Household Survey Data: Streamlined Analysis with ADePT Software (2016) by Ina Pietschmann, Steven Kapsos, Evangelia Bourmpoula, Zurab Sajaia, and Michael Lokshin

Simulating Distributional Impacts of Macro-dynamics—Theory and Practical Applications: Streamlined Analysis with ADePT Software (2014) by Sergio Olivieri, Sergiy Radyakin, Stainslav Kolenikov, Michael Lokshin, Ambar Narayan, and Carolina Sánchez-Páramo

Analyzing Food Security Using Household Survey Data: Streamlined Analysis with ADePT Software (2014) by Ana Moltedo, Nathalie Troubat, Michael Lokshin, and Zurab Sajaia

A Unified Approach to Measuring Poverty and Inequality—Theory and Practice: Streamlined Analysis with ADePT Software (2013) by James Foster, Suman Seth, Michael Lokshin, and Zurab Sajaia

Health Equity and Financial Protection: Streamlined Analysis with ADePT Software (2011) by Adam Wagstaff, Marcel Bilger, Zurab Sajaia, and Michael Lokshin

Assessing Sector Performance and Inequality in Education: Streamlined Analysis with ADePT Software (2011) by Emilio Porta, Gustavo Arcia, Kevin Macdonald, Sergiy Radyakin, and Michael Lokshin

For more information about Streamlined Analysis with ADePT software and publications, visit www.worldbankgroup.org/adept.

STREAMLINED ANALYSIS WITH ADePT SOFTWARE

Measuring Gender Equality

Josefina Posadas
Pierella Paci
Zurab Sajaia
Michael Lokshin

WORLD BANK GROUP

Contents

Contents

Contents

Boxes

Figures

Map

Tables

Contents

Foreword

Gaps between men and women permeate everyday life—and yet they are often difficult to pin down and quantify. Every year, countries around the world observe equal pay day, a symbolic day on which female earnings "catch up" with male earnings from the past year. However, calculating the gender gap in earnings can seem almost as daunting as efforts to close it, given a myriad of competing measures and computation methods.

This book seeks to help its readers navigate the sometimes confusing world of measuring and analyzing gender equality on the basis of household survey data. It is designed as a manual of ADePT Gender, a free software tool developed by the World Bank's Development Data Group and Gender Cross-Cutting Solution Area, which automates and simplifies the production of standardized tables and graphs related to the analysis of gaps between males and females. In addition, this book provides the core economic context needed to interpret—and sometimes challenge—measures of gender equality. Its primary audience is data analysts, who wish to perform hands-on analysis of household survey data to obtain a better understanding of the existing gender gaps within or across countries. However, other data users in government, media, or academia may also find it a useful read.

The ADePT Gender software is divided into two core modules. The first module produces a country gender diagnostic for the three core dimensions of gender equality highlighted in the 2012 *World Development Report*: human capital (or endowments), economic opportunities, and voice and agency. The second module zooms in on gender gaps in labor market outcomes, using more advanced decomposition techniques from the labor economics literature.

We hope this book will stimulate the analysis of country gender gaps and contribute to informed decision and policy making.

Caren Grown
Senior Director, Gender
The World Bank Group

Haishan Fu
Director, Development Data Group
The World Bank Group

Preface

Gender equality matters for both development outcomes and policy making. It is a core development objective in its own right but it is also smart economics as it enhances average productivity and improves prospects for the next generation and for the quality of societal policies and institutions.

However, differences between men and women are observed in several dimensions of social and economic life, and throughout the life cycle. The past 50 years have seen marked improvement in the lives of girls and women around the world. Across the globe, more girls and women are educated than ever before, more girls are in school than boys, and women make up nearly half of the global labor force. In some areas, however, progress toward reducing gender gaps has been more limited, especially among disadvantaged groups such as the poor, women and girls living in remote areas, or those belonging to minority groups.

As awareness of the importance of gender equality grows among researchers, development practitioners, and policy makers, so does the demand to better understand the patterns of progress and the nature and sources of persistent gaps. This information is fundamental to ensure that the limited resources are channeled to areas where progress has been harder to achieve and to priority areas of interventions. The increased availability of disaggregated statistics for men and women on many key development indicators is at the same time a reflection of, and fuel for, the growing interest in evidence-based, gender-sensitive policy making. However, access to data in itself is not enough to ensure better understanding of the magnitude, dynamics, and drivers of gender inequality, especially in the context of limited capacity, and even more limited resources. There is also a clear need for standard approaches, common methodologies, and analytical tools that facilitate the use of these data for systematic and comprehensive diagnostic work.

ADePT Gender is just such a tool. Building on the framework proposed by the *World Development Report (WDR) 2012: Gender Equality and Development*, ADePT Gender is designed to guide the broad and diverse gender and development community through the complexity of the diagnostics of gender inequality and its dynamics. The intuitive software consists of two parts. The first part uses simple statistics and tabulations to profile the extent and dynamics of gender inequalities across three dimensions— namely endowments, economic opportunities, and agency. The second part focuses on gender gaps in economic opportunities by analyzing gender disadvantages in the labor market and, in particular, wage inequality. Its focus is on being user-friendly and comprehensive, although not exhaustive.

This manual provides a guide to working with ADePT Gender with a particular emphasis on helping the wide community of users to interpret the large volume of statistical information generated by the software. Contrary to other ADePT modules, it does not detail the mechanisms behind gender differences in outcomes, as these are extensively covered in the *WDR 2012* and in its companion reports. Table 1.1 lists the main references available to the ADePT Gender users on the drivers of gender inequality and offers a short description of how they relate to the *WDR* framework.

ADePT Gender and this manual were made possible by the efforts of the many who have provided invaluable technical support and encouragement. This manual and the ADePT Gender module build on an earlier, more limited version of the software developed by Gisela García, Gayatri Koolwal, and Nistha Sinha. Andrea Atencio, Jenifer Golan, Francisco Haimovich, Giulia Mancini, Julieth Santamaria, and Chimedkham Zorigtbaatar went the extra mile in assisting us with data management and analysis of various countries and surveys in preparation for this version of the software and the manual. Thanks to their tenacious efforts, we have a tool that is flexible and user friendly, while covering a very wide range of indicators and dimensions. Particular thanks goes to our peer reviewers Georgia De Paoli, Elena Ferreras Carreras, and Gayatri Koolwal as well as to Isis Gaddis,

Eliana Rubiano Matulevich, and Elena Bardasi, who provided extensive comments at different stages during the development of the software and the preparation of this manual. The insightful feedback we received has raised the quality of both products and their interest and accessibility to a wider audience. Finally, we are grateful for the support we have received over the years from the management of the Gender and Development unit and, in particular, Mayra Buvinic, who supported the idea in its initial stages and Caren Grown, who oversaw the completion of the tool and the manual.

In finalizing ADePT Gender and this manual, we benefitted from the feedback on earlier versions received during training events in Armenia, the Lao People's Democratic Republic, and Timor-Leste, and from its use in selected poverty assessments. We thank Helle Buchave and Nistha Sinha for giving us these opportunities. Various presentations and training sessions during PREM Week 2012 and 2013 at the World Bank headquarters in Washington, DC, provided additional useful feedback. The invaluable support of the World Bank ADePT team in the technical aspects of the software development is acknowledged with thanks.

Abbreviations

ADePT   Automated DEC Poverty Tables
AIDS   acquired immune deficiency syndrome
BCG   Bacillus Calmette–Guérin (vaccination against tuberculosis)
CMC   century-month code
CPR   contraceptive prevalence rate
DHS   Demographic and Health Survey
DPT   diphtheria, pertussis, and tetanus (vaccination)
GER   gross enrollment rate
HIV   human immunodeficiency virus
ICLS   International Conference of Labour Statisticians
IHSN   International Household Survey Network
ILO   International Labour Organization
ISCED   International Standard Classification of Education
ISCO   International Standard Classification of Occupations
ISIC   International Standard Industrial Classification
LF   labor force
MMR   measles, mumps, and rubella (vaccination)
NER   net enrollment rate
OECD   Organisation for Economic Co-operation and Development
PISA   Programme for International Student Assessment

SPSS	Statistical Package for the Social Sciences (software package for statistical analysis)
Stata	data analysis and statistical software
STEP	Skills Toward Employment and Productivity
TIMSS	Trends in International Mathematics and Science Study
UN	United Nations
UNESCO	United Nations Educational, Scientific, and Cultural Organization
WDR	*World Development Report*
WHO	World Health Organization

PART I

Introducing ADePT
Gender Software

Part I of this book introduces the reader to ADePT software and the ADePT Gender module. ADePT software allows users to analyze microdata from sources such as household surveys to generate print-ready, standardized tables and charts. It can also be used to simulate the effect of economic shocks, farm subsidies, cash transfers, and other policy instruments on poverty, inequality, and labor. In this case, ADePT can be used to analyze and create standardized tables and charts to construct gender indicators. ADePT software can be customized to the user's needs. In the ADePT Gender module, the user can disaggregate data across men and women, as well as male versus female heads of household. The software can also disaggregate data across different geographic regions and socioeconomic and demographic backgrounds.

The software automates the analysis, helps minimize human errors, and encourages development of new economic analysis methods. ADePT supports datasets in Stata, the Statistical Package for the Social Sciences (SPSS), and tab-delimited text formats. ADePT incorporates Numerics by Stata (installed with ADePT) as its computational engine. For each run, ADePT produces one output file—containing the user's selection of tables and graphs, an optional original data summary, and errors and notifications—in

Microsoft Excel format. Optionally, tables of standard errors and frequencies can be added to a report. To learn more about the uses and requirements of ADePT software, the user may consult the *ADePT User Guide*.[1]

Chapter 1 introduces the software and the logic of the product. ADePT Gender uses the framework of the *World Development Report 2012: Gender Equality and Development* (World Bank 2012b) to organize the presentation of tables and graphs. Applying this framework is also recommended when writing the analysis of the results. This framework provides comprehensive coverage of all the dimensions of gender inequalities: endowments, economic opportunities, and agency. The results can then help identify areas for further analysis and priority actions. For instance, the systematic review of gaps helps answer such questions as:

- Should a country focus on addressing missing women or gender gaps in education?
- Is domestic violence a problem in the country?
- Are gender gaps in employment and wages important?
- How much of the gender gap can result from occupational segregation?

The next two chapters are intended to familiarize the user with ADePT Gender software. Chapter 2 helps the user understand how to install the program, upload the data, and fill in the variable fields. Chapter 3 helps the user prepare the data and introduces several variable definitions to ensure that the user has no misunderstanding in how the program interprets the data. All these definitions are based in standard practices and conventions adopted by international organizations such as the United Nations and the International Labour Organization. This step is critical for the validity of the results. Even when ADePT Gender software carries out some internal checks to establish the validity of the data, it is the user's responsibility to upload data that respond to the definitions of the variables requested by ADePT Gender and are suitable for interpreting the results correctly.

Note

1. Michael Lokshin, Sergiy Radyakin, Zurab Sajaia, and William Creitz. 2013. *ADePT User Guide*. Version 5 (Washington, DC: World Bank).

Chapter 1

Applying a Household-Centered Framework to Gender Analysis

Gender equality matters for its intrinsic and instrumental value. Gender equality matters intrinsically because the ability to live a life of one's choosing is a basic human right and should be available to anyone, regardless of one's sex or gender. Gender equality also matters because it contributes to economic efficiency and the achievement of other desirable development outcomes.

Gender equality can contribute to economic development in three ways. First, it can remove barriers that prevent women from accessing education, economic opportunities, and productive inputs that generate economic gains. Second, women's gains promote other desired development outcomes, such as increased economic productivity, as well as child nutrition, health, and education, which improve the welfare of future generations. Third, greater equality of female participation in community and political organizations leads to more inclusive and representative institutions, which contributes to development.

These messages have been discussed extensively among researchers, development practitioners, and policy makers. Recently, the *World Development Report (WDR) 2012: Gender Equality and Development* (World Bank 2012b) has resumed the conversation and contributed to establishing guidelines for how to analyze and measure gender equality in a comprehensive manner. This report not only exhaustively examined all types of outcomes related to gender equality but also advanced in bringing together findings and methodologies of analyses from economics and other social fields of studies, which are usually disconnected in this complex area of policy work. More important, this report also presented a set of policy actions for tackling gender inequalities.

ADePT Gender is designed to help this broad community working on gender equality and development to measure gender equality using the framework proposed in this influential report. With that purpose, this manual is organized in three parts: part I focuses on applying the framework introduced in the *WDR 2012: Gender Equality and Development* using simple statistics and tabulations across three dimensions, namely, endowments, economic opportunities, and agency; part II covers the output that produces a country gender diagnostic; and part III goes deeper in analyzing labor-market inequalities, particularly wage inequality.

This manual and ADePT Gender software refer to gender equality as the equality of outcomes between men and women, even if gender does not refer to men and women. Gender denotes the social, behavioral, and cultural attributes, expectations, and norms associated with being a woman or a man. Gender equality refers to how these aspects determine how women and men relate to each other and to the resulting differences in power between them. This approach is also consistent with that proposed by the *WDR* and is also applied by ADePT Gender.[1]

The rest of this chapter discusses how ADePT Gender uses the *WDR*'s framework. It is not the objective of this chapter to summarize the messages of the *WDR*. Given the wide impact of the product, there are multiple products used for its dissemination that the user can consult and that accommodate different users' needs, from quick overviews to extensive discussions.[2] The two following chapters provide information for working with the software. Chapter 2 introduces the ADePT software and the gender module, whereas chapter 3 describes the data sources that are suited for use in ADePT Gender. It also defines the concepts needed for proper data management that must be undertaken before using ADePT Gender.

Framework

Differences between men and women are observed in several dimensions of social and economic life and throughout the life cycle. The examples are numerous: in many countries, boys often have better health outcomes than girls and are more likely to achieve higher levels of education than girls. Such inequality persists later on in life: young women are more likely than young men to be unemployed, and a higher proportion of women compared with men do not participate in the labor force. These differences between men and women and between boys and girls are the result of complex interactions between households, markets, and formal and informal institutions. Sometimes, the inequalities may be detrimental to men: in various Caribbean countries, poor boys have less schooling than girls, as they drop out to work in agriculture; or in many eastern European countries, adult men have a low life expectancy associated with various life hazards and health problems.

One way to depict the complex interactions between households, markets, and institutions and their effects on equality of gender outcomes is to examine how households function. Families decide how much to spend on boys' and girls' education and health, how to allocate tasks inside and outside the household, and other matters that influence gender outcomes. This household-centered framework has proved useful for the economic analysis of gender equality and has been the basis of World Bank milestones in promoting gender equality in policy recommendations and allocation of resources.

Households make choices on the basis of preferences shaped by social norms, market incentives, and constraints that result from markets and formal institutions. The *WDR* summarizes these interactions in the simple diagram presented in figure 1.1. The interactions of households, markets, and institutions generate growth, which in turn contributes to gender equality as income and economic development alter some of the constraints. At the same time, greater gender equality contributes to economic efficiency and growth. The approach followed by ADePT Gender is to work over this framework and present a country diagnostic on gender equality that looks at gender outcomes from the perspective of households and individuals as household members. This is one way to condense the information concerning the interactions between households, markets, and institutions.

A country diagnostic on gender equality should be comprehensive, covering both social and economic issues. Following the *WDR*, ADePT Gender groups outcomes in three dimensions: human endowments (or capital), economic opportunities, and agency (box 1.1).[3] All of these aspects are interrelated and matter for individual welfare, gender equality, and economic development.

Building on the conceptual and empirical work of others, ADePT Gender was developed to maximize the use of household-level data and to create ready-to-print reports that allow users to easily visualize gender inequalities.

ADePT Gender is a tool for conducting country diagnostics using micro-data from different types of household surveys. The results allow users to identify broad areas for further analysis or for public action. At the same time, using the *WDR* helps take advantage of the report's in-depth analysis

Figure 1.1: *WDR* Framework for Analyzing Gender Equality

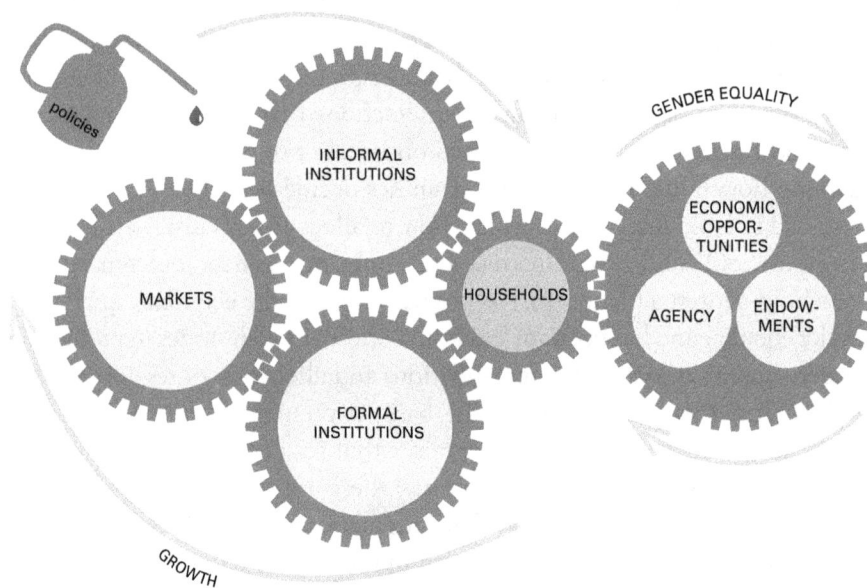

Source: World Bank 2012b.

Box 1.1: A Deeper Look at Agency

The term *agency* can be defined as the ability of individuals or groups to give voice to and act on their preferences and to influence outcomes that affect them and others in society. Agency is affected by and also affects individuals' ownership of and control over endowments and their access to economic opportunities (Kabeer 1999).

Within a household or partnership, one's relative power affects the strength of one's voice and influence in household decisions, such as how to spend or invest family resources. Similarly, at the community or societal level, the relative power of individuals and groups affects their ability to act on their preferences and to influence

(continued)

Box 1.1: A Deeper Look at Agency *(continued)*

outcomes in the economic, social, and political domains. The relative power of different members of society, which often differs systematically by gender, reflects a complex combination of one's personal characteristics, prevailing social norms, and the broader legal and institutional environments.

The ability to act on one's preferences, regardless of one's gender, and to translate those preferences into a desired outcome is a development objective in its own right. Development not only involves raising incomes or reducing poverty but also involves a process of expanding freedoms and choices available to all people (Sen 1999). Agency is a measure of a person's well-being, reflecting the ability to achieve as well as actual achievements (Sen 1992).

Source: Mason and others 2012.

and explanation of the mechanisms that generate the observed results. The *WDR* also concludes with a chapter containing a rich set of policy recommendations organized around the framework. It is recommended that the users of ADePT Gender software build on the lessons and policy recommendations of this report, as it complements this product.

Endowments

The term *endowment* refers to investments in nutrition, health, and education, beginning with the right to be born. The *WDR* chooses this term instead of human capital, a concept introduced by Gary Becker (1957), because it aims to capture differences that arise even before birth, and not just investments that take place during the life cycle.

Education and health investments have a huge effect on individuals' ability to function and reach their potential in life and society. Narrowing gender differences in endowments is important not only because all persons have the same right to health and education, but also because improvements in women's education and health will have positive effects on their children, which will in turn result in future economic growth. Evidence shows that a mother's nutritional status is positively associated with her children's health and survival, and a mother's education is positively linked to a range of health benefits for her children and to their educational attainment. There is no doubt that poor health outcomes in adulthood affect economic outcomes, which are reflected in health-related absences from the labor force, fewer work hours, and lower earnings.

ADePT Gender allows users to produce a set of tables that compare health and education outcomes for boys and girls and for men and women. The standardized graphs and charts produced include data that are most likely to be available in multitopic household surveys. Chapters 2 and 3 further detail how users of the ADePT software can choose independent variables to produce customized tables and charts.

Economic Opportunities

The term *economic opportunity* refers to access to both productive inputs and productive employment, and to the result of economic activities in the form of productivity and earnings.

For an economy to function at its maximum potential, women's skills need to be used productively. Instead, women's labor tends to be underused or misallocated. For example, women are more likely to occupy low-productivity occupations, do unpaid family work, or hold informal jobs. Many times, women have less access to productive assets, such as land and fertilizers, which in turn affects their productivity in self-employment as entrepreneurs and farmers. In agriculture, farms managed by women typically render lower yields than those operated by men, even if plots belong to the same household. That outcome is partly explained by different access to assets and agricultural inputs. In urban areas, female-managed firms tend to have lower levels of value added per worker. That is also explained by the fact that women often work predominantly in low-productivity sectors and have less access to credit.

These differences result from gender differences in endowments and in access to inputs, including time that men and women devote to household duties and market-paid activities, and from market and institutional failures. For example, differences in preferences—which may be specific to the individual but are also shaped by society—result in gaps in employment, occupations, and earnings and persist throughout the labor market.

ADePT Gender attempts to capture statistical differences between men and women in such outcomes as employment, unemployment, and occupational segregation. The software also allows users to explore differences in access to productive inputs, including both human capital and physical assets. Since women's constraints vary along the life cycle, these differences in outcomes are also provided for various age groups, marital status, and fertility outcomes.

Because ADePT Gender aims to understand gender differences in labor-market outcomes, part II of this manual is dedicated to producing measures of inequality in the labor market as well a set of standard decomposition methodologies that allow users to disentangle the contribution of differences in endowments—usually called the *composition effect*—and differences in labor market payoff of these endowments—usually called the *wage structure effect.*

Agency

The term *agency* refers to one's ability to make choices and to transform them into desired actions and outcomes. Agency can be exerted at the individual level, within the family, or in society (Kabeer 1999; Sen 1985; World Bank 2012b).

In household surveys, agency is typically measured through individuals' decision-making roles within the household, the community, or both, although their desired goals for different areas of decision making are usually not elicited. Independent of the income level or a country's economic development, women are less involved than men in decision making in the household, community, and society. In many countries, a large percentage of women do not have access to household resources or do not contribute to decisions about how to use household income. However, evidence shows that when women participate in household spending, greater household expenditures are devoted to items related to nutrition, health, and education, which later translate into better outcomes for children.

Conversely, in many countries, women do not participate in government, political parties, or even civil organizations, which perpetuates inequality. In politics, women's concerns are not represented if men cannot understand or defend female issues. Women also participate in weaker or even segregated networks, which makes it more difficult for them to participate in the institutional machine and to generate change. Most important, women and men internalize social norms and institutional incentives in ways that affect their expectations, aspirations, and choices. This in turn complicates the measurement of agency itself in surveys and the work of the analyst, as it becomes extremely complex—if not impossible—to disentangle "inherent" preferences from constraints that stem from markets and institutions.

To complicate matters even further, measuring agency is not simple, and agency is often confounded with other related concepts, such as empowerment.

Much has been written about measurement challenges and solutions for agency and empowerment (Annan and others 2016; Klugman and others 2014; Narayan 2005; World Bank 2012b). The agreement so far is that most of the available variables are weak proxies for agency. ADePT Gender uses the proxies for agency that are easily accessed by the user. Thus, the results on agency need to be interpreted bearing in mind the assumptions linking the proxy variables with the agency features they try to measure.

What This Manual Does and How to Use It

This manual provides a guide to working with ADePT Gender software and is intended to help the user interpret the results produced. As opposed to other ADePT modules, it does not detail the mechanisms that lead to gender differences in outcomes, as those are fully developed in the 2012 *WDR* as well as in its companion reports (see table 1.1). Moreover, the last

Table 1.1: Key Resources for ADePT Gender

Reference	Highlighted contribution
• *World Development Report 2012: Gender Equality and Development (WDR)* (World Bank 2012b)	The 2012 *WDR* takes stock of the evidence and develops a framework for analyzing gender equality, which ADePT Gender uses to organize output. The 2012 *WDR* provides a wealth of statistics that can be used as comparators/reference values of ADePT Gender's output. This report also provides a set of policy recommendations.
• *The World's Women 2010* (UN 2010)	This excellent report provides reference values for many indicators produced by ADePT Gender.
• *Global Gender Gap Report: 2014* (World Economic Forum 2014)	The 2014 report contains a wealth of indicators that can be used to provide reference values and complementary information from other sources.
Regional WDR companion reports	
• *Toward Gender Equality in East Asia and the Pacific* (Mason and others 2012)	The framework of the 2012 *WDR* is used to more deeply analyze countries of the East Asia and Pacific region. It provides reference values for many outcomes of ADePT Gender for those countries.
• *Opening Doors: Gender Equality and Development in the Middle East and North Africa* (World Bank 2013b)	The framework of the 2012 *WDR* is used to more deeply analyze countries of the Middle East and North Africa region. It provides reference values for many outcomes of ADePT Gender for those countries.
• *Work and Family: Latin American and Caribbean Women in Search of a New Balance* (Chioda 2016)	Using the household as the center of analysis and based on a rich set of household surveys for Latin America and the Caribbean, this report discusses many gender inequalities along the dimensions of the 2012 *WDR*. It also presents results on wage decompositions using Ñopo's methodology (see chapter 6).

(continued)

Table 1.1: Key Resources for ADePT Gender *(continued)*

Reference	Highlighted contribution
• *Enhancing Women's Voice, Agency and Participation in the Economy: Studies in Egypt, Jordan, Morocco, Tunisia and Turkey* (EBRD 2015)	A companion to the 2012 *WDR*, this report details five dimensions of agency in Egypt, Arab Rep.; Jordan; Morocco; Tunisia; and Turkey in relation to economic participation of women.
Thematic companion reports or related references	
• *Getting to Equal: Promoting Gender Equality through Human Development* (World Bank 2011b)	This companion report to the 2012 *WDR* analyzes in more detail the gender gaps in endowments.
• *On Norms and Agency: Conversations about Gender Equality with Women and Men in 20 Countries* (Munoz Boudet and others 2012)	This companion report to the 2012 *WDR* covers the background qualitative studies on social norms and agency and further discusses measurement issues for this dimension of the framework.
• *Voice and Agency: Empowering Women and Girls for Shared Prosperity* (Klugman and others 2014)	This report goes deeper into four of the five dimensions of agency described in the 2012 *WDR*—women's control over assets, control over family formation, freedom from domestic violence, and freedom of physical mobility.
• *Empowering Women: Legal Rights and Economic Opportunities in Africa* (World Bank 2011a)	This report analyzes the links between legal rights and a set of economic opportunities outcomes for African countries.
Country gender diagnostics using WDR framework	
• *Russian Federation Country Gender Assessment: Main Report* (Munoz Boudet and Posadas 2014)	Chapter 1 of the country gender assessment takes stock of gender inequalities over the three dimensions of outcomes proposed by the 2012 *WDR*. Most of the tables and graphs included in this chapter can be produced with ADePT Gender software.
• *Bosnia and Herzegovina: Gender Disparities in Endowments, Access to Economic Opportunities and Agency* (Cancho and Elwan 2015)	The country gender assessment takes stock of gender inequalities over the three dimensions of outcomes proposed by the 2012 *WDR*. Most of the tables and graphs included in this chapter can be produced with ADePT Gender software.
• *Country Gender Assessment: Economic Participation, Agency and Access to Justice in Jordan* (World Bank 2013a)	The report aims to assess gender imbalances in the areas of economic participation in the labor market, agency, and access to justice in Jordan. Many of the tables and graphs included in this assessment can be produced with ADePT Gender software.
• *Papua New Guinea: Country Gender Assessment for the Period 2011–2012* (World Bank 2012a)	The assessment describes the gender dimensions of Papua New Guinea's development challenges and strategies. Chapters 2 and 3 detail access to education and health as well as employment, livelihood, and economic resources, respectively. Many of the tables and figures included in these chapters can be produced using ADePT Gender software.
• *Vietnam: Country Gender Assessment* (World Bank 2011c)	The assessment highlights progress and challenges to gender equality in Vietnam over the past several decades. Several of the tables and figures produced in this report, particularly those in chapters 3 and 4, can be produced using ADePT Gender software.

Note: Dimensions of agency include (a) access to and control over resources, (b) freedom from the risk of violence, (c) freedom of movement, (d) decision making over family formation, and (e) a voice in society and influencing policy.

chapter of the *WDR* contains a rich set of policy recommendations based on the evidence collected from countries all over the world. The *WDR* companion reports build on the same framework and describe in detail the gender realities of countries in their regions or in a particular topic or dimension of the framework—education, jobs, or agency. ADePT Gender software users have this wealth of existing material at their disposal— table 1.1 lists several of the relevant references and country assessments, including a short description of how those documents relate to the *WDR* framework.

Moreover, since the launch of the *WDR* and in parallel to the development of ADePT Gender, a few countries have conducted individual country gender diagnostics that use the *WDR* framework and present tables and graphs similar to those produced by ADePT Gender software. Those country studies constitute excellent guides for ADePT Gender users, as they illustrate how to use and interpret ADePT Gender output.

The recommendation to the user is to work with the complementary studies when producing the report based on ADePT Gender output to have a rich description of the results and to link them to policy recommendations. Part II explains the main indicators produced to cover all the dimensions of gender equality. ADePT Gender software allows the user to produce many of the 52 minimum core gender indicators agreed by the United Nations Interagency and Expert Group on Gender Statistics.[4]

Notes

1. See box 1 in World Bank (2012b) for more details about the concept of gender in this setup.
2. The various dissemination outputs can be found on the website associated with the report (World Bank 2012b).
3. The definition of agency comes in the following paragraphs and more extensively in box 1.1.
4. For more details on the minimum core gender indicators, see the report of the International Household Survey Network (IHSN 2015) and the paper on mapping gender gaps by Buvinic, Furst-Nichols, and Koolwal (2014).

References

Annan, Jeannie, Aletheia Donald, Kathryn Falb, Gayatri Koolwal, and Markus Goldstein. 2016. "Measuring Women's Agency." Working Paper, Gender Innovation Lab, World Bank, Washington, DC.

Becker, Gary S. 1957. *The Economics of Discrimination.* Chicago: University of Chicago Press.

Buvinic, Mayra, Rebecca Furst-Nichols, and Gayatri Koolwal. 2014. "Mapping Gender Data Gaps." Data2X, Washington, DC. http://data2x .org/wp-content/uploads/2014/11/Data2X_MappingGenderDataGaps _FullReport.pdf.

Cancho, Cesar A., and Nihal Elwan. 2015. *Bosnia and Herzegovina: Gender Disparities in Endowments, Access to Economic Opportunities and Agency.* Washington, DC: World Bank. http://documents.worldbank.org /curated/en/2015/07/24811714/bosnia-herzegovina-gender-disparities -endowmentsaccess-economic-opportunities-agency.

Chioda, Laura. 2016. *Work and Family: Latin American and Caribbean Women in Search of a New Balance.* Washington, DC: World Bank. http:// siteresources.worldbank.org/LACEXT/Resources/informe_genero _LACDEF.pdf.

EBRD (European Bank for Reconstruction and Development). 2015. *Enhancing Women's Voice, Agency and Participation in the Economy: Studies in Egypt, Jordan, Morocco, Tunisia and Turkey.* London: EBRD. http:// www.ebrd.com/documents/comms-and-bis/enhancing-womens-voice -agency-and-participation-semed-and-turkey.pdf.

IHSN (International Household Survey Network). 2015. "How Well Are Gender Issues Covered in Household Surveys and Censuses? An Analysis Using the IHSN–World Bank Gender Data Navigator." http://ihsn.org/HOME/sites/default/files/resources/Gender_Issues_July -2015.pdf.

Kabeer, Naila. 1999. "Resources, Agency, Achievements: Reflections on the Measurement of Women's Empowerment." *Development and Change* 30 (3): 435–64.

Klugman, Jeni, Lucia Hanmer, Sarah Twigg, Tazeen Hasan, Jennifer McCleary-Sills, and Julieth Santamaria. 2014. *Voice and Agency: Empowering Women and Girls for Shared Prosperity.* Washington, DC: World Bank. https:// openknowledge.worldbank.org/handle/10986/19036.

Lokshin, Michael, Sergiy Radyakin, Zurab Sajaia, and William Creitz. 2013. *ADePT User Guide*. Version 5. Washington, DC: World Bank.

Mason, Andrew D., Reena Badiani, Trang Van Nguyen, Katherine Patrick, and Ximena Del Carpio. 2012. *Toward Gender Equality in East Asia and the Pacific: A Companion to the* World Development Report. Washington, DC: World Bank.

Munoz Boudet, Ana Maria, Patti Petesch, Carolyn Turk, and Maria Angelica Thumala. 2012. *On Norms and Agency: Conversations about Gender Equality with Women and Men in 20 Countries*. Washington, DC: World Bank. http:// documents.worldbank.org/curated/en/2012/01/17041656/norms-agency -conversations-gender-equality-women-men-20-countries.

Munoz Boudet, Ana Maria, and Josefina Posadas. 2014. *Russian Federation Gender Assessment: Main Report*. Washington, DC: World Bank. http:// documents.worldbank.org/curated/en/2016/04/19286033/russian -federation-gender-assessment-main-report.

Narayan, Deepa. 2005. *Measuring Empowerment: Cross Disciplinary Perspectives*. Washington, DC: World Bank.

Sen, Amartya K. 1985. "Well-Being, Agency and Freedom: The Dewey Lectures 1984." *Journal of Philosophy* 82 (4): 169–221.

———. 1992. *Inequality Re-Examined*. Oxford: Clarendon Press.

———. 1999. *Development as Freedom*. New York: Knopf.

UN (United Nations). 2010. *The World's Women 2010: Trends and Statistics*. New York: UN. http://unstats.un.org/unsd/demographic/products /Worldswomen/WW_full%20report_color.pdf.

World Bank. 2011a. *Empowering Women: Legal Rights and Economic Opportunities in Africa*. Washington, DC: World Bank. http://documents .worldbank.org/curated/en/2011/01/16394357/empowering-women -legal-rights-economic-opportunities-africa.

———. 2011b. *Getting to Equal: Promoting Gender Equality through Human Development*. Washington, DC: World Bank. http://siteresources.worldbank. org/EDUCATION/Resources/278200-1099079877269/547664 -1099080014368/Getting_to_equal.pdf.

———. 2011c. *Vietnam: Country Gender Assessment*. Washington, DC: World Bank. http://documents.worldbank.org/curated/en/2011/11/15470188 /vietnam-country-gender-assessment.

———. 2012a. *Papua New Guinea: Country Gender Assessment for the Period 2011–2012*. Washington, DC: World Bank. http://documents.worldbank

.org/curated/en/2012/12/17431121/papua-new-guinea-country-gender -assessment-period-2011-2012.

———. 2012b. *World Development Report 2012: Gender Equality and Development*. Washington, DC: World Bank. https://openknowledge .worldbank.org/handle/10986/4391.

———. 2013a. *Country Gender Assessment: Economic Participation, Agency and Access to Justice in Jordan*. Washington, DC: World Bank. http:// documents.worldbank.org/curated/en/2013/07/18423362/country-gender -assessment-economic-participation-agency-access-justice-jordan.

———. 2013b. *Opening Doors: Gender Equality and Development in the Middle East and North Africa*. Washington, DC: World Bank. http://documents. worldbank.org/curated/en/2013/02/17235637/opening-doors-gender -equality-development-middle-east-north-africa.

World Economic Forum. 2014. *Global Gender Gap Report: 2014*. Geneva: World Economic Forum. http://reports.weforum.org/global-gender-gap -report-2014.

Chapter 2

Working with ADePT Software

This chapter provides basic information about installing and using ADePT Gender. The instructions here are sufficient for performing a simple analysis. More information is available from the following sources:

- Detailed instructions for using ADePT are provided in the *ADePT User Guide*, which can be downloaded from http://www.worldbank .org/adept ▶ **Documentation**.
- Video tutorials are available at http://www.world bank.org/adept ▶ **Video Tutorials**.
- ADePT provides online help via the **Help** ▶ **Contents** command.
- For help using any ADePT module, see the appropriate chapters in this book or in another book in the *Streamlined Analysis with ADePT Software* series.
- Module-specific instructions, along with example datasets, projects, and reports, are available at http://www.worldbank.org/adept ▶ **Modules**.
- Example datasets and projects are installed with ADePT. They are located in the *example* subfolder in the ADePT program folder. Use the examples with the instructions in this chapter to familiarize your-self with ADePT operations.

Conventions Used in This Chapter

- Windows, buttons, tabs, dialogs, and other features you see on-screen are shown in **bold**. For example, the **Save As** dialog has a **Save** button and a **Cancel** button.
- Keystrokes are shown in SMALL CAPS. For example, you may be instructed to press the ENTER key.
- Menu commands use a shorthand notation. **Project ▶ Exit**, for example, means "open the **Project** menu and click the **Exit** command."

Installing ADePT

System Requirements

- A PC running Microsoft Windows XP (SP1 or later), Windows Vista, Windows Server 2003 and later, or Windows 7; ADePT runs in 32- and 64-bit environments.
- NET 2.0 or later (included with recent Windows installations), and all updates and patches.
- 80-megabyte disk space to install, plus space for temporary dataset copies.
- At least 512 megabytes of random-access memory (RAM).
- At least 1024 x 768 screen resolution.
- At least one printer driver must be installed (even if no printer is connected).
- Microsoft Excel for Windows (XP or later), Microsoft Excel Viewer, or a compatible spreadsheet program for viewing reports generated by ADePT.
- A Web browser and Internet access are needed to download ADePT. Internet access is needed for program updates and to load Web-based datasets into ADePT. Otherwise, ADePT does not require Internet access to run.

Installation

1. Download the ADePT installer by clicking the **ADePT Downloads** button at http://www.worldbank.org/adept.
   Launch the installer and follow the on-screen instructions.
   ADePT automatically launches after installation.

Launching ADePT

2. Click the ADePT icon in the Windows **Start** menu.
3. In the **Select ADePT Module** window, double-click the name of the module you want to use (see the up and down arrows in the bar at right in the screenshot below). To open a health module, double-click **Health;** then click **Health Financing** or **Health Outcomes**.

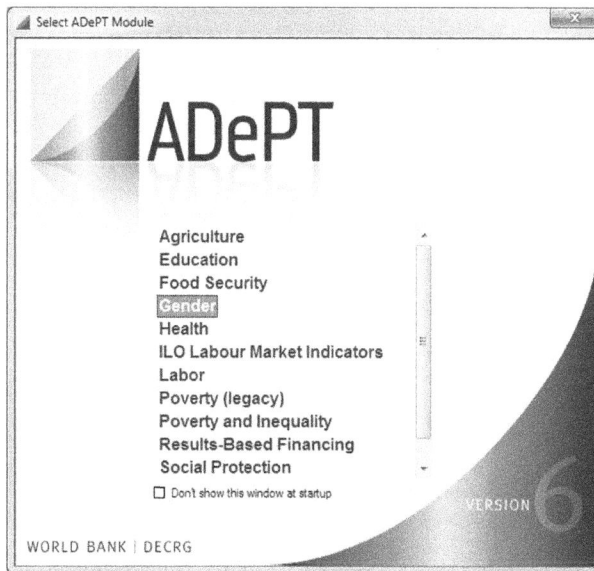

You now see the ADePT main window. (The example below shows ADePT configured with the gender module. The lower-left and upper-right panels will be different when another module is loaded.)

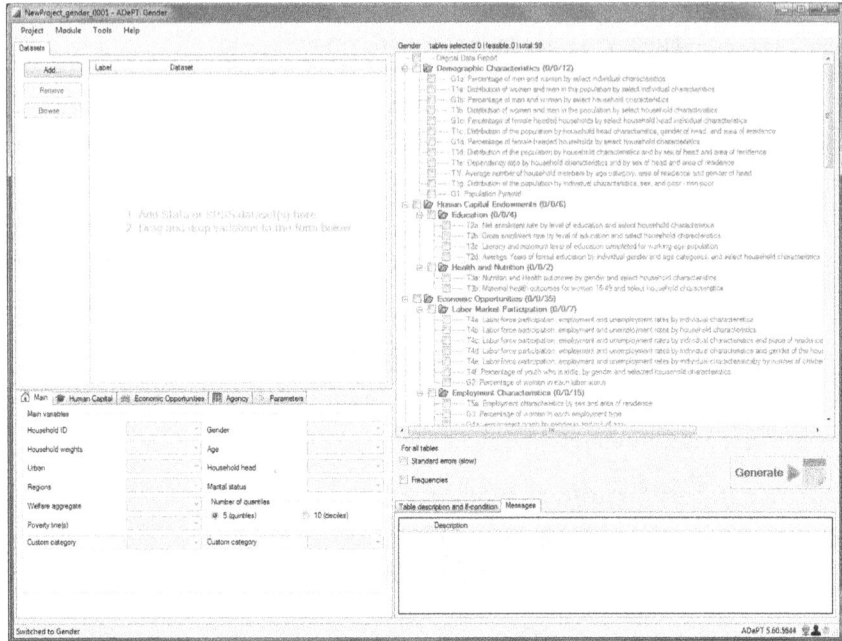

To switch to another module after launching ADePT:
Module ▶ Select Module....

In the **Select ADePT Module** window, double-click the name of the module you want to use.

Overview of the Analysis Procedure

There are four general steps to performing an analysis:

1. Specify one or more datasets that you want to analyze.
2. Map dataset variables to ADePT analysis inputs.
3. Select tables or graphs.
4. Generate the report.

Here is where you perform each step in the ADePT main window:

1. Click **Add** button to load.
Enter dataset year in **Label** column.

3. Select tables or graphs to be included in report.

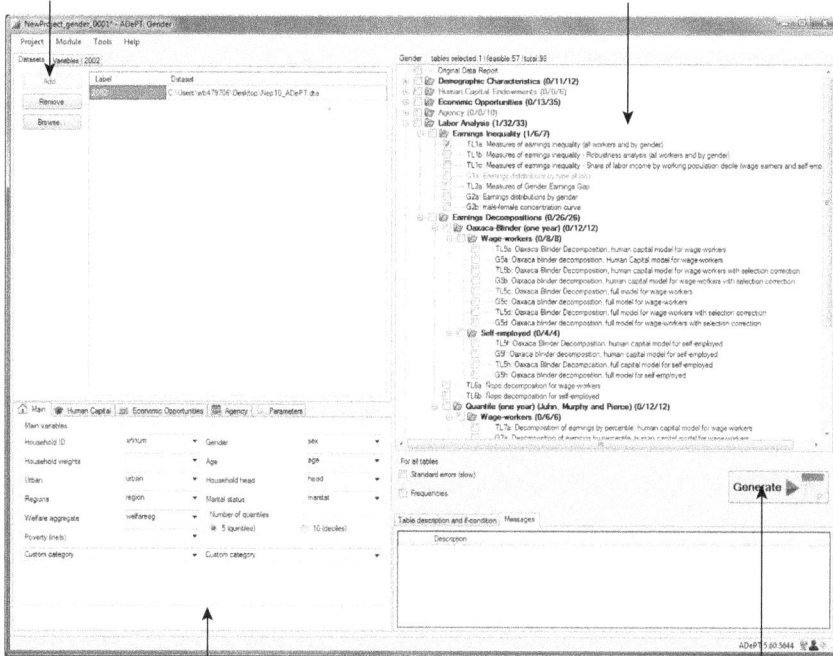

2. Map dataset variables to input variables by selecting dataset variables in drop-down lists.

4. Click **Generate**.

The next sections in this chapter provide detailed instructions for the four steps.

Specifying Datasets

Your first task in performing an analysis is to specify one or more datasets. ADePT can process data in Stata (*.dta*), SPSS (*.sav*), and tab-delimited text (*.txt*) formats.[1]

Operations in this section take place in the upper-left corner of the ADePT main window.

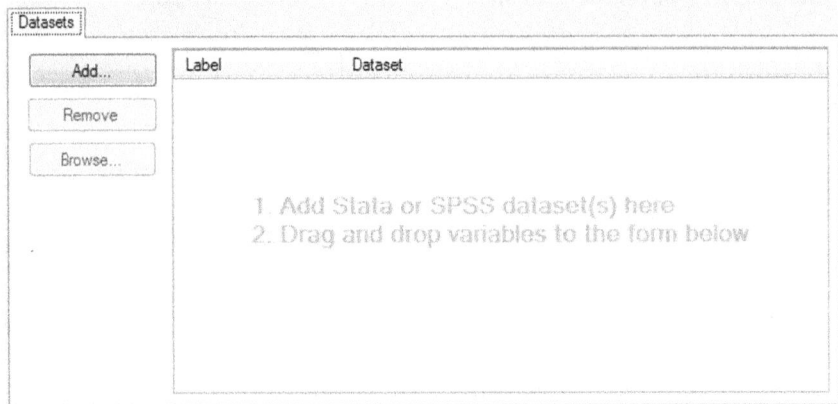

1. Click the **Add...** button.
2. In the **Open** dataset dialog, locate and click the dataset you want to analyze. Then click the **Open** button. The dataset is now listed in the **Datasets** tab.

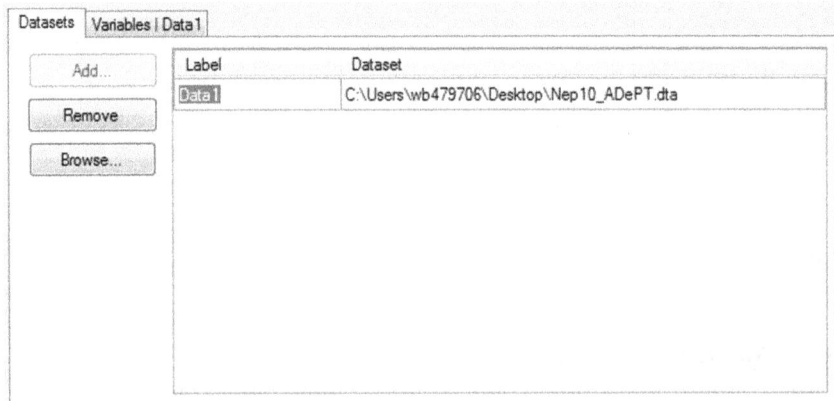

Tip: While learning to use ADePT, you may want to experiment with example data. You can find sample datasets in the *ADePT\Example* folder.

3. Specify a label for the dataset:

In the **Label** column, select the default label.

Type a label for the dataset. Recommendation: Label the dataset using the year the survey was conducted (for example, 2002). When labels are years, ADePT can calculate differences between surveys.

Press ENTER.

To remove a dataset: Click the dataset; then click the **Remove** button.

One dataset has been specified in this example.

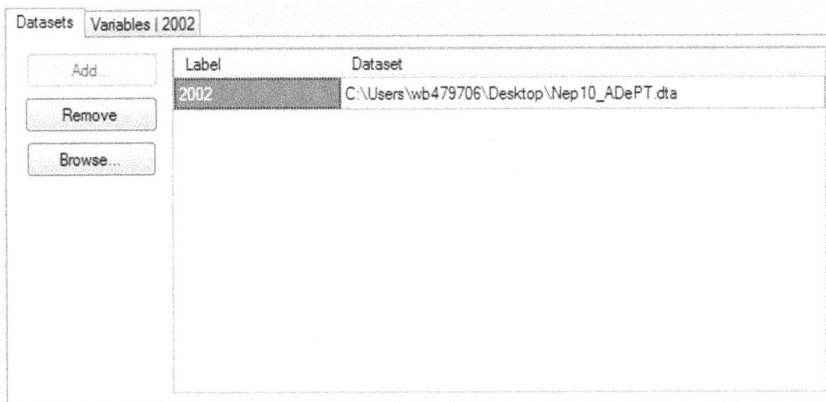

Datasets	Variables	2002		
Add...	Label	Dataset
Remove	2002	C:\Users\wb479706\Desktop\Nep10_ADePT.dta
Browse...		

Note: ADePT does not alter original datasets in any way. It always works with copies of datasets.

Mapping Variables

ADePT needs to know which variables in the dataset(s) correspond to the inputs to its calculations. You must manually map dataset variables to input variables.

Operations described in this section take place on the left side of the ADePT main window. These examples show the gender module loaded into ADePT, but the process is similar for the other modules.

There are two methods for mapping variables:

Method 1: In the lower input **Variables** tab, open the variable's list; then click the corresponding dataset variable, as shown here for the **urban** variable.

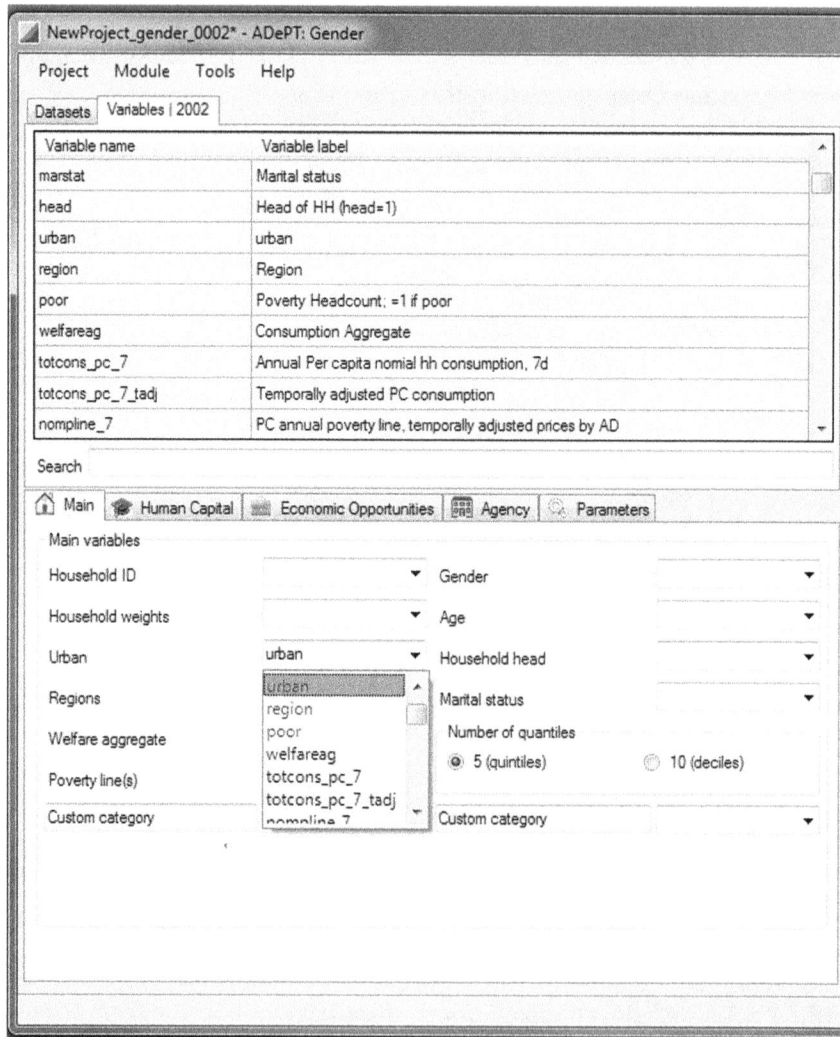

Method 2: In the upper dataset **Variables** tab, drag the variable name and drop it in the corresponding field in the lower input **Variables** tab.

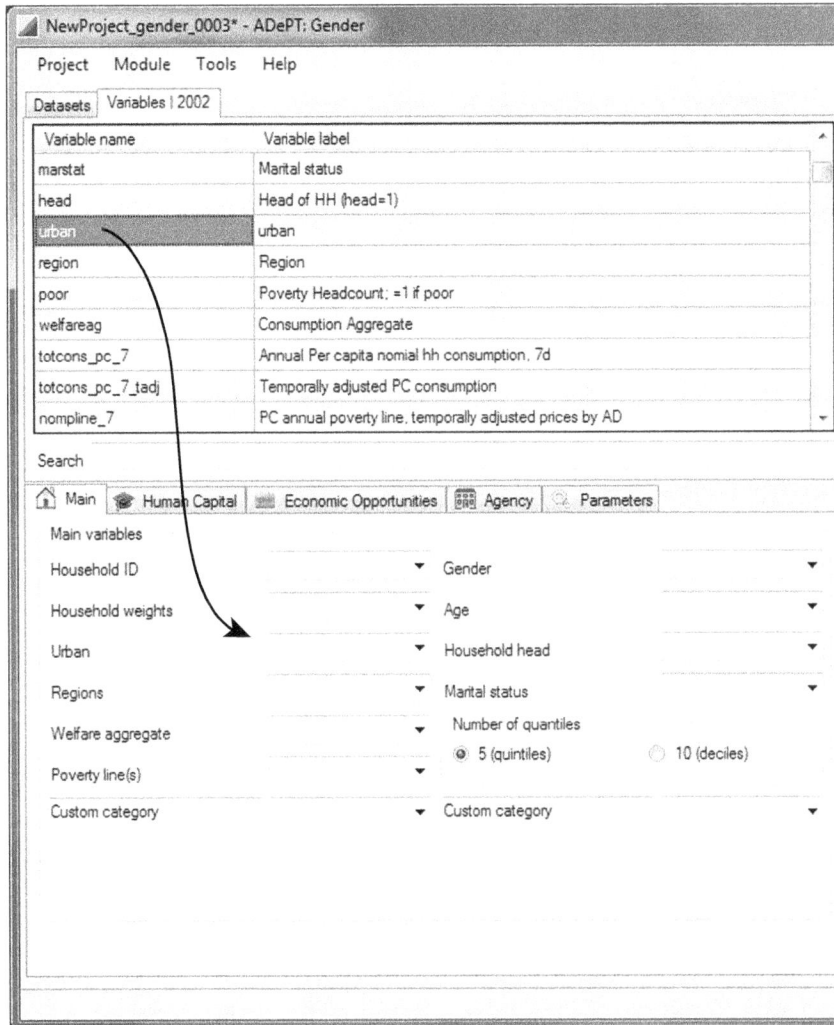

Note: You can also type dataset variable names in the input variable fields. The above methods are preferred, however, since typing may introduce spelling errors. A spelling error is indicated by the red exclamation point next to the input variable field.

To remove a mapping: Select the variable name in the input variable field, then press DELETE.

Some modules have multiple input variable tabs. The gender module, for example, organizes variables in four tabs.

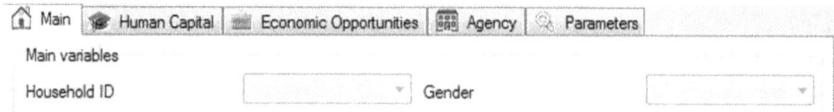

In some input variable fields, you can specify multiple dataset variables. Household ID, for example, may not be unique within a dataset because the same ID was assigned to a household in another region. In such cases, you can map multiple dataset variables to one input variable.

In this example, the **id** dataset variable has been mapped to the **Household ID** input variable.

The italic variable name indicates that this input variable field accepts multiple dataset variables. The **region** dataset variable can now be mapped to **Household ID** using either of the two methods described earlier.

ADePT uses this mapping to create its own internal household ID variable to uniquely identify each household.

Tip: Open the example project (**Project ▶ Open Example Project**) to see the result of mapping dataset variables to input variables.

Selecting Tables and Graphs

After mapping variables, you are ready to select the tables or graphs you want ADePT to generate.

Operations described in this section take place on the right side of the ADePT main window.

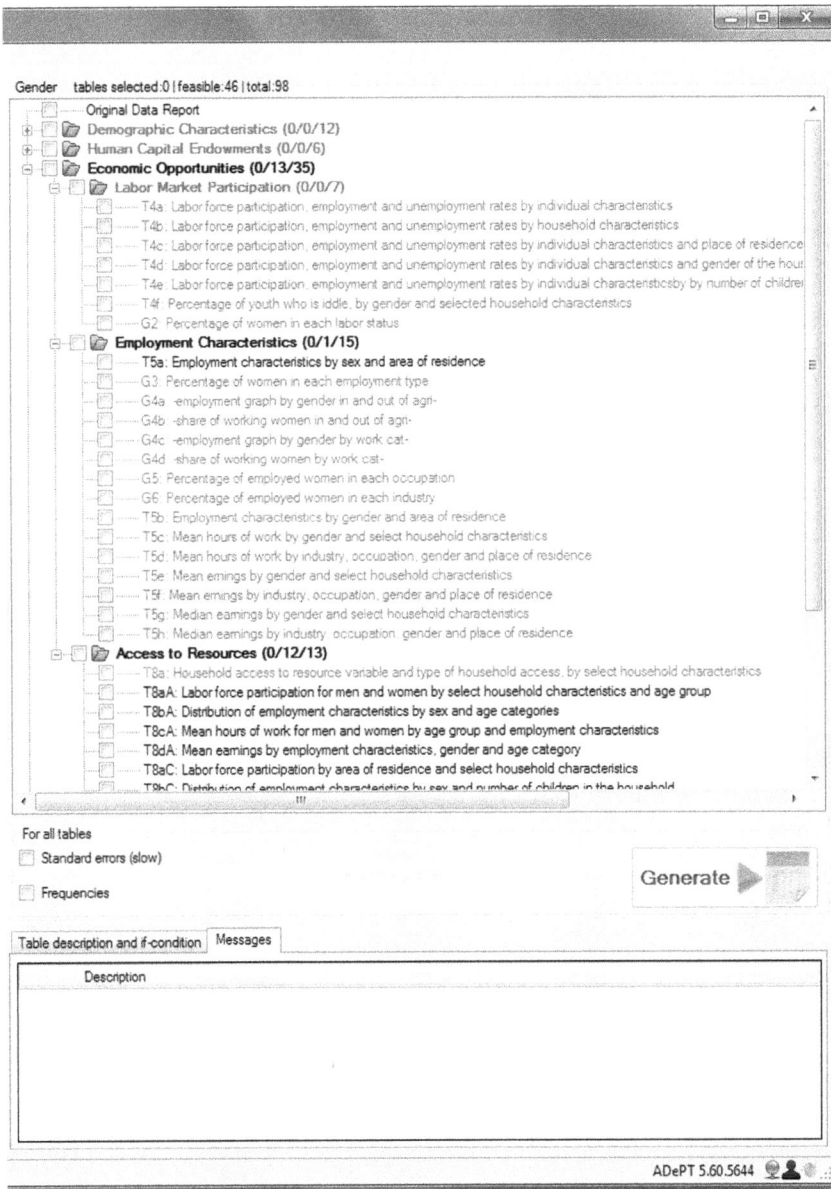

In the upper-right (outputs) panel, select the tables or graphs you want to generate.

Note: If a name is gray, it cannot be selected. These tables and graphs cannot be generated because no required variables have been specified.

To see a description of a table or graph: Click the name. Its description is displayed in the **Table description and if-condition** tab in the lower left corner of the ADePT window.

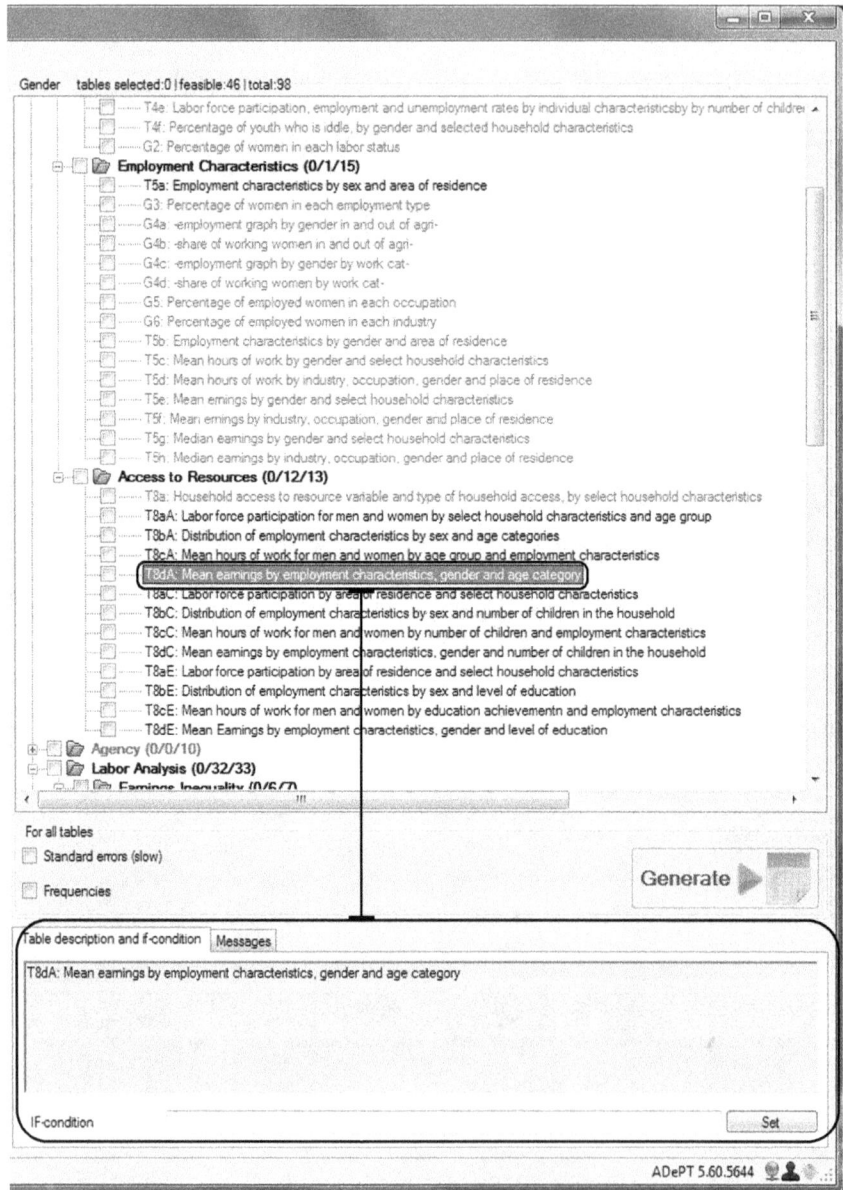

Generating the Report

Click the **Generate** button.

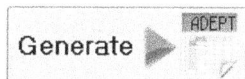

To stop calculating: Click the **Stop** button.

Examine items in the **Messages** tab. ADePT lists potential problems in this tab.

ADePT can identify three kinds of problems:

- **Notification** provides information that may be of interest to you. Notifications do not affect the content of reports generated by ADePT.
- **Warning** indicates a suspicious situation in the data. Warnings are issued when ADePT cannot determine whether the situation is impossible. Examples include the violation of parameters, the presence of potential outliers in the data, inconsistent data, and inconsistent category definitions. ADePT reports are not affected by warnings.
- **Error** prevents a variable from being used in the analysis. For example, a variable may not exist in a dataset (in this case, ADePT continues its calculations as if the variable was not specified).

If ADePT can match the problem to a particular variable field, that field is highlighted in the input **Variables** tab.

Correct problems as needed. Then, generate the report again.
Note: Notifications, warnings, and errors can negatively affect the results ADePT produces. Carefully review messages, and correct critical problems before drawing conclusions from tables and graphs.

Examining the Output

When its analysis is complete, ADePT automatically opens the results as a spreadsheet in Excel or Excel Viewer. The results are organized in multiple worksheets:

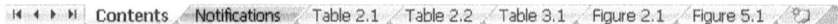

The **Contents** worksheet lists all the other worksheets, including titles for tables or graphs.

The **Notifications** worksheet lists the errors, warnings, and notifications that ADePT identified during its analysis. This worksheet may be more useful than the **Messages** tab in the ADePT main window, because the problems are organized by dataset.

Table worksheets display tables generated by ADePT.

Tip: ADePT formats table data with a reasonable number of decimal places. Click in a cell to see the data with full resolution in the formula bar.

Figure worksheets display graphs generated by ADePT.

Working with Variables

Viewing Basic Information about a Dataset's Variables

1. In the **Datasets** tab, click the dataset you want to examine.
2. Click the **Variables** tab.

Variable name	Variable label
age	Age (years)
rel2head	{1.04} Relationship to head
marstat	Marital status
head	Head of HH (head=1)
urban	urban
region	Region
poor	Poverty Headcount; =1 if poor
welfareag	Consumption Aggregate
totcons_pc_7	Annual Per capita nomial hh consumption, 7d
totcons_pc_7_tadj	Temporally adjusted PC consumption
nompline_7	PC annual poverty line, temporally adjusted prices by AD
pline_7	PC annual total poverty line, temporally adjusted national prices; 7d
doi	Date of interview (CMC)
wt_ind	Individual weights
wt_hh	Household weights
dob	Dato of birth (CMC)
eduatt	Education Attainment
edunone	None/Less than primary
eduprim	Primary completed
edusec	Secondary completed

Datasets | Variables | 2002

Search

To search for a variable: In the **Search** field, type a few characters in the variable name or variable label.

To view statistics for a variable: Double-click the variable name or variable label. This operation opens the **MultiDataset Statistics** window for that variable.

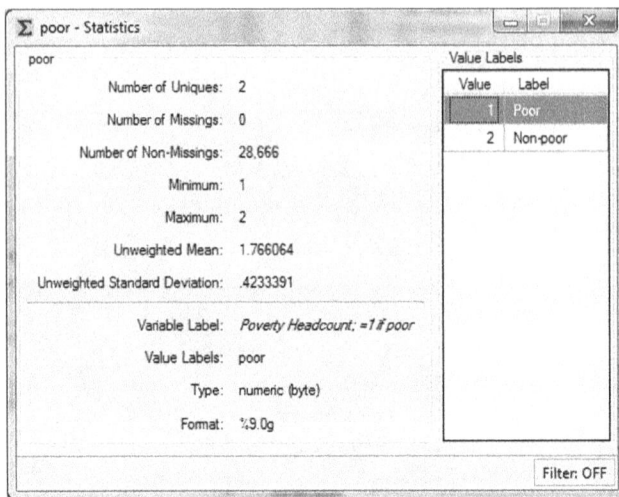

Viewing a Dataset's Data and Variable Details

1. In the **Datasets** tab, click the dataset you want to examine.
2. Click the **Browse...** button. This operation opens the **ADePT Data Browser**.

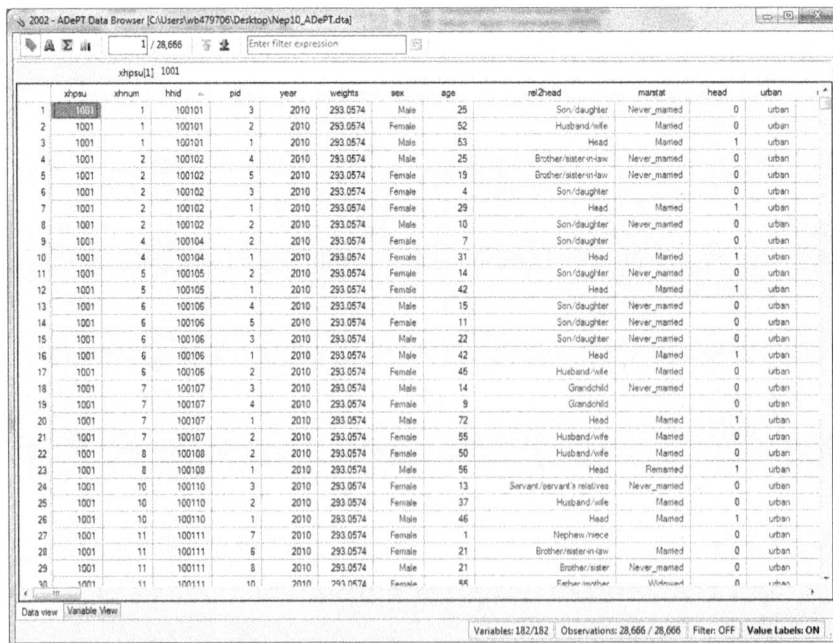

The **Data Browser** lists observations in rows and organizes variables in columns.

To see underlying data: Click the **Hide value labels** button.

To see value labels: Click the **Show value labels** button.

To view a variable's statistics:

Click in the variable's column.

Click the **Show statistics...** button.

To view detailed information about the dataset's variables: Click the **Variable view** tab on the bottom left of the **Data Browser**.

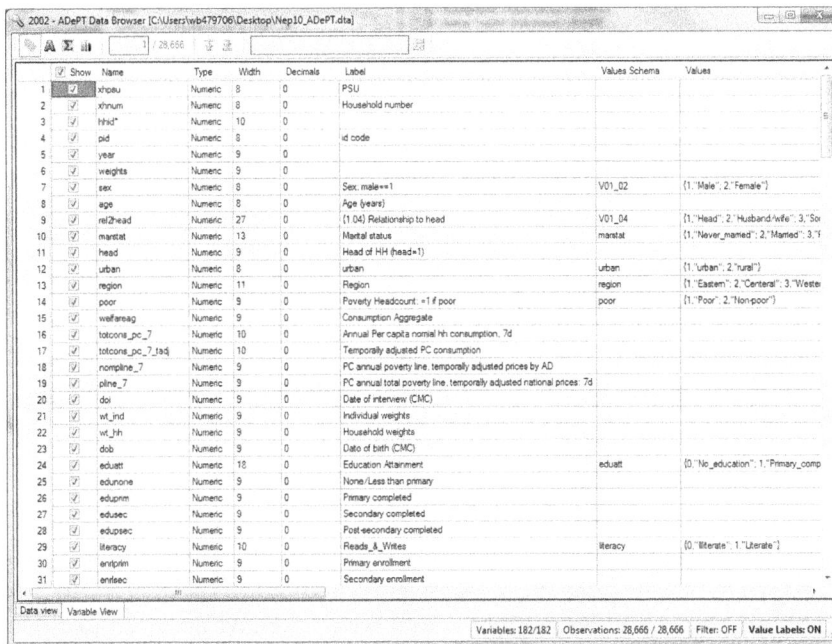

*To hide or show variable columns in the **Data view** tab:* In the **Variable view** tab, click the checkbox next to the variable name.

Tip: The *ADePT User Guide* describes other functions available in the **Data Browser**.

Generating Variables

You can create new variables based on the variables present in a dataset. This process might be useful for simulating the effects of changes in parameters on various economic outcomes.

1. In the **Datasets** tab in the main window, click the dataset you want to modify.
2. Click the **Variables | [dataset label]** tab.
3. Right-click in the table; then click **Add or replace variable...** in the pop-up menu.
4. In the **Generate/replace variable** dialog:
   a. In the **Expression** field, define the new variable using the following syntax:

      <new_variable_name> = <expression> [if <filter_expression>],

   where

<new_variable_name>	is a unique name not already in the dataset(s),
<expression>	calculates new data for the variable, and
<filter_expression>	(optional) filters observations that are used in the calculation.

   (See the "Variable Expressions" section below for more information.)
   b. Optional: Activate the **Apply to all datasets** option.

      Note: If you load multiple datasets but do not generate the new variable for all datasets, you will be unable to use the new variable in calculations. However, you may want to generate a different new variable for each dataset in the project.
   c. Click the **Generate** button.
   d. In the **Information** dialog, click the **OK** button.

The new variable will be listed in the **Variables | [dataset name]** tab, and in the **Data Browser**. If the variable was generated for all loaded datasets, it will appear in the drop-down lists in the input **Variables** tab.

When you save a project, variable expressions are saved with the project, and the variables are regenerated when you open that project. Generating new variables does not change original datasets.

Replacing Variables

You can replace an existing numeric variable by following the instructions in "Generating numeric dataset variables," but in the **Generate/replace variable** dialog (step 4a above), specify an existing variable name instead of a new variable name.

As with generated variables, these expressions are saved with a project, and the variables are regenerated when you open the project. Replacing variables does not change original datasets.

Variable Expressions

The following operators can be used in expressions:

Operator				Description
+	–	*	/	Basic mathematical operators
abs	sign			
=	==			Equality check operators
^	pow	sqrt		Exponent (for example, x^2 is x squared), power (for example, pow(4,2) is 42 = 16) and square root
round	truncate			Shortening operators
min	max			Range operators
ceiling	floor			

Variable expressions can include constants, and strings can be used for variables that are of the string type.

Expression examples are as follows:

$x = 1$	Sets all variable x observations to 1
$x = y + z$	Sets variable x observations to y observation plus z observation
$x = y = 1$	Sets variable x observations to 1 (true) if y is 1, otherwise sets to 0 (false)
$x = 23$ if $z ==$.	Sets variable x observations to 23 if z is missing (.), otherwise sets to .
$x = Log(y)$ if $z = 1$	Sets variable x observations to log of y observation if z is 1, otherwise sets to .
$s =$ "test"	Sets all variable x observations to the string "test"

Deleting Variables

You can remove variables from the working copy of a dataset that ADePT uses for its calculations. This operation does not change the original dataset. Native variables, as well as generated and replaced variables, can be deleted.

1. In the dataset **Variables** tab, right-click in the row containing the variable you want to delete; then click **Drop variable [variable name]** in the pop-up menu.
2. In the **Confirmation** dialog, click the **Yes** button.

Setting Parameters

Some modules have a **Parameters** tab next to the input **Variables** tab. In the **Parameters** tab, you can set ranges, weights, and other module-specific factors that ADePT will apply during its processing. A **Parameters** tab may also have input variable fields for mapping dataset variables.

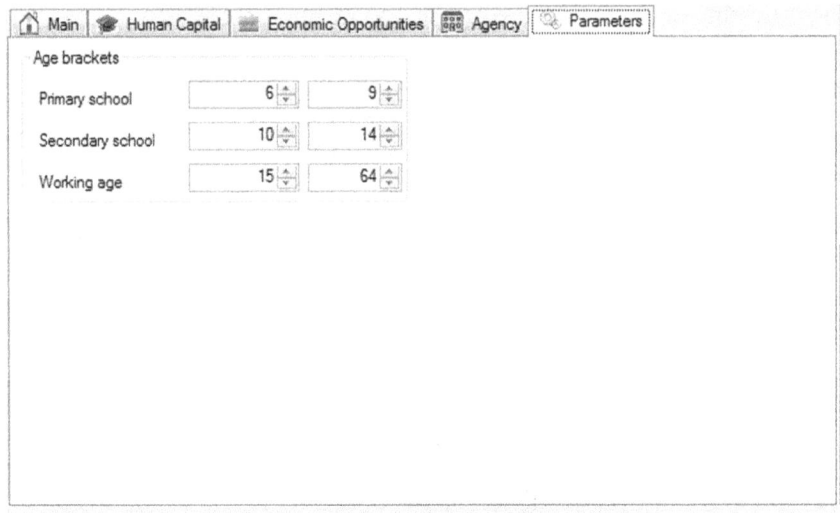

The mechanics for setting parameters are straightforward: activate options, set values, and select items in drop-down lists. The analytical reasons for setting parameters can be found elsewhere in this book or in the appropriate book in the *Streamlined Analysis with ADePT Software* series.

Working with Projects

After specifying datasets and mapping variables, you can save the configuration for future use. A saved project stores links to datasets, variable names, and other information related to analysis inputs. Projects do not retain table and graph selections, corresponding if-conditions, and choices for frequencies and standard errors, as they are related to analysis outputs.

To save a project:

1. **Project ▶ Save project** or **Project ▶ Save as... .**
2. In the **Save as** dialog, select a location and name for the project; then click the **Save** button.

To open a saved project:
1. **Project ▶ Open project...** .
2. In the **Open** dialog, locate and select the project; then click the **Open** button.

ADePT supports Web-based projects and datasets.
To open a Web-based project:
1. **Project ▶ Open web project...** .
2. In the **Open web project** dialog, enter the project's URL; then click the **OK** button.

To add a Web-based dataset:
1. In the **Datasets** tab, SHIFT-click the **Add...** button.
2. In the **Add web dataset** dialog, enter the dataset's URL; then click the **OK** button.

Adding Standard Errors or Frequencies to Outputs

To calculate standard errors: Before clicking the **Generate** button, activate the **Standard errors** option.

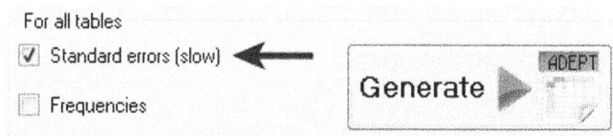

Calculating tables with standard errors takes considerably more time than calculating tables without them. A good approach is to obtain the result you want without standard errors and then generate final results with standard errors.

To calculate frequencies: Before clicking the **Generate** button, activate the **Frequencies** option.

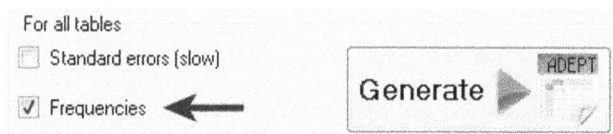

Tables with frequencies show the unweighted number of observations that were used in the calculation of a particular cell in a table. No significant additional time is needed to calculate frequencies.

Results of standard error and frequency calculations associated with a table are provided in separate worksheets, labeled **SE** and **FREQ**, within the output report.

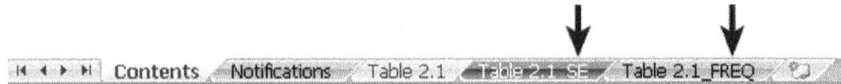

Applying If-Conditions to Outputs

The purpose of if-conditions is to include observations from a particular subgroup of a population in the analysis. The inclusion condition is formulated as a Boolean expression—a function of the variables that exist in the dataset. Each particular observation is included in the analysis if it satisfies the inclusion condition (the Boolean expression evaluates to value **true**). In many cases, the conditions we use are quite simple. Consider the following examples:

If-condition	Interpretation
urban=1	Only those observations that have the value of variable **urban** equal to **1** will be included in the analysis.
region==5	Only observations from the **region** with code **5** are included in the analysis.
age_yrs>=16	Only those individuals who are age 16 or older are included in the analysis.
sland!=0	Exclude from analysis those individuals who are not landowners (given that the variable **sland** denotes the area of the land owned).

1. In the list of tables and graphs, click the table or graph name.
2. Enter the if-condition at the bottom of the **Table description and if-condition** tab (see list of operators below).

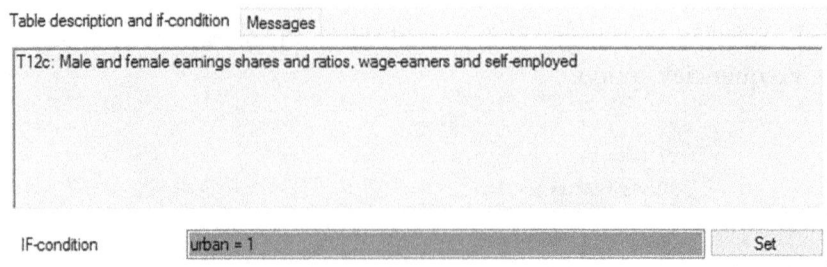

If-condition operators:

Operator	Description
=	Equal
==	Equal
>=	Greater than or equal
<=	Less than or equal
!=	Not equal
&	Logical AND
|	Logical OR
inlist(<variable>,n_1,n_2,n_3,...)	Include only observations for which <variable> has values n_1,n_2,n_3,...
inrange(<variable>,n_1,n_2)	Include observations for which <variable> is between n_1 and n_2
!missing(<variable>)	Exclude observations with missing values in <variable>

3. Click the **Set** button. A table or graph that has an if-condition is highlighted.

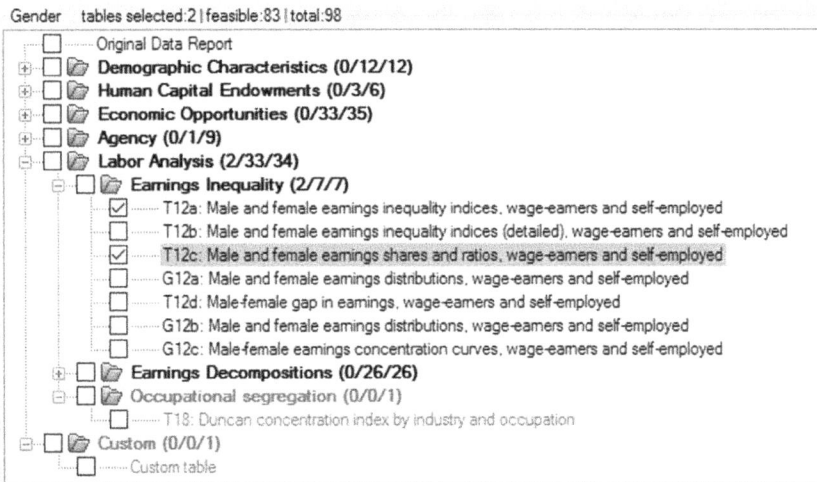

Gender   tables selected:2 | feasible:83 | total:98

```
      □ ......... Original Data Report
  ⊞ □ 🗀 Demographic Characteristics (0/12/12)
  ⊞ □ 🗀 Human Capital Endowments (0/3/6)
  ⊞ □ 🗀 Economic Opportunities (0/33/35)
  ⊞ □ 🗀 Agency (0/1/9)
  ⊟ □ 🗀 Labor Analysis (2/33/34)
      ⊟ □ 🗀 Earnings Inequality (2/7/7)
              ☑ ...... T12a: Male and female earnings inequality indices, wage-earners and self-employed
              □ ...... T12b: Male and female earnings inequality indices (detailed), wage-earners and self-employed
              ☑ ...... T12c: Male and female earnings shares and ratios, wage-earners and self-employed
              □ ...... G12a: Male and female earnings distributions, wage-earners and self-employed
              □ ...... T12d: Male-female gap in earnings, wage-earners and self-employed
              □ ...... G12b: Male and female earnings distributions, wage-earners and self-employed
              □ ...... G12c: Male-female earnings concentration curves, wage-earners and self-employed
      ⊞ □ 🗀 Earnings Decompositions (0/26/26)
      ⊟ □ 🗀 Occupational segregation (0/0/1)
              □ ...... T18: Duncan concentration index by industry and occupation
  ⊟ □ 🗀 Custom (0/0/1)
      □ ......... Custom table
```

Generating Custom Tables

You can add a custom table to ADePT's output.

1. **Tools ▸ Show custom table** tab.
2. In the lower-left panel's **Custom table** tab, activate the **Define custom table** option.

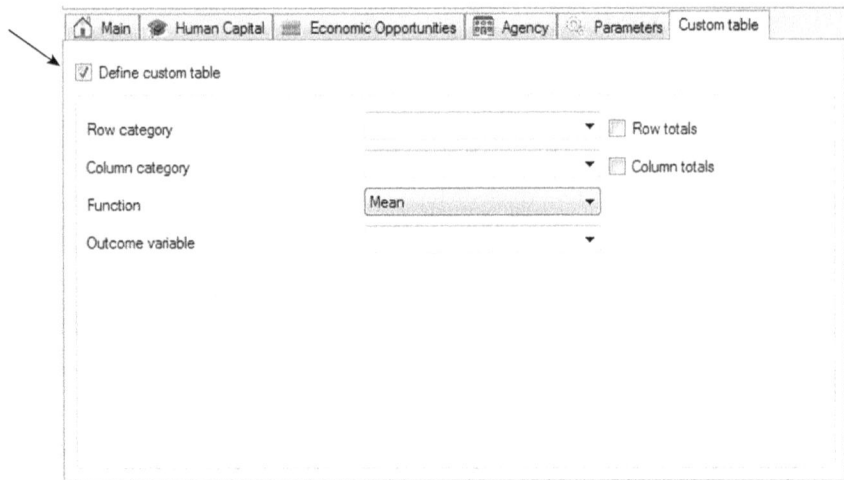

Design the table by selecting items in the drop-down lists and by activating the options as desired.

The **Custom table** tab in the lower-right corner of the ADePT main window displays a simple preview of your table design. This preview enables you to interactively modify the table to suit your needs.

In the outputs panel:

1. Scroll to the bottom of the list.
2. Select **Custom table**.

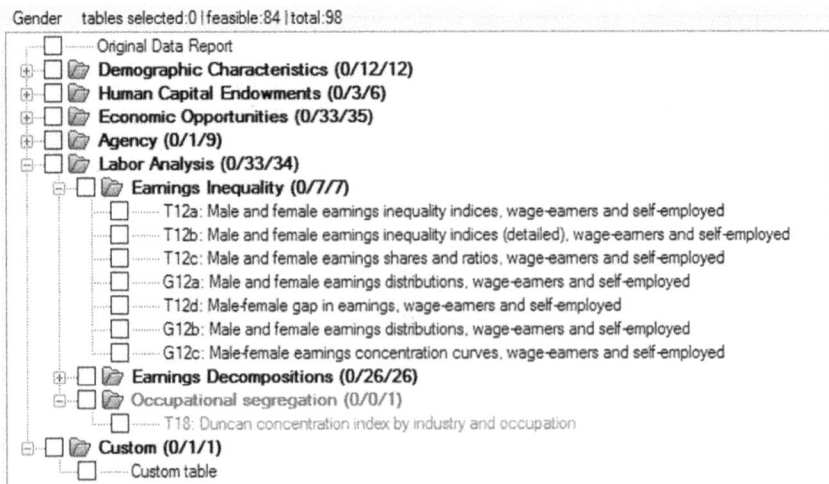

The custom table will be included in the report generated by ADePT.

Note

1. Stata files have to be Version 9 or later.

Chapter 3

Data Preparation

This chapter describes the data requirements for producing the complete set of tables and graphs available in ADePT Gender. ADePT Gender requires the user to prepare the data. Data preparation can be done using statistic or econometric packages, such as Stata or the Statistical Package for the Social Sciences (SPSS). ADePT Gender is also capable of creating variables, though its power to do so is limited compared with econometric packages. This chapter does not explain how to create variables; it only describes the data characteristics and the variable definitions to be uploaded in ADePT Gender.[1] It also briefly discusses methodological measurement issues of some of the key variables and provides key references for further reading.

ADePT Gender uses data of individuals or persons, which can be found in many household surveys, such as the Living Standards Measurement Surveys, Demographic and Health Surveys (DHS), Labor Force Surveys, and other multitopic surveys. Without data of individuals to identify their gender, ADePT Gender cannot produce any output. If the household survey collects the data in separate modules—and thus data files—with observations at the individual and household level, all data need to be combined into a single data file with observations at the individual level before uploading them to the ADePT Gender software. However, data files from different years or countries do not need to be merged and can be uploaded to ADePT one at a time.

The data fields to be completed in ADePT Gender software are of two types: (a) fields that describe the individual and the household and (b) fields that contain outcomes of interest. The first group includes the variables that define the relevant groups of the population the user is interested in analyzing, and they are filled in under the **Main** tab and the **Parameters** tab. The second group includes outcome variables that are filled in under three tabs: **Human Capital**, **Economic Opportunities**, and **Agency**. As the different fields are completed, ADePT works out which tables and graphs are feasible to produce.

The rest of the chapter describes each of the variables to be populated in ADePT Gender's fields. The book uses different typefaces to indicate a **field** or a **tab** name that is fixed in ADePT software and a *variable* name that is completed by the user. It is fundamental that the user understands the definition that ADePT Gender expects for each variable in order to correctly interpret the tables and graphs. The definition of the variable might require the user to manipulate data depending on the format of the raw survey data before loading it into ADePT Gender software. The complete list of field variables and definitions is also summarized in appendix A. In addition, ADePT Gender provides a short description of the input variable in the status bar (see screenshot 3.1).

Notice that ADePT Gender does not perform any data cleaning. However, the software provides information about the data in order to help the user identify potential problems. Thus, the user is responsible for evaluating the quality of the data and therefore the quality of the final output. ADePT Gender performs various internal and background checks on each of the variables filled in, but it does not eliminate observations. The user must perform this task outside ADePT Gender software, if necessary. It is recommended that the user eliminate all observations from the sample that have no positive sample weight and the observations with missing values for a few key variables, such as gender and age. It is also recommended that the user eliminates households with no identifiable household head from the sample. As a rule of thumb, the eliminated observations should be no more than 5 percent of the total sample covered by the survey. If the missing information affects a larger percentage of the sample, the user should find additional information to assess the validity of the data. For example, the user can conduct additional statistical analysis on the eliminated observations in order to determine the reliability of data and thus of the results. It is good practice to produce a log of these deletions.

Screenshot 3.1: Variable Definition Hint

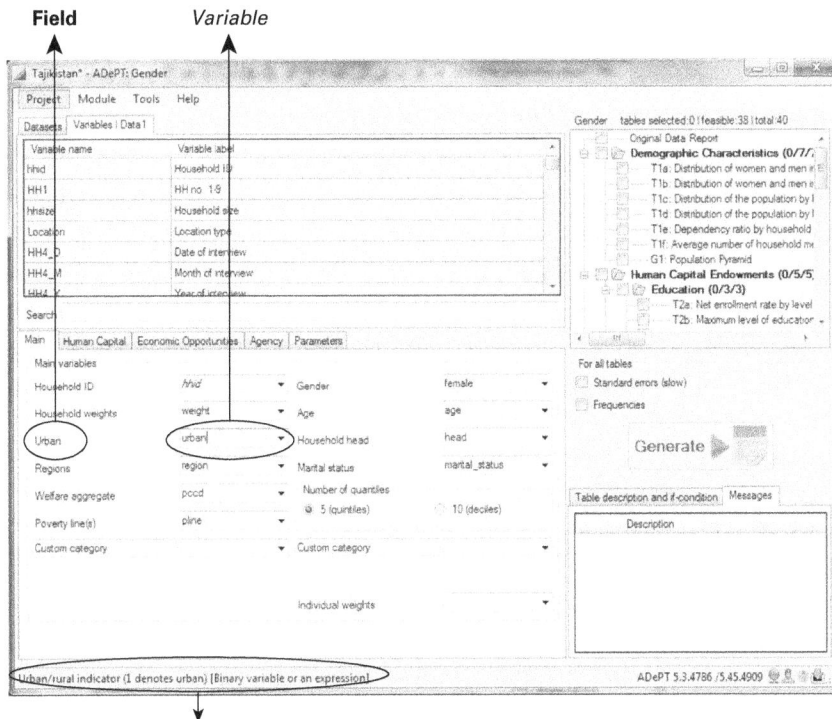

A description of the input variable is shown in the status bar.
The description appears as the cursor moves onto the **field**
name or when the scroll-down menu is opened.

Household Surveys

Different types of household surveys can be used in ADePT Gender. Survey
instruments are designed with a variety of main objectives. They thus cover
issues to varying extents and might be representative of different population
groups. For example, labor force surveys are fielded with the main objective
of measuring employment and unemployment rates; they have good coverage of employment variables and are usually representative of the working-
age population. Demographic and health surveys aim to measure outcomes
indicated by their name. They have poor coverage of labor market performance and often oversample women of reproductive age. These surveys are
collected by national statistics offices, either alone or with the support of

the Demographic and Health Survey Program.[2] An additional resource for understanding gender indicators is the International Household Survey Network (IHSN) study based on an analysis of the IHSN–World Bank Gender Data Navigator database on coverage of gender data and specific types of surveys (IHSN 2015).

However, most surveys serve many purposes, such as providing data to complete national accounts, providing weights for consumer price indexes, and so on. Many countries—in particular, those with the support of the World Bank—developed multitopic surveys such as the Living Standards Measurement Surveys, which was originally designed to monitor poverty and inequality but has evolved to collect a wide range of indicators. The number of tables and graphs that ADePT Gender generates depends on the variables populated and thus on the survey instrument. Table 3.1 shows the most common household survey instruments and their usual coverage of gender topics that allow populating ADePT Gender fields.

ADePT Gender's template cannot accommodate microdata surveys in which the sampling unit is not the household. For example, this is the case with Enterprise Surveys, which have firms as the unit of observation.[3] However, some of these surveys have employee modules where the unit of observation is the firm employee and that distinguish between male and female employees. Although ADePT Gender is not designed to work with

Table 3.1: Usual Topic Coverage of Survey Instruments

Topic and survey instrument	Demographic and health survey	Labor force survey	Multitopic survey[a]	Household budget survey
Endowments				
Education	***	*	**	*
Health and nutrition	***		*	
Maternal health	***			
Economic opportunities				
Labor market participation	*	***	**	*
Job characteristics		***		
Access to resources	*		**	*
Voice, agency, and participation				
Control over resources	**		*	
Freedom of movement	**			
Decision making over family formation	**		*	
Violence against women	**			
Voice and participation			*	

Note: The qualification of the coverage is relative; in other words, it was done comparing the average coverage of the other survey instruments and using as a reference the variables needed to populate ADePT Gender fields. *** = excellent coverage; ** = good coverage; * = weak coverage.
a. For example, Living Standards Measurement Surveys.

these data, some of the tables and graphs can be produced with them, as long as the variable definitions satisfy the requirements of ADePT Gender fields.

Main Variables

ADePT Gender uses data files with the observations at the individual level. Some of the variables vary by individual (such as a person's age) and others vary by household (such as place of residence or the welfare aggregate). Some of the variables require no data preparation and thus can be loaded directly into ADePT Gender (for example, age). Other variables demand very little manipulation and can be created in ADePT Gender (for example, employment). Finally, a few variables are complex, and it is recommended that the user construct them using econometric or statistic packages before loading the data into ADePT Gender software (for example, the welfare aggregate).

Next, we discuss each of the variables to be completed in ADePT Gender as well as some concepts behind these definitions.

Sample Weights

As opposed to census data, in which all the units of the universe are interviewed, surveys select a random sample of the population, and thus sample weights are necessary to make the estimates representative of the (country) population. Given that the data are loaded at the individual level—all persons in a household—ADePT Gender requires only household weights, which will automatically be used to produce weighted results representative of the country's population. The **Household weights** field should be completed with a continuous variable that indicates the estimated expansion factor of each household in the country population.

Household weights are needed because the sampling design does not necessarily select households with equal probability. If all households were selected with equal probability, all of them would have the same weight. However, because of cost and accuracy reasons, the probability of being selected likely differs across households (Deaton 1997). When selection probabilities differ, each household in the survey stands proxy for or represents a certain number of households in the population. Consequently, when the sample is used to calculate estimates of the population, it is necessary to weight the sample data. In other words, the weighted averages used "undo" the sample design to obtain estimates that match the population. The rule here is to weight according to the reciprocal of the sampling probabilities, because households with low or high probabilities of selection stand proxy for a large or small number of households in the population.

Surveys often include more than one type of weight. They might have individual weights (or person-specific weights) and household weights. If the survey comes from a stratified sample, the data can include strata weights. If the survey is longitudinal (that is, follows the same individual or household over time), the survey may have cross-sectional weights, longitudinal weights, or both. Each of these weights makes the observations representative of different populations. ADePT Gender assumes that the weights used for each observation are representative of the total population, and the explanations of how to interpret tables and graphs in chapters 4 and 6 refer to this case.[4] Box 3.1 describes the basics of sampling design to understand how probabilities of being selected in the survey might vary across households.

Box 3.1: Sampling Design

The typical household survey collects data from a national sample of households that are randomly selected from a national list. That list is called the *survey frame*. The frame is usually the national population census; however, some countries use administrative data. Often, the survey frame does not cover the total population. The term *coverage* refers to completeness of the survey frame compared with the total population. Certain groups of the population are likely to be excluded from the sampling frame, such as the homeless, members of the armed forces, seasonal migrants, people in jail, workers who live in factories, and college students.

Partial coverage of the survey frame will result in differences between actual and estimated statistics. However, this result is typical of household surveys and should not prevent the data from being used. Users simply need to bear in mind the population that the survey will represent, that is, the population that is covered by the frame.

In addition to noncoverage, users need to consider *nonresponse*: those households that either refuse to join the survey (unit nonresponse) or that do not answer specific modules or questions (item nonresponse). If nonresponse is associated with certain observable or nonobservable characteristics, users need to take that into account when making inferences from survey estimates. For example, women subject to domestic violence might be more likely not to participate in a survey simply because they do not want to open the door and be seen by strangers. In this case, the survey would underestimate the prevalence of domestic violence because of nonresponse or nonparticipation.

(continued)

Box 3.1: Sampling Design *(continued)*

The simplest household survey design would be one in which (a) a reliable, up-to-date list of all households in the population exists; (b) the design assigns an equal probability to each household selected from the list to participate in the survey; and (c) all households asked to participate actually do so. Under this design, each household has the same weight, since all of them represent the same number of households in the population. However, surveys tend to be more complex, as discussed by Deaton (1997). Most of the time, surveys rely on a two-stage sampling design. However, in any of these cases, we need to know only the weight of each household to generate statistics that represent the country.

To generate statistics that are valid for population subgroups, the sampling design needs to stratify the population. The most common design has two stages. In the first stage, *clusters*—groups of households determined by geographic location or another characteristic—are selected. In the second stage, households are selected within each cluster. This type of survey has many advantages with regard to costing and visits. Note that in two-stage sampling, we can still have households that have the same probability of being selected, if clusters are selected with a probability proportional to the number of households in each cluster.

Stratification converts a sample from one national population into a sample from many populations. Stratification guarantees enough observations to have estimates by group. For example, suppose we are interested in knowing the percentage of female-headed households in urban and rural areas. Without stratification, we would run two surveys, one for each population—urban and rural. However, with stratification, we might run a single survey in which the national values are obtained by a weighted average of the urban and rural populations, where the weights are the proportion of rural and urban households in the total population. The precision of this combined estimate is assessed (inversely) from its variance over replications of the survey. Because the two components of the survey are independent, the variance of the overall mean will be the sum of the estimates from each stratum. Hence, the variance depends only on the within-stratum component and not the between-strata component.

Although stratification typically enhances the precision of sampling estimates, the clustering of the sample will reduce it.

Source: Deaton 1997.

Household Information

Household

A household is a person or group of people who usually live and eat together. The standard definition of *household* is a group of people who live together, pool their money, and share at least one meal (UN 2008b).

However, more recent revisions of this definition have removed the condition of sharing a meal (UN 2008b).[5] Household members typically share a residential unit and have organized economic production and consumption. In many countries, sharing extends to inheritance and child rearing. Members might not be related. *Household* is not synonymous with *family*, which is a social institution that is characterized by common residence, economic cooperation, and reproduction.

This definition of household has four main exceptions. First, unrelated individuals may share a dwelling to minimize housing costs. Second, one house might have two families who use different rooms and do not share a budget. Third, servants might live in the same household and even share meals, but they have different budgets. Fourth, renters or pensioners may share meals with the owner of the house, but they also have different incomes. In all four cases, separate households should be considered even if all the people reside in the same dwelling and share meals.

The other main concern when identifying household members is to avoid counting one person twice when they reside in more than one dwelling. This situation might arise when households split, that is, when household members migrate (especially seasonally), or when members move to study somewhere else. As Beaman and Dillon (2012) show, using different definitions has consequences for measuring household welfare and production, which are variables that ADePT Gender uses to define groups for comparing gender outcomes.

ADePT Gender must specify a household identification variable, or a series of variables, that uniquely identifies the household in the dataset. They are filled in under **Household ID**. Numeric variables used for **Household ID** are expected to be integers; this is the only internal check performed by the software. ADePT Gender cannot produce any table if this variable (or set of variables) is not completed.

Place of Residence

Two fields are used to create groups to examine differences by place of residence. The field **urban** needs to be completed with a variable that takes a value of 1 when the household resides in an urban area. The field **region** needs to be completed with a categorical variable that codes the household's region of residence. This variable can be defined following the political division of the country or any other relevant division the user considers of interest, such as ethnographic division, level of development, climate, and so on. ADePT Gender checks that the variables have the numerical properties expected.

Welfare Aggregate

ADePT Gender analyzes the differences in outcomes across population groups that have different standards of living. Two fields are used to describe a household's welfare. The first requires a continuous variable that measures household well-being. This variable is completed in the **Welfare aggregate** field and is used to construct quintiles or deciles of the population, according to the option selected in the **Number of quantiles** field. The second uses a poverty line to divide the population between poor and nonpoor. The **Poverty line** field requires a number that is the minimum amount—according to the welfare indicator—that an individual needs to be out of poverty.[6] Both variables (the ones that populate the **Welfare aggregate** and the **Poverty line** fields) should be expressed in the same unit of measure. For example, if the value of the poverty line variable is per capita, then the welfare aggregate variable should also be per capita; if the value of the poverty line variable is per adult equivalent, then the one corresponding to the welfare aggregate should also be per adult equivalent.

Most commonly, there are three direct measures of household well-being: income, consumption, and expenditures. *Income* refers to the earnings of all household members from productive activities, plus the sum of all current transfers. The earnings from productive activities include wages and salaries, sales of home-produced goods (including farming), and rents from land and assets. *Consumption* is the sum of the value of food and nonfood items consumed by the household. Consumption is usually retrieved from consumption recall modules or consumption diaries. Price indexes are often used to adjust for spatial and temporal differences in cost of living. *Expenditure* is the sum of all household expenses, both food and nonfood items. It is similar to consumption, but it has some conceptual differences. First, using expenditures excludes the consumption of items that were not part of a market transaction (for example, own-produced agricultural goods). This difference can be large in those countries with high levels of home production. Second, expenditures record a transaction and thus are subject to measurement error if the time of transaction differs from the time of consumption. This problem arises mostly with durables, which are bought in one period but consumed over several periods.

Income and consumption measures differ, since consumption can also come from borrowing (or past savings), and income can be used to accumulate savings. In addition, each of these variables has its own measurement problems. For income, it is difficult to accurately measure all possible sources of income, especially in countries with high levels of informality, either in wage employment or in self-employment.[7]

When direct measurements of welfare are unavailable, the user can construct a welfare index using proxy variables. Welfare indexes can be constructed in different ways. One way is to use principal components analysis to construct a "wealth" index using information on asset and land-ownership as well as household characteristics.[8] However, the user must bear in mind that mechanic correlations can be generated between the outcomes of interest and these composite indexes of welfare, if the same variables are used as outcomes and as inputs into the composite index. Other less frequently used measures include direct reports of household well-being.[9]

Individual Information

Gender, Age, and Marital Status

The word *gender* is a social construct that includes male, female, transgender, and third gender, and the word *sex* refers to biological and anatomical differences between male and female. ADePT Gender software, however, does not include transgender and does not differentiate between the terms *sex* and *gender*, even using them interchangeably. The reason for these omissions is simply the limitations in the survey data: the datasets used in ADePT do not code these characteristics, and the objective of the software is to analyze surveys from the highest number of countries possible (screenshot 3.2).

The **Gender** field needs to be completed with an indicator variable that identifies male or female and takes a value of 1 for males. ADePT Gender performs background checks to ensure that each individual's gender is identified by the variable filled in, and that the variable takes only two values.

The **Age** field expects a continuous integer variable that indicates the age of each household member. This variable is used to construct age groups

Screenshot 3.2: Fields in Main Tab

Household characteristics fields   Individual characteristics fields

relevant for the analysis. By default, ADePT Gender software constructs broad categories that reflect the stages of life that matter for the gender analysis: youth (15–24), adult reproductive age (25–49), adulthood (50–64), and elderly (65 years of age and older). However, ADePT Gender is capable of setting finer or different age groups if desired by the user.

Another concern is that in some very poor contexts, respondents might not know their own age or, if there is only one respondent, the age of other household members. To avoid this problem, many surveys also collect information about date of birth, as it may be easier for some elderly respondents to remember their date of birth rather than their age. Data preparation might require calculating the age using date of birth instead of respondent values. In these cases, it is recommended that users perform basic tabulations to see whether any spikes occur in age responses (usually in round numbers like 20, 30, and 40), since these are not part of ADePT Gender internal checks. ADePT Gender verifies that the populated variable is a continuous positive integer between 0 and 99.

The **Marital status** field expects a variable that indicates whether or not household members are in a marital union, and if not, the main cause of its dissolution. Users can define the categories of this variable according to their country context and survey options. For example, polygyny is still common. However, if the prevalence of a certain marital status is low or not relevant for the study, users might decide to consider only one large group referred to as "under a marital union." ADePT Gender tests only for whether the populated variable is categorical.[10]

Household Head

Head of household is a complex concept. The head of household is supposed to be the person that the other members of the household acknowledge as head. The head has primary authority and responsibility for household affairs. However, in cases where such authority and responsibility are not vested in one person, special rules may be needed to identify the head of household.[11] In some surveys, the interviewer asks respondents to identify the head of household. In other countries, like the United States, it depends on how the household files taxes. In other surveys, head of household does not denote any particular role and is the code that the interviewer gives the oldest male of working age or the member responding to the questionnaire.

As with the definition of household, the definition of its head has consequences for measuring outcomes. For example, Fuwa (2000) examines how poverty incidence for female-headed households varies for different definitions of female-headed households in Panama. In particular, he compares de jure female-headed households—where women declared themselves as the head—with de facto female-headed households—where the woman is working, and the present male spouse is not; or where the woman is present in the household, and the husband is away for work. Fuwa finds that the poverty incidence varies across these definitions, even when compared with households of similar composition.

The **Household head** field expects a binary variable that takes a value of 1 for the individual that is identified as the head of household. ADePT Gender checks that one of the variable's two values is 1, that only one household member is coded as head, and that the household head is at least 15 years old.

Custom Category

ADePT Gender allows the user to add custom variables that can be used to further tabulate the results. A custom variable can provide a household characteristic (that is, with a common value for all the individuals in the household) or an individual one. Examples of the former could be whether the household head is absent part of the year because of seasonal work outside the city,[12] whether pensioners are in the household,[13] or whether a household member receives cash transfers.[14] Examples of individual variables include race or ethnicity.[15] Another significant household characteristic to include may be households with individuals who have disabilities, who likely require additional time and resources for their care.

If a custom individual field is completed, additional rows will be added in the tables where the outcomes are presented by individual characteristics, such as ADePT tables 1a and 1c. If a custom household field is completed, additional rows will be added in the tables where the outcomes are presented by household characteristics, such as ADePT tables 1b and 1d.

Outcome Variables

Variables that reflect outcomes are grouped into three categories following the three main dimensions proposed by the *World Development Report*—human capital (or endowments) (screenshot 3.3), economic opportunities, and agency. We discuss each concept in turn.

Human Capital

Education

ADePT Gender examines gaps in access to education for boys and girls—measured by school enrollment or attendance—and gender gaps in education attainment for the adult population. Both access to and completed education outcomes require binary variables by level of education—primary, secondary, and postsecondary. For adults (or those who have completed their education), ADePT Gender also offers the option to assess gaps in literacy. Literacy is the "ability to identify, understand, interpret, create, communicate and compute, using printed and written materials associated with varying contexts" (UNESCO 2006).[16] Most surveys identify literacy levels through specific questions that assess whether respondents know how to read and write.[17] For finer gender gaps in completed education, ADePT Gender also allows the user to input years of education.

Screenshot 3.3: Fields in the Human Capital Tab

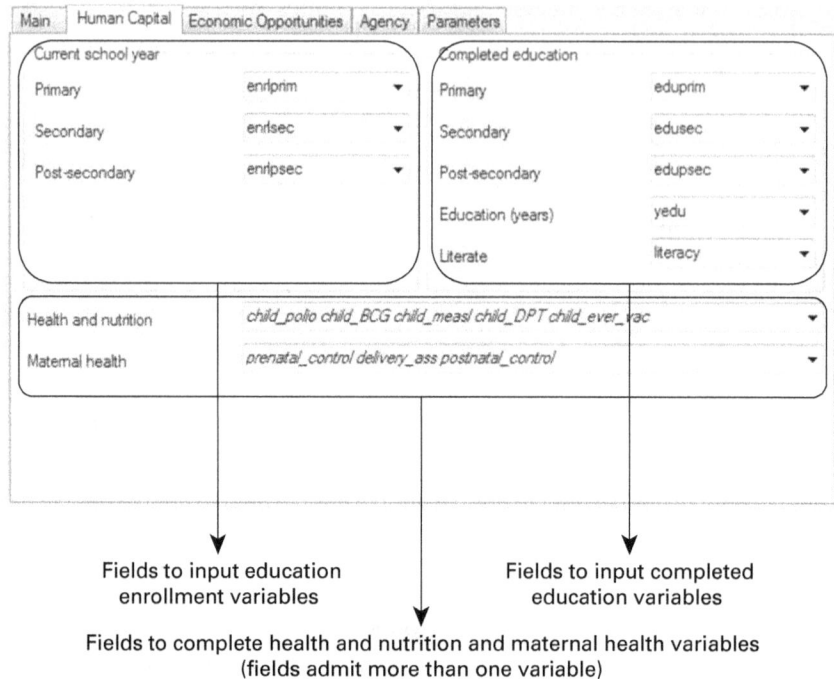

Fields to input education
enrollment variables

Fields to input completed
education variables

Fields to complete health and nutrition and maternal health variables
(fields admit more than one variable)

Levels of education are classified by the International Standard Classification of Education (ISCED), adopted by the General Conference of the United Nations Educational, Scientific, and Cultural Organization.[18] Primary education (ISCED 1), sometimes called elementary education, refers to programs normally designed to give students a sound basic education in reading, writing, and mathematics, along with an elementary understanding of other subjects, such as history, geography, natural science, social science, art, and music. Religious instruction may also be featured. Secondary education refers to programs of lower (ISCED 2) and upper (ISCED 3) secondary education. Lower secondary education continues the basic programs of the primary level, but the teaching is typically more subject focused, requiring more specialized teachers for each subject area. In upper secondary education, instruction is often organized along more in-depth subject lines, and teachers typically need an advanced degree or more subject-specific qualification.

One caveat when looking at the variables on current education is that although school enrollment and school attendance are both used to ascertain school participation, they are two different issues. Household surveys usually collect data on household members' school attendance, whereas administrative data—generated from school records—yield information on school enrollment. A child may be enrolled in school but not be attending at the time of the interview. As a result, school enrollment data tend to overstate the effective student population. School attendance at the time of the interview is a more reliable indicator of the proportion of students actually attending school.[19]

Tertiary education refers to a wide range of programs with more advanced educational content. The first stage of tertiary education (ISCED 5) refers to theoretically based programs intended to qualify a student to enter (a) an advanced research program that is practical, technical, or occupation specific; or (b) a profession with high skill requirements. The second stage of tertiary education (ISCED 6) refers to programs devoted to advanced study and original research.

Postsecondary nontertiary education (ISCED 4) refers to programs that, regarding their content, cannot be considered tertiary from an international point of view. These programs might be considered postsecondary in a national context, but they are not significantly more advanced than programs classified as ISCED 3, a level that should be completed before being enrolled in ISCED 4. Some countries do not have ISCED 4 programs. We recommend caution when uploading the human capital variables by checking the country ISCED mapping (see box 3.2 for an example from Panama).[20] The ADePT user has the option to pool the levels corresponding to ISCED 4, 5, and 6 into one variable and upload it in the **Postsecondary** field or to reserve this category for tertiary education only, if it makes more sense in the country context.

All the fields in ADePT Gender that are related to the current level of school enrollment expect binary variables that take a value of 1 if the individual is enrolled in that level.[21] The same arguments apply to the fields related to completed education, and the variables take a value of 1 to indicate the highest level achieved. For example, if a person has started but not completed college, he or she will have a value of 1 for the variable indicating the secondary level of education. ADePT Gender performs internal checks of these variables, so that no person is coded with two different levels of education.

Box 3.2: Mapping Panama's Education System to the International Standard Classification of Education

Panama's education system is divided into five levels: preschool, basic, presecondary, secondary, and superior. The first four levels correspond to International Standard Classification of Education (ISCED) levels 0, 1, 2, and 3, respectively, and the superior levels exist in several programs that can be classified as ISCED 4, 5, or 6.

The secondary level can be accomplished in two ways: the first and most common is called academic secondary education, and the second is called technical and professional education. The two options have the same duration and prerequisites and correspond to ISCED 3 programs. However, it is a common mistake to classify technical and professional education as ISCED 4 or 5 since, in the national surveys, it is presented as a separate level, and its name could be easily confused with an ISCED 5 program.

Like Panama, several other countries have domestic labels of education that might be misleading, even for national practitioners. For this reason, we recommend checking the *country ISCED mapping* variable before classifying the specific country levels at the data preparation stage.

Source: Panama 1997.

Nutrition and Health

Data on nutrition and health that are disaggregated by gender are not widely available from household surveys. Thus, ADePT Gender has been designed to let users accommodate the existing data. As opposed to other outcomes for which ADePT Gender requires specific variables, users can fill in the fields with outcomes of their choice and have the option to have outcomes for boys and girls, men and women, and women of reproductive age. The section that follows provides examples of variables that can be used as outcomes.

Users can fill in as many variables as they want in the **Health and nutrition** field, as long as they are available for both sexes. These variables can refer to outcomes relevant for children, such as being inoculated with BCG (Bacillus Calmette–Guérin vaccine against tuberculosis), DPT (diphtheria, pertussis, and tetanus), MMR (measles, mumps, and rubella), or all three. Alternatively, the variables can be anthropometric outcomes, such as age for height, weight for height, and age for weight. The field can also be populated with variables that describe adults' health, such as human immunodeficiency virus (HIV) and alcohol consumption.

Instead, the **Maternal health** field expects variables that pertain only to women's reproductive health. Thus, ADePT Gender will compute the statistics only for women of reproductive age—15 to 49 years old. Examples of outcomes of interest related to maternal health are whether a woman received assistance when delivering a child, prenatal care, and postnatal care. Prenatal care and postnatal care include the services that health care providers give to a pregnant woman before and just after the birth of her infant, respectively. Delivery assistance is usually provided by a skilled birth attendant. Ensuring quality maternity care can save the lives of women and newborns. These services require an accredited health professional—such as a midwife, doctor, or nurse—who is proficient in the skills needed to manage normal (uncomplicated) pregnancies, childbirth, and the immediate postnatal period. Such professionals are also trained to identify and manage complications in women and newborns and to refer them to specialists.

Other important health and maternal health outcomes are more difficult to assess using household survey data. The most important are life expectancy at birth, infant mortality (by gender), and maternal mortality. These outcomes are usually constructed using information from vital statistics records. However, Demographic and Health Surveys collect information to calculate a few of them. Maternal mortality is the death of a woman while pregnant or within 42 days of terminating a pregnancy—irrespective of the duration of the pregnancy—from any cause related to or aggravated by the pregnancy or its management, excluding accidental or incidental causes. To facilitate the identification of maternal deaths in circumstances in which cause of death attribution is inadequate, a new category has been introduced: pregnancy-related death.[22]

For the variables populated in **Health and nutrition** and in **Maternal health**, ADePT Gender checks only nonmissing values for the relevant populations; that is, it checks the variables that are available for men and women for the former field and that are available only for women ages 15–49 in the latter.

Economic Opportunities

Labor Status

The analysis of economic opportunity is limited to the *working-age population*. The minimum age range for defining the working-age population needs to be specified by the user according to national circumstances, such as the minimum age for admission to employment and the extent of child labor. These circumstances vary so greatly among countries that it is impossible to specify any universally applicable minimum age limit at the international level. By default, ADePT Gender assumes that the working-age population is between 15 and 64 years of age. The user can define the limits through the **Parameters** tab (see below). Tables for outcomes on economic opportunities will be computed only for the working-age population.

According to the International Labour Organization (ILO) 1982 guidelines, which most national statistical agencies continue to use as a reference to date, individuals are *employed* if they worked for at least one hour during the previous seven days (a) for a wage, (b) in a household enterprise or on a farm, or (c) as an unpaid apprentice or trainee. The definition also includes all persons who had a job or enterprise during that period but were temporarily absent from it—persons who during the reference period were sick, on vacation, on maternity leave, on strike, or temporarily laid off (Hussmanns 2007; ILO 1982). However, the International Conference on Labour Statisticians' 2013 change in the definition of employment will also affect employment modules going forward by classifying employment as work for pay. That change may affect comparability of estimates over time.

Measuring employment in developing countries, in particular for women, is especially difficult when many income-generating activities are performed outside of markets. Respondents may not think of such activities as "work" or "employment." To help respondents understand the concept of work, employment modules usually include a series of questions that ask about different kinds of work (work on own farm, nonfarm household enterprise, and wage employment), as well as reasons for temporary absences from a job. It is recommended that such questions come with examples to help respondents understand the range of activities to which the interviewer is referring (Anderson Scheffner 2000). In addition, the user should be aware of who the respondent of the labor module is, since it has been found that responses depend on how and to whom questions are asked (Bardasi and others 2011).

A person of working age is *unemployed* if during the period of reference—usually one week—he or she was not employed, was available for work, and was actively seeking work,[23] which is understood as taking concrete actions in a specified recent period to seek employment. The period of reference for seeking employment does not have to coincide with the reference period of employment. The ILO abstains from making recommendations about the length of the reference period, or whether the reference periods used for employment and unemployment have to coincide. Some countries might prefer to have longer reference periods (one month or four weeks) based on the idea that lags in the process of obtaining a job can exceed the reference period for employment (Hussmanns 2007).

The other condition that requires clarification is being available for work. Availability for work means that, if given a work opportunity, a person is able and ready to take the job and start working. The idea behind this condition is to eliminate people like students, who might be looking for a job at a later date—for example, after graduation. The condition also excludes those who cannot accept work because of certain impediments, such as family responsibilities, illness, or other commitments. The ILO makes no recommendations regarding the time reference for this condition either, and it does not have to coincide with any of the previous reference periods.

A related concept is *underemployment*, which refers to a less extreme situation of partial lack of work. Underemployment captures the idea that a person is willing to work more hours, referred to as time-related underemployment. Two concepts are measured by underemployment: the number of persons in time-related underemployment and the intensity of underemployment. A person is considered underemployed if he or she (a) is willing to work additional hours, (b) is available to work more hours, and (c) is not working more than a certain number of hours (or days) during the reference period—in order to avoid extra hours or any other unusual circumstances. The intensity of underemployment refers to the gap in hours (or days) of work and the threshold fixed as normal hours of work.[24]

If a person of working age is neither employed nor unemployed, he or she is said to be *out of the labor force*. Thus, every person of working age in the sample has to be employed, unemployed, or out of the labor force.

In some cases, the labor status variable is already coded by the national statistics office. However, there are other cases in which the user needs to code these variables before loading the data into ADePT Gender software. ADePT Gender requires the user to complete the **Employed** and **Unemployed** fields and assumes that all persons of working age that are neither employed nor unemployed are out of the labor force. ADePT Gender does not explicitly include a space for underemployed. Users interested in this type of employment should work with the ADePT Labor module.

Even if the definitions above can be found in most household surveys, the user should be aware that the ILO changed the official definition of employment in 2013 (ILO 2013). The transition toward this new definition will take time, as it first has to be tested in several countries before it is applied worldwide. Box 3.3 describes it in more detail. It should be noted that even though the definition of employment has changed, the ADePT Gender software can still be used to assess labor status in line with the new definitions, as long as the *employment* variable is defined according to the new standards.

Box 3.3: Revised ILO Statistical Standards for Measuring Employment and Work

In October 2013, the 19th International Conference of Labour Statisticians (ICLS)—which makes recommendations on selected topics of labor statistics to the governing body of the International Labour Organization (ILO)—adopted the resolution concerning statistics of work, employment, and labor underuse (hereafter referred to as the new ICLS standards). The resolution revises previous international statistical standards and guidelines for labor market statistics.

An important element of the new ICLS standards is to narrow the definition of *employment* to work performed for pay or profit. Unlike in the previous definition, the production of goods for one's own consumption (particularly subsistence agriculture) is now excluded from the employment category (see table B3.3.1 for a schematic overview). In addition, the 2013 resolution introduces a new category of *work*, which recognizes all productive activities—paid and unpaid—and proposes several measures of labor underuse.

Once fully implemented, the new ICLS standards are expected to have significant implications for the measurement of employment and labor force participation at the aggregate level, but especially for the large share of the population in developing countries who are engaged in subsistence activities, especially women and the rural poor.

- Under the revised definition of *employment*, farmers who produce only for subsistence purposes are no longer counted as employed and are considered to be out of the labor force. Given the large number of workers—especially women—involved in these activities in low-income countries, the revised standards are likely to result in significantly lower estimates of employment and labor force participation.

- Services produced for own final use (such as childcare and eldercare, food preparation, and other household chores), which are often performed by women and were not captured by the previous employment definition, are now recognized as *work* under the category own-use production. Full and separate measurement of women's participation in these unpaid activities allows a more comprehensive assessment of their overall workload.

It is important to note that the new definition of *employment* is narrower and the new definition of *work* broader than that of the 2008 System of National Accounts (SNA) frontier, as the latter includes own-produced goods but not own-produced services (see table B3.3.1). Hence, attention must be taken when comparing employment statistics to National Accounts production estimates.

(continued)

Box 3.3: Revised ILO Statistical Standards for Measuring Employment and Work (continued)

Table B3.3.1: Comparison of New and Previous Definitions

	Productive activities						Nonproductive activities[a]
	Market units		Nonmarket units (government, nonprofit)		Households (producing for own final use)		
	Goods	Services	Goods	Services	Goods	Services	
Previous activity scope for "employment"							
New activity scope for "employment"							
New concept of "work" = productive activities							
Activities in the SNA production boundary							
Activities in the SNA general production boundary							

Source: Diez de Medina and Benes 2014.
Note: SNA = System of National Accounts.
a. For example, sleeping, learning, own creation, begging, stealing.

Work Characteristics

The measures of labor force participation are as important as the characteristics of the work. Women might be as likely as men to engage in economic activities, especially in very poor countries, but their economic opportunities are very different. The disparities in economic opportunity can be analyzed only by looking at the type of work they do in more depth. The **Work category** field can be completed by a categorical variable that can take several values, depending on the country context. At a minimum, it should differentiate between wage work and self-employment, but it can also accommodate other work classifications, such as unpaid or family work.

Self-employed refers to working for oneself. Self-employed people work for themselves instead of an employer, drawing income from a trade or business that they operate. To be self-employed is not necessarily the same as being a business owner; many self-employed people conduct the day-to-day operations of the business as managers, as line workers, or as both. A business owner may or may not work in the business and is not required do so. Self-employed persons without workers are known as *own-account workers*. Self-employed persons who employ family members are known as *household enterprises*.

Wage workers or *paid employees* are those who hold jobs in which the basic remuneration is not directly dependent on the revenue of the employer.

Paid employees include regular employees, workers in short-term employment, casual workers, outworkers, seasonal workers, and other categories of workers who hold paid jobs. Paid employees are not own-account workers, contributing family workers, members of worker cooperatives, or workers unclassifiable by status (ILO 2012).

A finer category, called the International Classification of Status in Employment, uses a scale according to the type of contract the person has with other people or organizations when performing a particular job. The type of contract is determined by the type of economic risks and authority that are involved when doing the job. The International Classification of Status in Employment consists of the following groups:

- *Employees*, who receive basic remuneration not directly dependent on the revenue of the employer—among whom countries may need and be able to distinguish "employees with stable contracts" (including "regular employees");
- *Employers*, who are self-employed—that is, whose remuneration depends directly on the (expectation of) profits derived from the goods and services produced—and who engage one or more person to work for them as "employees" on a continuous basis;
- *Own-account workers*, who are self-employed and do not engage "employees" on a continuous basis;
- *Members of producer cooperatives*, who are self-employed in a cooperative producing goods and services, where the members participate equally in making major decisions concerning the cooperative;
- *Contributing family workers*, who hold jobs in an establishment operated by a relative, whose degree of involvement in its operation is too limited to be considered a partner; and
- *Workers not classifiable by status*, for whom insufficient relevant information is available, or who cannot be included in any of the preceding categories.

The ILO monitors *employment vulnerability* and the corresponding gender gap, in which vulnerable employment comprises own-account workers and contributing family workers. ADePT Gender allows the user interested in exploiting this differentiation to input the categorical variable that best reflects the country context and needs. However, users should be aware that the differentiation between these two categories is subject to measurement errors, since the distinction between own-account and family workers can be unclear.

Informality

The term *informality* means different things to different people, but its connotation as a type of work is almost universally negative. It refers to unprotected workers, inadequate regulation, low productivity, unfair competition, evasion of the law, underpayment or nonpayment of taxes, and working "underground" or in the shadows (Perry and others 2007). Informality can refer to the worker as well as the firm, if both workers and firms do not integrate (or at least not fully) the state's role as regulator and public service provider in their economic activities. There are three main types of informality: (a) firms that can be formal or informal; (b) firms that can be partly formal and partly informal; and (c) workers, who can be formal and informal in the way in which they operate in the labor market. These margins are not exhaustive and are related to each other, but they cover much of the discussion (Perry and others 2007).

Thus, the final definition of *informality* depends on two aspects or margins. The *intrafirm margin* refers to firms that are partially informal across several dimensions—because (a) they underreport sales, (b) they are partially compliant with all registration requirements (firms might be registered at the municipal level but not at the national level), (c) they underreport wages (wages are partly paid on the books and partly off the books), or (d) they are partially compliant with labor regulations (firms can have just a part of their workforce compliant with labor regulations). The *intersectoral margin* of firms is the threshold that divides formal firms from informal ones and relates to whether workers are covered by labor legislations. A formal firm can be regarded as one that complies with all the labor, business, and tax regulations. However, such legislation often does not reach or cover microfirms, which are then by definition considered informal. Many times, people consider informal workers as those who are not covered by labor legislation, including those in microfirms.

The ILO defines informal employment as (a) own-account workers and employers working in their own informal sector; (b) enterprises with at least some market production that are unregistered or small in the number of persons employed (for example, fewer than five employees); (c) all contributing family workers; (d) employees who hold informal jobs, that is, employees not covered by legal protection or social security or unentitled to other employment benefits, such as paid annual or sick leave; (e) members of informal producer cooperatives (not established as legal entities); and (f) own-account workers who produce goods exclusively for final use by their household (if considered employed). Table 3.2 provides a schematic framework of the definition.

However, in practice, data limitations shape the definition of informality. Not all labor force surveys collect information about the status of the firm or employer, and employees do not necessarily know whether the firm they work for complies with all the regulations. Thus, many times, countries and policy makers define formality according to whether a firm or employer has any of the following nonexclusive criteria: (a) offers permanent as opposed to temporary contracts, (b) offers written as opposed to oral contracts, (c) provides pension coverage, or (d) provides health coverage. Other benefits of formal jobs—such as vacations or maternity or sick leave—are seldom incorporated in the analysis. The user thus needs to assess the quality of the variable that can be constructed using the available information.

ADePT Gender expects the user to fill in the **Formal status** field with a binary variable (or expression) that takes a value of 1 if the worker is formal. The only background check performed by the software consists of assessing whether one of the two values of the variable is equal to 1.

Table 3.2: ILO Conceptual Framework: Informal Employment

Production by type	Job by status in employment								
	Own-account workers		Employers		Contributing family workers	Employees		Members of producer cooperatives	
	Informal	Formal	Informal	Formal	Informal	Informal	Formal	Informal	Formal
Formal sector enterprises					1	2			
Informal sector enterprises[a]	3		4		5	6	7	8	
Households[b]	9					10			

Source: Hussmanns 2004.
Note: Cells shaded in dark gray refer to jobs that by definition do not exist in the type of production unit in question. Cells shaded in light gray refer to formal jobs. Unshaded cells represent the various types of informal jobs. Informal employment: cells 1–6 and 8–10. Employment in the informal sector: cells 3–8. Informal employment outside the formal sector: cells 1, 2, 9, and 10. ILO = International Labour Organization.
a. As defined by the 15th International Conference of Labour Statisticians 1993 (excluding households that employ paid domestic workers).
b. Households that produce goods exclusively for their own use and households that employ paid domestic workers.

Sector of Employment and Occupation

Knowing the sector of the economy and the occupations in which men and women are employed is as important as knowing if they are employed, unemployed, or out of the labor force.

Sector refers to the type of economic activity in which workers are involved. It refers to the main activity of the firm, enterprise, or establishment as opposed to the main activity of the worker, which is the *occupation*. Sectoral classification is usually collected in the data using detailed industry classifications. The ILO recommendation is to follow the International Standard Industrial Classification (ISIC) for all economic activities.[25] The scope of ISIC covers all (or almost all) productive activities—that is, economic activities within the production boundary of the System of National Accounts (EC and others 2008). These economic activities are subdivided into a hierarchical, four-level structure of mutually exclusive categories, which facilitates data collection, presentation, and analysis at detailed levels of the economy in an internationally comparable, standardized way. The categories at the highest level are called *sections*, which are alphabetically coded categories intended to facilitate economic analysis. The sections subdivide the entire spectrum of productive activities into broad groupings, such as agriculture, forestry, and fishing (section A); manufacturing (section C); and information and communication (section J). The classification is then organized into successively more detailed categories, which are numerically coded: two-digit divisions, three-digit groups, and, at the greatest level of detail, four-digit classes.[26]

ADePT Gender works with three fields that capture different levels of detail, with different purposes. The **Broad sector** field should be completed with a categorical variable that differentiates agriculture, industry, and services.[27] The **Sector** field should be completed with a categorical variable that offers more detail on the activity—for example, the one-digit ISIC. Finally, the **Detailed sector** field should be completed with a detailed sector classification, such as the four-digit ISIC, and is used to compute industry segregation indexes. The **Agriculture** field expects a bivariate variable to denote employment in the agriculture sector. This variable can include farmwork but also off-farm work in agriculture—for example, everything captured under ISIC section A according to the fourth ISIC revision (UN 2008a). *Industry* is commonly defined as ISIC sections B to F; thus, it includes mining, manufacturing, utilities, and construction. The *services* category includes all other ISIC sections (for example, ISIC sections G–U).

Similar to the industry classification, there is an *occupation* classification. The most widely used classification is the International Standard Classification of Occupations (ISCO) produced by the ILO.[28] ISCO is a tool for organizing jobs into a clearly defined set of groups according to the job's tasks and duties. Its main aim is threefold: (a) to provide a basis for international reporting, comparison, and exchange of statistical and administrative data about occupations; (b) to provide a model for the development of national and regional classifications of occupations; and (c) to establish a system that can be used directly in countries that have not developed their own national classifications. As opposed to sector, ADePT Gender has only one field to complete with occupation. The field **Occupation** requires a categorical variable like the one-digit ISCO.

ADePT Gender expects categorical variables for the **Broad sector**, **Sector**, **Detailed sector**, and **Occupation** fields. ADePT Gender performs no background checks except for the variable input into the **Broad sector** field, for which ADePT Gender ensures that it only takes three values.

Work Intensity

Work intensity is measured in two ways: (a) by differentiating full-time and part-time jobs and (b) by looking directly at the number of hours worked. Both variables have complexities that are worth discussing.

Many household surveys include a question about the full-time or part-time status of respondents' employment. The ILO Part-Time Work Convention (1994, no. 175) defines a part-time worker as an employed person whose normal hours of work are fewer than those of comparable full-time workers (ILO 2004). Part-time work can be identified through a question or through the number of hours worked. Asking a direct question has advantages and disadvantages. On the one hand, it reflects the job requirements with regard to time, which might be different from the number of hours worked. On the other hand, a self-assessment is subject to biases, since workers might be unaware of how many hours constitute a full-time job in their country. For example, the threshold between part-time and full-time work is 30 hours per week in Canada, Finland, and New Zealand; 35 hours in Australia, Japan, and the United States; and 37 hours in Norway (Messenger 2004).

Another measure of work intensity is the *hours of work* per week (or equivalent period of reference) that are spent on activities that contribute to the production of goods and services. The *normal* hours of work are those that workers are expected to spend on work activities during a short reference period, such as one day or one week, as stipulated in laws, regulations, collective agreements, arbitral awards, or establishments' rules or customs. The *usual* hours of work are the average hours worked during a reference period, like the past calendar year. The hours *actually* worked are the hours spent on work activities during a specified reference period, such as the past week. These are presented as a list of elements of a day of work or work components and include (a) productive time (hours actually worked during normal periods of work and any additional time worked that is generally paid at a higher rate than normal rates, such as overtime); (b) time spent on ancillary activities (time spent at the workplace on such tasks as repairs and maintenance, preparation and cleaning of tools, and preparation of receipts, time sheets, and reports); (c) unproductive time spent in the course of the production process (time spent at the place of work waiting or standing by for such reasons as lack of workload, breakdown of machinery, accidents, or time spent at the place of business during which no work is done but for which payment is made under a guaranteed employment contract); and (d) resting time (time corresponding to short rest periods at the workplace, including tea and coffee breaks). The definition explicitly excludes paid time not worked, such as paid annual leave, paid public holidays, paid sick leave, meal breaks, and time spent on travel from home to work and vice versa.

Surveys typically ask either the usual number or the actual number of work hours. Actual hours are preferred if the user is interested in exploring how the number of work hours varies over the year, for example, to study seasonality. Usual hours, in contrast, are less influenced by short-term fluctuations. If the interviewer asks for the number of hours of work for each separate job, the users should sum the hours of work from all jobs.

Another variable that can be used to indicate work intensity is the *number of weeks worked* during a period of reference (such as the past calendar year or past 12 months). As with the number of hours, the phrasing of the question can refer to the normal, the usual, or the actual weeks worked in a reference period. This question can be important if women are more likely than men to have temporary jobs or to hold jobs that have long out-of-work periods (such as teachers and farmers).

ADePT Gender analyzes the full-time or part-time labor status and the number of hours worked, which are to be completed in the **Full time** and **Hours** fields, respectively. The **Full time** field can be filled in with the minimum number of hours required to be considered a full-time worker. A related issue that ADePT Gender does not explicitly include—though it can be analyzed through the use of custom variables or tables—is scheduling. This aspect can be critical for gender analysis, since women's household responsibilities might constrain their access to jobs that require night shifts or unusual work hours.

Scheduling work hours relates to the periods of the day, week, or month when work is done, such as in the morning, afternoon, or evening; from Monday to Friday; on weekends; as overtime; and so on. Scheduling work hours can be combined with the hours of work and information on their fixed or variable nature to derive a vast number of different working time arrangements. These relate to schedules that are different from regular full-time working schedules—that is, where workers are required by their employer or choose to work (a) less or more than full time, (b) only part of the year, (c) only part of the week, (d) at night, and (e) on weekends, in addition to starting or ending at different times and having variable daily or weekly schedules as part of flexible schedules or as part of "annualized" working schemes, which fix working time over a long period of one year, allowing weekly schedules to vary.

Labor Income

Several concepts related to labor income need to be differentiated (Ehrenberg and Smith 2009). For paid employees, differences are made among wages, earnings, and income.[29]

The concept of *wage rates* relates to the basic price of a unit of labor, before adding any bonuses for overtime, shift work, or family allowance and before deducting contributions for social security schemes or advanced tax payments. Wage rates can be expressed in units of time, such as an hour, a week, or a month, or as piece rates. It is the smallest of all pay concepts and applies only to workers in paid employment.

The concept of *earnings* typically relates to the pay that employers provide directly to their employees regularly during a specified reference period. It includes basic pay for time worked or work done, as well as for time not worked, such as vacation, holiday, and sick leave. It also includes other payments granted by the employer for various reasons, such as overtime work, hazard payments, regular bonuses, and fringe benefits, such as family allowances. However, it excludes all irregular bonuses, even if they are provided by the employer. Like time rates, earnings are recorded gross of social security contributions or tax deductions.

The concept of *income related to paid employment* is the most comprehensive measure of workers' remuneration. In addition to earnings, it includes all irregular bonuses and payments and all social security benefits received from the employer directly or from a social security scheme, if they are related to employment. These include family and education allowances, as well as sick and maternity benefits. They also include benefits received by those who are no longer employed, such as unemployment benefits, pensions, and invalidity benefits. All of these social benefits will be part of income from paid employment only insofar as workers received them because they participated in work activities. In countries with general social security systems, whereby family and other allowances are provided independently of work activities, these allowances are not part of income related to paid employment. To avoid double counting, these benefits are recorded net of contributions the worker makes to social security schemes.

The **Earnings** field should be completed with the total earnings as per the above definition and summing the earnings from multiple jobs. ADePT Gender expects a continuous variable and will check only for usual nonresponse values, such as negative values or 9999. The most important requirement is to have consistency in the reference period of the variables used for the **Earnings** and **Hours** fields.

Access to Resources

Productive assets determine the scale of production, investment, and growth. Farmers depend on land, labor, water, seeds, fertilizer, pesticides, machinery, and other inputs to produce crops. Entrepreneurs require labor and—depending on the business's size and sector of operation—capital for investment. Access to credit is crucial for farmers and entrepreneurs. Despite women's diverse and fundamental roles in agricultural and nonagricultural activities, women tend to have more limited access to productive assets, as well as inputs and services. Women also face additional constraints on their use of time, which are often tied to local norms and beliefs. ADePT Gender gives the user the flexibility to decide which outcomes to measure (screenshot 3.4).

Screenshot 3.4: Economic Opportunities Tab

Fields to input work characteristics variables

| Main | Human Capital | Economic Opportunities | Agency | Parameters |

Economic status and work characteristics

Work characteristics

Employed	empld	▾
Unemployed	unempld	▾
Work category	work_type	▾
Public sector employment	public_emp	▾
Formal status	informal=0	▾
Full time	fullt	▾

Occupation	occupation	▾
Sector	industry_3_cat	▾
Broad sector	industry	▾
Detailed sector	industry_detailed	▾
Agriculture	agric	▾
Earnings	inc1_wage	▾
Hours	hrs_pmt	▾

Access to resources

| Resource | credit_prim | ▾ |

Fields to input labor status variables

Fields to input resource variables (admits more than one variable)

The **Resources** field can be completed by one or many categorical variables. The variables are expected to have a missing value if the household does not have access to or ownership of the resource, and positive integers are used to indicate the three types of ownership, access, or use of the resource: (a) only man, (b) only woman, or (c) both man and woman. It is up to the user to decide whether the variable should be restricted to all men and all women in the household or to the husband and wife. The following section offers examples and clarifies some measurement issues that are common to all candidate variables.

Household versus individual: Many household surveys collect information on access to assets at the household level. This approach implicitly assumes that the resources are equally shared or that consensus exists within the household on the allocation and use of resources. However, this approach does not do justice to the reality of different spheres of decision making within households and intrahousehold inequalities in access to resources. Even when surveys ask questions about individual versus joint asset ownership, caution is warranted if this information is gathered from a single respondent in the household, usually a self-identified

"most knowledgeable" household member. In particular, different perceptions about ownership rights within the household may exist. Women
may provide different responses when interviewed together with their
partners, or household members may hide resources from each other.
A recent survey experiment in Uganda under the UN Evidence and
Data for Gender Equality initiative—which seeks to improve measurement of asset ownership from a gender perspective—sheds light on these
issues by comparing different interviewing modalities. The results, though
preliminary, suggest that reported ownership rates for a broad range of
physical and financial assets increase significantly if all adult household
members are interviewed individually (and alone) compared with interviewing a single household member (Kilic and Moylan 2016).

Access to versus use of resources: Not using a resource does not necessarily mean that someone did not have access to it; it simply means that it
was not optimal for the person to use it. This difference matters when we
analyze financial services, which include managing financial transactions
(including borrowing, saving, making payments, and having insurance).
Having *access* to finance is not the same as *using* finance; it is having the
possibility of using a financial service (Cull and Scott 2009). Having access
to finance therefore implies the absence of price and nonprice obstacles
regarding financial services. It also implies that measuring access to
finance requires a combination of information on current use of formal and
informal financial services, savings, payments, insurance, unmet demand,
and details on all types of barriers faced by men and women, households,
and firms (Demirgüç-Kunt, Beck, and Honohan 2008). However, it is
more likely to have indicators that measure *use of financial services*—for
example, having bank accounts or loans from either formal or informal
institutions.[30]

Ownership or management of productive resources: Ownership and management of productive resources are very different concepts. *Land rights* are
those property rights that pertain to real estate—that is, land. Because land
is a limited resource and property rights include the right to exclude others,
land rights are a form of monopoly. Landownership matters because it can
be used as collateral to buy assets or to get a loan. It might also be indicative
of intrahousehold bargaining power (Quisumbing and Maluccio 2003).
However, from the viewpoint of inputs necessary for an income-generating
activity, what matters is whether women can make decisions about how
land is used; about the use of inputs such as fertilizer, pesticides, poultry,

and so on (Croppenstedt, Goldstein, and Rosas 2013); and about the use of the output generated by the land.

Agency

The *World Development Report* on gender equality and development (World Bank 2012) proposes five outcomes or expressions of agency, all of which are closely associated with a woman's ability (or inability) to make choices. These outcomes are related and often overlap; as a result, a woman's ability to choose and act at any point in time partly reflects foundations laid earlier in her life, often starting in childhood.[31] Household surveys can cover many of the indicators of each of these expressions, though users should exercise caution when using and interpreting these types of variables (see chapter 4 of this book).

Marriage and Fertility

One of the expressions of agency is a woman's ability to decide when and whom to marry, when and how many children to have, and when to leave a marriage. ADePT Gender translates this concept into specific indicators. The **Age at first marriage** field should be completed with a continuous integer variable. Surveys like the DHS that contain fertility histories usually include this type of question. Ideally, it should be retrieved from a direct question, such as "When did you start living with your first husband/partner? In what month and year was that?" Surveys often instead ask, "In what month and year did you start living with your husband/partner?" The latter question captures only the length of the current marriage and does not necessarily indicate a woman's ability to decide the timing of marriage, because previous marriages are taken into consideration. The DHS includes all the relevant information.

Another indicator is average age at first birth. Again, the user should complete the field using a direct question, as opposed to computing the variable using the age of the oldest child. If the woman had a miscarriage or any of her children had died, the latter "estimated" variable would bias the indicator upward. ADePT Gender expects a continuous integer variable in the **Age at first birth** field.

A woman's control over when to have children and how many to have can be measured in several ways. The total fertility rate as well as the age-specific fertility rate will serve this purpose. To compute these two rates, the user needs to know the mother's date of birth and the birth dates of all the children who were born alive. ADePT Gender computes these rates using the DHS's method. Thus, ADePT Gender requires the date of the interview (**Interview date** field), the mother's date of birth (**Mother's birth date** field), and the birth dates of all the children (**Children's birth dates** field) in century-month code format (CMC). For example, consider a woman interviewed in December 2001 who was born in May 1970. Her CMC date of interview would be $12 \times (2001 - 1900) + 12 = 1224$. Her CMC date of birth would be $12 \times (1970 - 1900) + 5 = 845$.

WDR's *Five Dimensions of Agency*

Given the scarce availability on agency outcomes, ADePT Gender lets the user select variables. The only requirement is that the mean of the variable (or set of variables) to be completed in the field **Agency** has an economic meaning (screenshot 3.5). Hence, they have to be either bivariate variables

Screenshot 3.5: Fields in the Agency Tab

Four (out of five) dimensions of agency identified in the *World Development Report* and that can be described or proxied with household surveys

75

with values of 0 or 1 or continuous variables. Examples of variables from the DHS for expressions of agency are as follows:

- *Control over resources*: "Who usually decides how the money you earn will be used: mainly you, mainly your husband/partner, or you and your husband/partner jointly?" "Who usually decides how your husband's/partner's earnings will be used: you, your husband/partner, or you and your husband/partner jointly?" "Who usually makes decisions about your health care: you, your husband/partner, you and your husband/partner jointly, or someone else?" "Who usually makes decisions about major household purchases?" "Who usually makes decisions about making purchases for daily household needs?" Of course, this expression of agency is closely related to the **Resources** field in the **Economic opportunities** tab.
- *Ability to move freely*: "Who usually makes decisions about visits to your family or relatives?" "In the past 12 months, how many times have you been away from home for one or more nights?"
- *Decision making over family formation*: "Would you say that using contraception is mainly your decision, mainly your husband's/partner's decision, or do you decide together?"
- *Freedom from the risk of violence*: The DHS has a module on domestic violence that focuses mainly on physical abuse. However, a comprehensive assessment of domestic violence will include physical, sexual, psychological, and economic violence (UN 2014).
- *Ability to have a voice in society and influence policy*: Most of the time, these variables are collected at a different level. For example, the indicators on political participation come from administrative data on parliamentary representation. The information is collected via community questionnaires. However, very few of these sources have sex-disaggregated information. Although scarce, in some cases, household surveys include questions that can be used to construct indicators, such as whether they are members of cooperatives and other community associations. One example is the Indonesia Family Life Survey, which includes a module on community participation and such questions as "Have you participated in a community association meeting in the past 12 months?" "How many community association meetings have you participated in during the past 12 months?"

When choosing variables related to voice and agency, the user needs to bear in mind some characteristics that affect their interpretation. Variables can be (a) direct versus indirect measures of voice and agency, (b) intrinsic versus extrinsic, or (c) universal versus context specific.[32]

Direct versus indirect: Direct measures of voice and agency aim to capture increases in an individual's ability to achieve goals and control his or her life. Indirect, or proxy, measures of voice and agency traditionally focus on the possession of resources necessary for agency or the determinants of being empowered—such as education or asset ownership—rather than on empowerment itself. For example, decision-making variables are more direct measures of agency, whereas indicators of asset ownership are more indirect measures. Although the general recommendation is to use direct measures as much as possible, it would be useful to explore further how direct measures correlate with indirect measures.

Intrinsic versus extrinsic: The intrinsic variables capture the value that people give to voice and agency, whereas the extrinsic variables relate to what people can do with those skills and abilities independently of the value they assign to them.

Universal versus context specific: Voice and agency are context-specific concepts, since they are highly determined by socioeconomic, cultural, and political conditions. Currently, some initiatives feature indicators that can be compared across contexts and time, such as the Assets Project and the Women's Empowerment in Agriculture Index (see chapter 8).

Parameters

Several age brackets relevant for the analysis vary from country to country. ADePT Gender allows the user to define age brackets according to the specific circumstance or the interest of the analyst, as explained in the following section (screenshot 3.6).

General Age Brackets

Several tables in ADePT Gender present statistics for subgroups of the population defined by age. By default, ADePT Gender divides the population into five main groups: (a) children ages 0–14; (b) youth ages 15–24; (c) the adult population with women still in their fertility years, ages 24–49; (d) the adult

Screenshot 3.6: Fields to Be Completed in the Parameters Tab

Main	Human Capital	Economic Opportunities	Agency	Parameters

Age brackets

Primary school	6	9
Secondary school	10	14
Working age	15	64

population with women past their fertility years, ages 50–64; and (e) the elderly population, age 65 and older. These age brackets are detailed enough to earmark the main aspects of a woman's life cycle. However, some users might be interested in analyzing certain groups in more detail, for example, teenagers ages 13–19 or elderly people between 65 and 70 years old. This analysis can be done using customized tables.

Youth

According to the United Nations World Population Statistics, the fastest-growing population is that of 15- to 24-year-olds who are also considered *youths*. An increase in this age group could result in high unemployment rates, if countries are unable to create jobs to meet the fast-growing labor force. High youth unemployment can discourage job searching among those ages 15–24. In addition, high youth unemployment can put downward pressure on employment and earnings in many countries (World Bank 2012). ADePT Gender generates some statistics that refer explicitly to this demographic group.

Education

As explained earlier, years of education and the entrance age for primary education can vary from country to country. The number of years of education at each level can be tailored using the **Primary school** and **Secondary school** fields.

Working-Age Population

The minimum age for legal work, as well as the retirement age, varies from country to country. The user has the option to define the relevant age brackets for the working-age population using the **Working age** field. The general recommendation is to use the minimum age of legal work as the lower limit and the age of retirement as the upper limit. If these bounds do not coincide with the available information from the survey, the user should correct them to reflect the age of the people to whom the labor module was administered.

Notes

1. The use of ADePT Gender software is explained in chapter 2. A detailed explanation of the software's capabilities is provided by Lokshin and others (2013).
2. For more details, see the DHS Program website, http://www.measuredhs.com/Who-We-Are/About-Us.cfm.
3. Enterprise Surveys can be downloaded at http://www.enterprisesurveys.org.
4. For further details on how to compute and understand basic concepts related to sampling weights, the user can consult Deaton (1997), particularly, chapter 1.
5. The latest revision of UN recommendations for conducting surveys and censuses eliminated the condition of sharing one meal a day, and instead it focuses on one-person households and multiperson households. A household may be either (a) a one-person household, that is, a person who makes provision for his or her own food or other essentials for living without combining with any other person to form part of a multiperson household; or (b) a multiperson household, that is, a group of two or more people living together who make common provision for food or other essentials for living. The people in the group may pool their resources and have a common budget; they may be related or unrelated persons or a combination of both related and unrelated. This arrangement exemplifies the "housekeeping" concept. Some countries use a concept different from the housekeeping concept, namely, the "household-dwelling" concept, which regards all persons living in a housing unit as belonging to the same household. According to this concept, there is one household per occupied

housing unit. Therefore, the number of occupied housing units and the number of households occupying them are equal, and the locations of the housing units and households are identical. Countries should specify in their census reports whether they used the "housekeeping" or the "household-dwelling" concept of a private household (UN 2008b, paragraph 2.108).

6. Notice that ADePT Gender admits only a single variable, as opposed to ADePT Poverty, where the **Poverty line** field can be filled with more than one variable,.

7. For a discussion of the advantages and disadvantages of each of these measures, see Deaton and Zaidi (2002).

8. See the Demographic and Health Surveys Program's "Wealth Index" web page for a description of the construction of the wealth index, http://www.dhsprogram.com/topics/wealth-index/Wealth-Index -Construction.cfm.

9. Examples of direct variables could be those that evaluate household well-being, such as the Cantril ladder used by Gallup's World Poll (Cantril 1965; Gallup 2009).

10. *Categorical* means that each category represented by the variable takes an integer or alphanumeric combination.

11. One reason why the term *head of household* is a complex concept is that the title does not necessarily correlate with household decision making. For example, if a woman's husband migrates for work, she may be considered the de facto head of household, although other male family members—such as an older son, father-in-law, or another adult male family member—may be making household financial decisions. Data analysts and policy makers should therefore consider the reasons why certain women become heads of households and consider this variation when looking at this group.

12. For an application of such a variable, see the Country Gender Assessment of Lesotho.

13. This variable might be relevant for eastern European countries; see Sattar (2012) for examples.

14. For example, in Mexico, whether or not the household is a beneficiary of PROGRESA (Programa de Educación, Salud, y Alimenación), a program to alleviate poverty.

15. *Ethnicity* is defined as large groups classified by cultural factors, such as nationality, culture, ancestry, language, and beliefs. Ethnicity is a variable

that in certain contexts could be defined at the household level or at the individual level, if there are interracial marriages and within-household differences in ethnic affiliation.

16. For a detailed discussion on the definition of literacy, see UNESCO (2006), chapter 6.

17. Literacy level can be determined by different methods: (a) by respondents reporting their literacy level (self-declaration), (b) by another individual—typically, the head of the household—reporting on the literacy level of household members (third-party assessment), and (c) by the number of years of schooling completed determining the "literate" from the "'nonliterate" (educational attainment proxy), which varies from country to country, ranging from one year up to eight years but typically four or five years of schooling. However, all of these methods are subject to measurement error and difficulty in the cross-country comparison. To respond to this problem, surveys and censuses started to use direct measures of literacy in the 1990s. These methods range from the interviewer giving a card to the respondent to evaluate his or her own literacy level to more complex skills measurement surveys, such as PISA (Programme for International Student Assessment), TIMSS (Trends in International Mathematics and Science Study), and STEP (Skills Toward Employment and Productivity). For more details on this discussion, see UNESCO (2006, 2015).

18. The current version of the ISCED was adopted in 1998 and is called ISCED 1997. For more details consult UNESCO (1997).

19. A more detailed discussion of the differences between enrollment and attendance can be found in the ADePT education manual (Porta and others 2011).

20. The ISCED 1997 mappings are available at http://www.uis.unesco.org /Education/ISCEDMappings/Pages/default.aspx.

21. Or expressions that ADePT interprets as binary variables.

22. For more details, see WHO (2010).

23. The three conditions must hold to be considered unemployed.

24. The underemployment rate is the number of underemployed persons as a percentage of the number of employed persons (Hussmanns 2007). The rate of volume of time-related underemployment is the ratio between the volume of time-related underemployment and the potential time for work of employed persons, calculated as the sum of the

total hours actually worked by employed persons and the volume of time-related underemployment (Hussmanns 2007).

25. The ISIC has four revisions: ISIC Revision 2 (1968), Revision 3 (1990), Revision 3.1 (2002), and Revision 4 (2008). The details of each classification and the correspondence among revisions can be found at http://unstats.un.org/unsd/cr/registry/isic-4.asp.

26. For more details, see UN (2008a).

27. If users consider it appropriate for the country context, they could use the alternative classification of economic sectors: (a) the primary sector comprising agriculture, mining, and forestry; (b) the secondary sector comprising manufacturing and construction; (c) the tertiary sector comprising services, such as retail sales, entertainment, and financial services; and (d) the quaternary sector comprising intellectual activities like education.

28. ISCO was first adopted in 1957 and is also known as ISCO-58. The classification was revised many times and is superseded by ISCO-68 (1966), ISCO-88 (1987), and ISCO-08 (2007). More details can be found at http://www.ilo.org/public/english/bureau/stat/isco/isco08/index.htm.

29. Definitions are taken from the ILO "Income Statistics" web page, http://www.ilo.org/global/statistics-and-databases/statistics-overview-and-topics/income/lang--en/index.htm. All definitions refer to a gross concept of remuneration.

30. Good questions have a definite reference period (such as, within the past year or past six months).

31. See chapter 4 of World Bank (2012) for a proper definition of each dimension of agency and more details on these concepts.

32. This discussion is based on Alkire and others (2012).

References

Alkire, Sabina, Ruth Meinzen-Dick, Amber Peterman, Agnes Quisumbing, Greg Seymour, and Ana Vaz. 2012. "The Women's Empowerment in Agriculture Index." OPHI Working Paper 58, Oxford Poverty and Human Development Initiative, Oxford University.

Anderson Scheffner, Julie. 2000. "Module for Chapter 9: Employment." In *Designing Household Survey Questionnaires for Developing Countries: Lessons from Ten Years of LSMS Experience*, edited by Margaret Grosh and Paul Glewwe, 147–250. Washington, DC: World Bank.

Bardasi, Elena, Kathleen Beegle, Andrew Dillon, and Pieter Serneels. 2011. "Do Labor Statistics Depend on How and to Whom the Questions Are Asked? Results from a Survey Experiment in Tanzania." *World Bank Economic Review* 25 (3): 418–47.

Beaman, Lori, and Andrew Dillon. 2012. "Do Household Definitions Matter in Survey Design? Results from a Randomized Survey Experiment in Mali." *Journal of Development Economics* 98 (1): 124–35.

Cantril, Hadley. 1965. *The Pattern of Human Concerns*. New Brunswick, NJ: Rutgers University Press.

Croppenstedt, Andre, Markus Goldstein, and Nina Rosas. 2013. "Gender and Agriculture: Inefficiencies, Segregation, and Low Productivity Traps." Policy Research Working Paper 6370, World Bank, Washington, DC. https://openknowledge.worldbank.org/handle/10986/13171.

Cull, Robert, and Kinnon Scott. 2009. "Measuring Household Usage of Financial Services: Does It Matter How or to Whom You Ask?" Policy Research Working Paper 5048, World Bank, Washington, DC.

Deaton, Angus. 1997. *The Analysis of Household Surveys: A Microeconometric Approach to Development Policy*. Baltimore: Johns Hopkins University Press.

Deaton, Angus, and Salman Zaidi. 2002. "Guidelines for Constructing Consumption Aggregates for Welfare Analysis." Living Standards Measurement Study Working Paper 135, World Bank, Washington, DC.

Demirgüç-Kunt, Ash, Thorsten Beck, and Patrick Honohan. 2008. *Finance for All: Policies and Pitfalls in Expanding Access*. Washington, DC: World Bank.

Diez de Medina, Rafael, and Elisa Benes. 2014. "Redrawing the Boundaries: From Employment and Unemployment towards Work and Labour Underutilization." International Labour Organization, Geneva.

EC, IMF, OECD, UN (European Commission, International Monetary Fund, Organisation for Economic Co-operation and Development, United Nations), and World Bank. 2008. *System of National Accounts: 2008*. New York: EC, IMF, OECD, UN, and World Bank. http://unstats.un.org/unsd/nationalaccount/sna2008.asp.

Ehrenberg, Ronald G., and Robert S. Smith. 2009. *Modern Labor Economics*. 10th ed. Boston: Pearson/Addison-Wesley.

Fuwa, Nobuhiko. 2000. "The Poverty and Heterogeneity among Female-Headed Households Revisited: The Case of Panama." *World Development* 28 (8): 1515–42.

Gallup. 2009. "Understanding How Gallup Uses the Cantril Scale." http://www.gallup.com/poll/122453/Understanding-Gallup-Uses-Cantril-Scale.aspx?version=print.

Hussmanns, Ralf. 2004. "Measuring the Informal Economy: From Employment in the Informal Sector to Informal Employment." Working Paper 53, International Labour Organization, Geneva.

———. 2007. "Measurement of Employment, Unemployment and Underemployment: Current International Standards and Issues in Their Application." International Labour Organization, Geneva. http://www.ilo.org/global/statistics-and-databases/WCMS_088394/lang--en/index.htm.

IHSN (International Household Survey Network). 2015. "How Well Are Gender Issues Covered in Household Surveys and Censuses? An Analysis Using the IHSN–World Bank Gender Data Navigator." http://ihsn.org/HOME/sites/default/files/resources/Gender_Issues_July-2015.pdf.

ILO (International Labour Organization). 1982. "Resolution Concerning Statistics of the Economically Active Population, Employment, Unemployment and Underemployment, Adopted by the 13th International Conference of Labour Statisticians." http://www.ilo.org/public/english/bureau/stat/download/res/ecacpop.pdf.

———. 1993. "Report of the Conference," Fifteenth International Conference of Labour Statisticians. Geneva, January 19–28. http://www.ilo.org/public/libdoc/ilo/1993/93B09_65_engl.pdf.

———. 2004. "80 Years of ILO Statistical Standard Setting," Seventeenth International Conference of Labour Statisticians, Geneva, November 24–December 3, 2003. http://www.ilo.org/public/english/bureau/stat/download/articles/2004-1.pdf.

———. 2012. *Measuring Informality: A Statistical Manual on the Informal Sector and Informal Employment.* Geneva: ILO.

———. 2013. "Resolution Concerning Statistics of Work, Employment and Labour Underutilization." Presented at the Nineteenth International Conference of Labour Statisticians, Geneva, October 2–11. http://www.ilo.org/wcmsp5/groups/public/---dgreports/---stat/documents/normativeinstrument/wcms_230304.pdf.

Kilic, Talip, and Heather Moylan. 2016. "Methodological Experiment on Measuring Asset Ownership from a Gender Perspective (MEXA)."

Technical report, World Bank, Washington, DC. http://siteresources
.worldbank.org/INTLSMS/Resources/3358986-1423600559701/MEXA
_Technical_Report.pdf.

Lokshin, Michael, Sergiy Radyakin, Zurab Sajaia, and William Creitz. 2013. *ADePT User Guide*. Version 5. Washington, DC: World Bank.

Messenger, Jon C., ed. 2004. *Working Time and Workers' Preferences in Industrialized Countries: Finding the Balance*. London and New York: Routledge.

Panama, Government of. 1997. "ISCED Mapping." Ministry of Education, Panama City. http://www.uis.unesco.org/Education/ISCEDMappings /Pages/default.aspx.

Perry, Guillermo, William F. Maloney, Omar S. Arias, Pablo Fajnzylber, Andrew D. Mason, and Jaime Saavedra-Chanduvi. 2007. *Informality: Exit and Exclusion*. Washington, DC: World Bank.

Porta, Emilio, Gustavo Arcia, Kevin Macdonald, Sergiy Radyakin, and Michael Lokshin. 2011. *Assessing Sector Performance and Inequality in Education*. Washington, DC: World Bank.

Quisumbing, Agnes, and John A. Maluccio. 2003. "Resources at Marriage and Intrahousehold Allocation: Evidence from Bangladesh, Ethiopia, Indonesia, and South Africa." *Oxford Bulletin of Economics and Statistics* 65 (3): 283–327.

Sattar, Sarosh. 2012. *Opportunities for Men and Women in Emerging Europe and Central Asia*. Washington, DC: World Bank.

UN (United Nations). 2008a. "International Standard Industrial Classification of All Economic Activities (ISIC), Rev 4." Statistical Papers Series M, no. 4, New York.

———. 2008b. *Principles and Recommendations for Population and Housing Censuses Revision 2*. New York: UN. http://unstats.un.org/unsd/publication /seriesM/seriesm_67Rev2e.pdf.

———. 2014. *Guidelines for Producing Statistics on Violence against Women: Statistical Surveys*. New York: UN.

UNESCO (United Nations Educational, Scientific, and Cultural Organization). 1997. "International Standard Classification of Education: ISCED 1997." Paris. http://www.unesco.org/education/information /nfsunesco/doc/isced_1997.htm.

———. 2006. *Education for All: Literacy for Life*. Paris: UNESCO. http:// unesdoc.unesco.org/images/0014/001416/141639e.pdf.

————. 2015. *Education for All 2000–2015: Achievements and Challenges*. Paris: UNESCO. http://unesdoc.unesco.org/images/0023/002322/232205e.pdf.

WHO (World Health Organization). 2010. *World Health Statistics, 2010*. Geneva: WHO.

World Bank. 2012. *World Development Report 2012: Gender Equality and Development*. Washington, DC: World Bank. https://openknowledge .worldbank.org/handle/10986/4391.

PART II

Producing a Country Gender Diagnostic

Part II of this manual guides the user through the ADePT output that feeds into a country gender diagnostic. This is the set of tables and graphs that describe the three dimensions of gender inequality highlighted by the 2012 *World Development Report* (*WDR*) framework: human endowments, economic opportunities, and agency.

Chapter 4 provides guidance on how to produce and interpret the tables and graphs. Using the household surveys from Nepal and Panama, the chapter discusses selected tables and graphs to show the user how to interpret them. Chapter 5 provides additional information about theoretical models and statistical techniques that aid the interpretation of results.

This organization aims to help different audiences to quickly access necessary inputs and outputs. Users familiar with quantitative analysis and gender issues can consult chapter 4, whereas users less familiar with quantitative analysis or the economic angle of gender issues should consult chapters 4 and 5.

How to Interpret the Results of the Country Gender Diagnostic

This chapter discusses how to interpret the results of the tables and graphs produced by ADePT Gender, which aspires to be as comprehensive as possible, while using a minimum set of key variables. At the same time, it leaves the door open to further customization to fully exploit the richness of the data on hand. ADePT Gender can be used for diagnostics, for tracking progress over time, and for evaluating country performance with respect to peer countries. In addition, many of the statistics here are part of the 52 minimum core gender indicators identified by the United Nations (UN) Inter-Agency and Expert Group on Gender Statistics.[1] It also helps to highlight needs for further analysis in areas that have persistent gender inequality or knowledge gaps. The set of tables and graphs also allows users to identify gaps in gender-relevant data.

The country gender diagnostic aims to answer such questions as: Are female infants as likely as male infants to be born in a country? Do female and male infants receive the same attention and care? Are girls as likely as boys to attend school? Are women as engaged in paid work as men? And if so, do they have access to the same jobs and payment for their work and education? How much can differentiated access to productive assets such as land and credit be associated with the gaps in economic opportunities for men and women? Do women and men have equal decision-making power in the household and in society? These are among the questions that this chapter will help the user answer using simple statistical tools.

The output produced is by nature descriptive. However, in combination with the broader economic literature, it can help the user to infer which mechanisms are most likely to produce those outcomes. If needed, the user can pursue further analysis to establish causal links and measure the effects from different drivers of change. These needs may arise (a) because the user is interested in disentangling different mechanisms that could be working simultaneously, (b) because it is an area of high priority, or (c) because a unique opportunity exists to measure a policy's effect (via a quasi-natural experiment, for example).

The diagnostic uses simple basic tabulations to describe the differences between men and women in the main outcomes and by relevant population subgroups. Progress in some domains is tempered by the sobering realities that women face in others (World Bank 2012).

This chapter is divided into four parts. The first discusses how to place gender in the country's demographic context. Tables and graphs present the distribution of women across the country's main demographic and regional groups. The following three sections describe gender differences in outcomes in the three main domains identified by the *WDR 2012: Gender Equality and Development*: human capital (or endowments), economic opportunities, and agency (see chapter 1). Each section is organized in the same way. The content of the output produced by ADePT Gender is first presented. Next, basic concepts are introduced that help illustrate the content of the tables and graphs. The last section describes how to interpret the output.

When interpreting the results, the user should bear in mind that different values of the statistics for men and women do not necessarily reflect the existence of gender gaps. These differences might not be statistically significant; they might result from lack of precision[2] of the estimates to be confident—from a statistical point of view—of the existence of such difference. The user interested in assessing whether the difference is statistically significant needs to conduct additional tests. These tests—discussed more extensively in appendix A—can be carried out by simple math calculations based on ADePT Gender outputs (means and standard deviations) or by using standard statistical software packages.

Two datasets are used to provide the user with practical examples of output and as reference to interpret the results: (a) the Nepal Living Standards Survey for 1996, 2003, and 2010 and (b) the Panama Living

Standard Measurement Study for 2008.[3] All results are based on the definitions discussed in chapter 3. Applying the same definitions to all datasets is key to ensure comparability across countries. Only selected tables and graphs are described in detail in the chapter as an illustration.

Demographic and Regional Characteristics

Content

This section guides the reader through seven tables (tables 1a–1g) and five graphs (figures 1a–1e) that show the distribution of women across different groups of the population, defined by either individual or household characteristics. Generally, the graphs show the share of women within each group, whereas tables show the distribution of men and women according to individual and household characteristics. ADePT Gender tables 1a and 1b show the distribution of men and women according to such characteristics, respectively. Tables 1c and 1d show the distribution of the population by the household head's gender and individual characteristics and by the household head's gender and select household characteristics, respectively. Figures 1a–1d show the share of women (or women heads of household) for each of the groups defined in tables 1a–1d. Finally, detailed information on household composition and age composition is provided in tables 1e and 1f and figure 1e. Some examples from specific country datasets are also presented below.

Concepts

When preparing gender diagnostics or examining gender disadvantages within the context of poverty assessments, labor market studies, or other analytical country work, it is important to ascertain whether women are disproportionately represented among certain demographic, regional, or income groups. This is because gender inequalities tend to be amplified for *severely disadvantaged populations*, even when women have the same potential and right as men to a full, meaningful life. Across and within countries, gender gaps widen at lower incomes. And in the poorest economies, gender gaps are even larger. In general, the benefits of economic growth have not accrued equally to all men and women of a society. Household poverty can mute the effect of national development, and gender differences—even if shared by all—often compound or exacerbate other types of exclusion, such as geography and ethnicity. Understanding the degree of overlap between gender disparities and other vulnerabilities is fundamental for correctly interpreting gender differences in outcomes. For example, in some countries, gender disparities remain significant only for those who are poor. In both India and Pakistan, although boys and girls from the top income quintile participate in school at similar rates, the bottom income quintile has a gender gap of almost five years (World Bank 2012). In the former Yugoslav Republic of Macedonia, Roma women are considerably less likely than non-Roma women to work (Angel-Urdinola and Macias 2008; Gamberoni and Posadas 2012).

Often, certain population groups are more vulnerable to *external shocks*—economic, political, and institutional—which can erase gender equality gains or cause reversals, with welfare losses for boys and men. For example, economic shocks in many poor Latin American countries result in boys leaving school at young ages. Such adverse circumstances early in life can have long-lasting effects, even irreversible ones. Moreover, when it comes to gender equality, it seems that countries or population groups often fall in either *virtuous or vicious circles*, or "sticky gets stickier," as the World Bank (2012) puts it. Progress in one dimension of gender can multiply the effects of other dimensions. Under this hypothesis, it is useful to understand which groups of the population may fall into virtuous or vicious circles.

Missing Women

Basic demographic analysis helps explore the high rates of missing women and adult male mortality. The term *missing women* highlights a country's excess female mortality that results from different behaviors, preferences, and exposure to health risks: (a) prenatal sex preferences that translate into "stopping behavior"[4] and sex-selective abortions, (b) excessive female mortality in early childhood, (c) maternal mortality, and (d) higher human immunodeficiency virus (HIV) risks. Age-specific mortality rates differ between males and females because of various biological and behavioral factors. Although female life expectancy exceeds male life expectancy in high-income countries, in poor-income countries, women, especially young women and girls, die at higher rates than men. To a large degree, the reason is the lack of access to health services, in particular, those related to reproductive health. However, sex-selective abortions are also an important factor in some countries.

A combination of three factors led to falling numbers of female births (World Bank 2012). First, fertility started to drop as female education and returns to the labor market increased. Second, new technologies allow pre-natal sex screening to become widespread and available to all sectors of society. Third, the preference for sons remains unchanged, and families that want to have only two children strongly prefer to have at least one son.

Population Pyramids and Demographic Transitions

Population pyramids typically consist of two back-to-back bar graphs, with the population plotted on the *x*-axis and age on the *y*-axis. One graph shows the number of males, and the other shows females in a particular population in five-year age groups (also called cohorts). Males are conventionally shown on the left and females on the right, and they may be measured by raw number or as a percentage of the total population. Demographic structures are classified by four types: (a) demographic explosion, (b) demographic window of opportunity, (c) demographic implosion, and (d) demographic hourglass.[5] See figure 4.1 for a plot of each type.

It is important to understand the population's demographic composition for policy making and other issues. Gender inequality affects demographic processes, which in turn further affect economic outcomes (Buvinic, Das Gupta, and Casabonne 2009). For example, if a country is transitioning from a demographic explosion to a demographic window of opportunity, it should ensure that the present cohort of girls will be ready to participate in the labor market when they become adults.

Population pyramids allow *missing women* to be identified when the imbalance is acute. For instance, an asymmetric population pyramid may suggest differences in sex ratios at birth, mortality differences by gender, or gender-differentiated migration patterns. However, as described above, males and females of different ages face different survival probabilities, so that the quantification of missing women requires more complex computations and the use of model life tables from countries expected to have little or no sex discrimination as benchmark (Klasen and Wink 2003; World Bank 2012).

Household Composition

The term *household composition* refers to the description of household members by gender and age. Before analyzing the results, it is important to

Figure 4.1: Demographic Typology

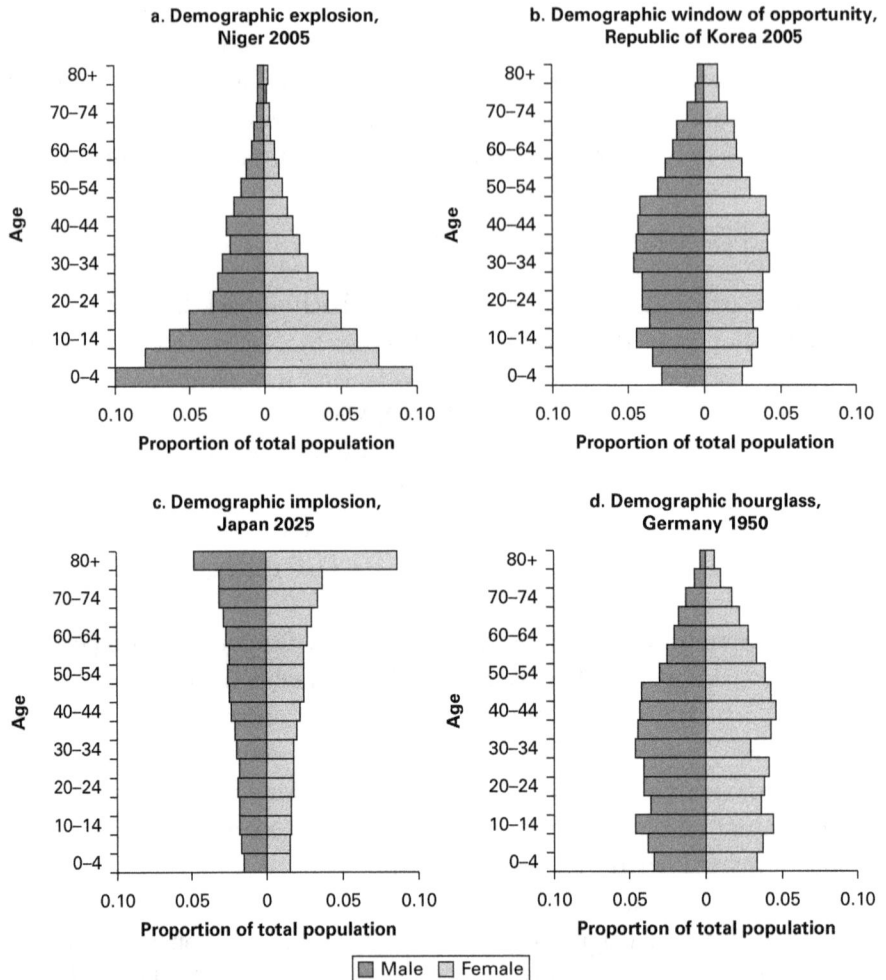

a. Demographic explosion,
Niger 2005

b. Demographic window of opportunity,
Republic of Korea 2005

c. Demographic implosion,
Japan 2025

d. Demographic hourglass,
Germany 1950

Male   Female

Source: Buvinic, Das Gupta, and Casabonne 2009.

understand whether household composition differs across vulnerable groups to assess household differences in access to resources and other constraints. Two types of indicators are usually used that present the same type of information but in different contexts—dependency ratio and a direct description of household members' age and gender.

The dependency ratio is an indicator intended to capture the household's potential—from a demographic perspective—to earn income. Table 1e shows the dependency ratio, defined as

$$Dependency\ ratio = \frac{\left(\begin{array}{c} number\ of\ HH\ members\ ages\ 0\ to\ 14\ + \\ number\ of\ HH\ members\ 65\ and\ older \end{array}\right)}{number\ of\ HH\ members\ ages\ 15\ to\ 64} \times 100.$$

As the ratio increases, the burden on the household's productive members to support the economically dependent—children and elderly—also increases. This effect results in direct impacts on household expenditures, in particular, on expenses related to health and education. The dependency ratio is typically higher for female-headed households, because women often assume headship when the working-age male is absent. Thus, at the aggregate level, the dependency ratio needs to be analyzed jointly with the percentage of the population in female-headed households and with their heads' characteristics.

Two other indicators are used in the literature but are not included in ADePT Gender. They are the child dependency ratio and elderly dependency ratio:

$$Child\ dependency\ ratio = \frac{number\ of\ HH\ members\ ages\ 0\ to\ 14}{number\ of\ HH\ members\ ages\ 15\ to\ 64} \times 100,$$

$$Elderly\ dependency\ ratio = \frac{number\ of\ HH\ members\ 65\ and\ older}{number\ of\ HH\ members\ ages\ 15\ to\ 64} \times 100.$$

Interpreting the Results

ADePT Gender figures 1a–1d are all interpreted in the same way. They show the percentage of women or female heads for different groups of the population defined using individual or household characteristics. For example, ADePT Gender figure 1a shows the percentage of women in each of five age groups—children, youth, reproductive-age adults, mature adults, and elderly. Figure 4.2 reproduces ADePT Gender figure 1b and shows that in Panama in 2008, more women than men lived in female-headed

Figure 4.2: ADePT Gender Figure 1b, Panama 2008

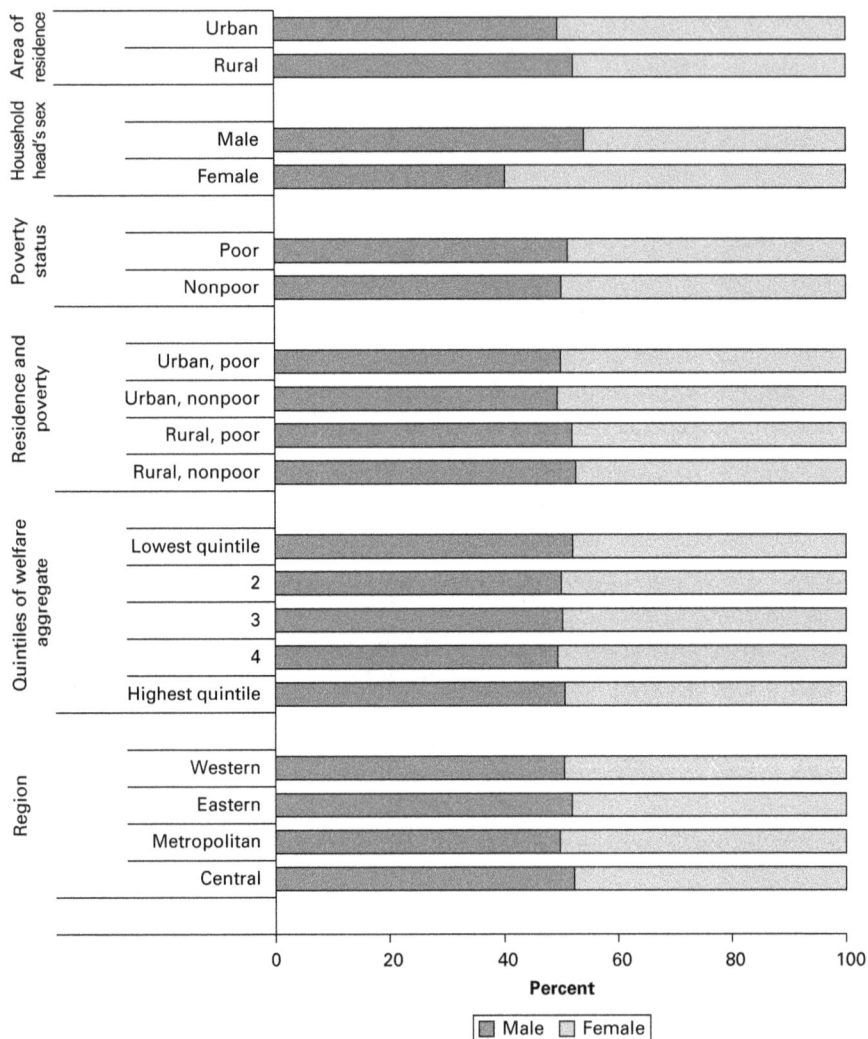

Source: Based on ADePT Gender using the Panama 2008.

households (60 percent versus 40 percent, respectively). In male-headed households, the gender balance is more even (54 percent versus 46 percent, respectively).[6]

ADePT Gender tables 1a–1d also show the distribution of certain groups of the population among categories defined by a certain characteristic.

The population group being analyzed is indicated in the column head, and the categories among which the group is distributed are indicated in the rows in successive blocks. Take, for example, ADePT table 1a. It examines three population groups—total country population, men, and women—and three individual characteristics—age, marital status, and completed education. The top left block indicates the distribution of the total country population by age categories, whose sum is the total population, that is, 100. ADePT table 1d examines other population groups—male- and female-headed households, alone (for the total country population), and combined with two characteristics typically found to exacerbate the gender imbalances—rural and poor populations. As before, these groups are combined with other characteristics—household area of residence, household poverty status, the combination of residence and poverty status, household quintile, and region of residence—indicated in the table rows.

ADePT figures 1a and 1b and ADePT tables 1a and 1b analyze men and women by select individual (figure 1a and table 1a) and household (figure 1b and table 1b) characteristics. ADePT Gender figures 1c and 1d and ADePT Gender tables 1c and 1d analyze female- and male-headed households by select individual characteristics of the head (figure 1c and table 1c) and the household (figure 1d and table 1d). The characteristics used to define the groups of ADePT figures 1a–1d are aligned with the characteristics used in ADePT tables 1a–1d.

Women are often, though not always, *overrepresented in vulnerable groups*, such as female-headed, poor, and rural households. In the case of Panama, a larger fraction of women live in female-headed households than in male-headed households (31 percent versus 21 percent, ADePT table 1b). Whether this difference is mechanical (that is, resulting from the fact that no or fewer male adults are present in female-headed households) depends on the definition of household head (see chapter 3) and on the country context. In Panama, more men than women live in rural households (37 percent versus 34 percent, table 4.1 that corresponds with ADePT table 1b), though this difference is not statistically significant.[7] The percentage of women living in poor households is low compared with other countries. Table 4.2 lists 65 countries grouped by region and by the three ranges of the percentage of poor that are women. No difference exists in the poverty status of the household. It should be noted that because the welfare measures are at the household level, such analysis ignores any differences in resource allocations among household members.

Table 4.1: ADePT Gender Table 1b, Panama 2008

Table 1b: Distribution of Males and Females in the Population across Selected Household Characteristics

		Gender	
	All	Male	Female
Total	**100.0**	**100.0**	**100.0**
Area of residence			
Urban	64.3	63.0	65.5
Rural	35.7	37.0	34.5
Gender of household head			
Male	73.7	79.0	68.3
Female	26.3	21.0	31.7
Poverty status			
Poor	32.7	33.2	32.2
Nonpoor	67.3	66.8	67.8
Residence and poverty status			
Urban, poor	11.4	11.2	11.5
Urban, nonpoor	52.9	51.8	54.0
Rural, poor	21.4	22.0	20.7
Rural, nonpoor	14.4	15.0	13.8
Quintile of welfare aggregate			
Lowest quintile	20.0	20.6	19.3
2	20.0	19.8	20.2
3	20.0	19.9	20.1
4	20.0	19.6	20.4
Highest quintile	20.0	20.1	19.9
Region			
Western	19.7	19.7	19.6
Eastern	2.7	2.8	2.6
Metropolitan	58.0	57.2	58.8
Central	19.6	20.3	18.9

Source: Based on ADePT Gender using Panama 2008.
Note: The complete ADePT output for Panama 2008 and Nepal 2011 can be found on the ADePT website, under the tab for "Gender," at http://go.worldbank.org/0GA4FDMQY0.

Hence, any disproportionate share of women living in poor households reflects solely demographic patterns. If gender gaps in the allocation of resources among household members were considered, gender gaps in poverty rates would be considerably more pronounced in some country contexts.

Moreover, in general, there are *overlapping vulnerabilities*. For example, women are more likely to live in poor households and in female-headed households, and female-headed households may also be more likely to be poor.[8] Or women may be more likely to live in female-headed households, and female-headed households may be more likely to be headed by an elderly woman. For example, in Panama, 25 percent of women and 17 percent of men live in female-headed households, and 70 percent of

Table 4.2: Countries by Share of Women in Total Population Living in Poor Households, 1999–2008

Below 50 percent			50–54 percent				55–61 percent	
Africa	Asia	Latin America and the Caribbean	Africa	Asia	Latin America and the Caribbean	More developed regions	Asia	More developed regions
Benin	China	Panama	Burkina Faso	Bhutan	Belize	Belgium	Cyprus	Austria
Mali	Philippines	Paraguay	Cameroon		Bolivia	Denmark	Armenia	Bulgaria
			Cabo Verde		Brazil	Finland		Czech Republic
			Congo, Rep.		Chile	France		Estonia
			Congo, Dem. Rep.		Colombia	Germany		Iceland
			Guinea		Costa Rica	Greece		Italy
			Kenya		Dominican Republic	Hungary		Latvia
			Niger		Ecuador	Ireland		Lithuania
					El Salvador	Luxembourg		Norway
					Guatemala	Malta		Slovak Republic
					Haiti	Netherlands		Slovenia
					Honduras	Poland		United States
					Jamaica	Portugal		
					Mexico	Romania		
					Nicaragua	Serbia		
					Peru	Spain		
					Uruguay	Sweden		
					Venezuela, RB	United Kingdom		

Source: UN 2010.
Note: Year is the latest available in the period of reference.

female-headed households are headed by a woman with no education, as opposed to 43 percent of male-headed households (ADePT tables 1b and 1c for Nepal, not shown[9]). Hence, women might be at a disadvantage for being in a female-headed household and in a household whose head has no education. Users should interpret results with caution when overlapping vulnerabilities exist, since the confounding effects prevent drawing conclusions about which factors are more oppressive.

Also, overlapping vulnerabilities might mutually reinforce each other. In general, women tend to have less access to resources, tend to be unprotected by legislation, or are subject to social norms that affect their agency, which in turn affects economic opportunities. For example, in Panama, female-headed households are more likely to be headed by widows. If widowed or divorced women have less access to resources because of inheritance or divorce laws, then gender disparities in outcomes might be a consequence of women's unequal access to resources upon marriage dissolution and may not be due to the fact that women are household heads (Buvinic and Gupta 1997; World Bank 2012).

Thus, if the data allow, it is useful to complement the output of ADePT Gender with a description of the factors that are pushing women to fall into each vulnerable group—for example, what causes them to become heads of households. Women might become heads because of marriage dissolution or because husbands had to migrate for a job or are unemployed. The consequences in each case are very different for household well-being. Female-headed households with migrant husbands might receive remittances—and thus are less likely to be poor—whereas female-headed households with unemployed husbands depend on female earnings only—and thus are more likely to be poor. In other words, the percentage of female-headed households might be endogenous to other factors, either economic or social. If there is a large percentage of female-headed households, users should consider additional custom variables, such as whether the husband is present or his labor status, to obtain cross-tabulations and further examine the factors behind the phenomenon.

Household Composition

Table 4.3 (that corresponds to ADePT table 1e) shows a higher dependency ratio in female-headed households than in male-headed households—78 for male-headed households and 89 for female-headed households. Tabulation

Table 4.3: ADePT Gender Table 1e, Panama 2008
Table 1e: Dependency Ratio by Selected Household Characteristics and by Male- and Female-Headed Households: Total, Rural, and Poor Households

	Total		Rural		Poor	
	Male	Female	Male	Female	Male	Female
Total	**78.0**	**88.9**	**98.1**	**107.8**	**120.5**	**126.2**
Area of residence						
Urban	64.8	83.0			113.7	131.2
Rural	98.1	107.8	98.1	107.8	123.4	121.3
Poverty status						
Poor	120.5	126.2	123.4	121.3	120.5	126.2
Nonpoor	56.3	72.0	60.8	82.1		
Residence and poverty status						
Urban, poor	113.7	131.2	—	—	113.7	131.2
Urban, nonpoor	54.9	70.6	—	—	—	—
Rural, poor	123.4	121.3	123.4	121.3	123.4	121.3
Rural, nonpoor	60.8	82.1	60.8	82.1	—	—

(continued)

Table 4.3: ADePT Gender Table 1e, Panama 2008 *(continued)*

	Total		Rural		Poor	
	Male	*Female*	*Male*	*Female*	*Male*	*Female*
Quintile of welfare aggregate						
Lowest quintile	132.9	129.2	134.3	128.3	132.9	129.2
2	88.8	112.7	86.7	104.9	98.7	122.7
3	66.6	82.9	67.6	89.4	—	—
4	58.8	67.1	54.2	65.3	—	—
Highest quintile	38.5	54.2	38.3	53.0	—	—
Region						
Western	98.7	108.7	114.0	124.0	138.8	132.4
Eastern	111.4	125.8	112.0	131.4	121.9	166.0
Metropolitan	68.1	84.5	89.1	104.1	117.9	132.2
Central	79.5	81.7	84.1	91.1	103.4	107.3

Source: Based on ADePT Gender using Panama 2008.
Note: Individual (population) weights. This table is representative of the national population. — = not applicable.

of the household head's marital status (not shown, ADePT table 1c) further suggests that most female-headed households are a consequence of marriage dissolution.

ADePT Gender output shows the household composition in more detail by calculating the average number of household members by gender and age in ADePT table 1f. As with ADePT tables 1c–1e, the averages are presented for the total population and separately for rural and poor households, each time distinguishing between male- and female-headed households. For example, in Panama, on average households have 3.7 members, one adult male, one adult female, and most likely three children, with relatively equal probability of having boys and girls (table 4.4). Very few households have elderly men and women. Reference values of dependency ratios can be found in UNFPA (2011).

Population Pyramids

Additional details on the demographic composition of the population are important for understanding other issues. ADePT figure 1e illustrates the population pyramid for Nepal, which shows a decrease in the number of young men ages 20 to 45, which might reflect international migration (see figure 4.3). Figure 4.4 shows population pyramids for Azerbaijan and Armenia, which have among the highest levels of missing women in the

Table 4.4: ADePT Gender Table 1f, Panama 2008

	Total			Rural		Poor	
	Total	Male	Female	Male	Female	Male	Female
Total	**3.7**	**3.8**	**3.5**	**4.1**	**3.7**	**5.4**	**5.2**
1	0.8	1.0	0.5	0.9	0.5	1.0	0.6
2	0.8	0.8	1.0	0.7	0.9	0.9	1.0
3	0.3	0.3	0.3	0.3	0.3	0.5	0.5
4	0.3	0.3	0.3	0.3	0.3	0.4	0.5
5	0.4	0.4	0.3	0.5	0.4	0.7	0.7
6	0.3	0.3	0.3	0.4	0.4	0.7	0.7
7	0.2	0.2	0.2	0.3	0.2	0.5	0.4
8	0.2	0.2	0.2	0.3	0.2	0.4	0.4
9	0.1	0.2	0.1	0.2	0.1	0.2	0.1
10	0.1	0.1	0.3	0.1	0.3	0.1	0.3

Source: Based on ADePT Gender using Panama 2008.
Note: Individual (population) weights. This table is representative of the national population. Adult men and adult women include head of household. If the number of adult men in a male-headed household is 1, this means he is the head.

Figure 4.3: ADePT Gender Figure 1e, Nepal 2010–11

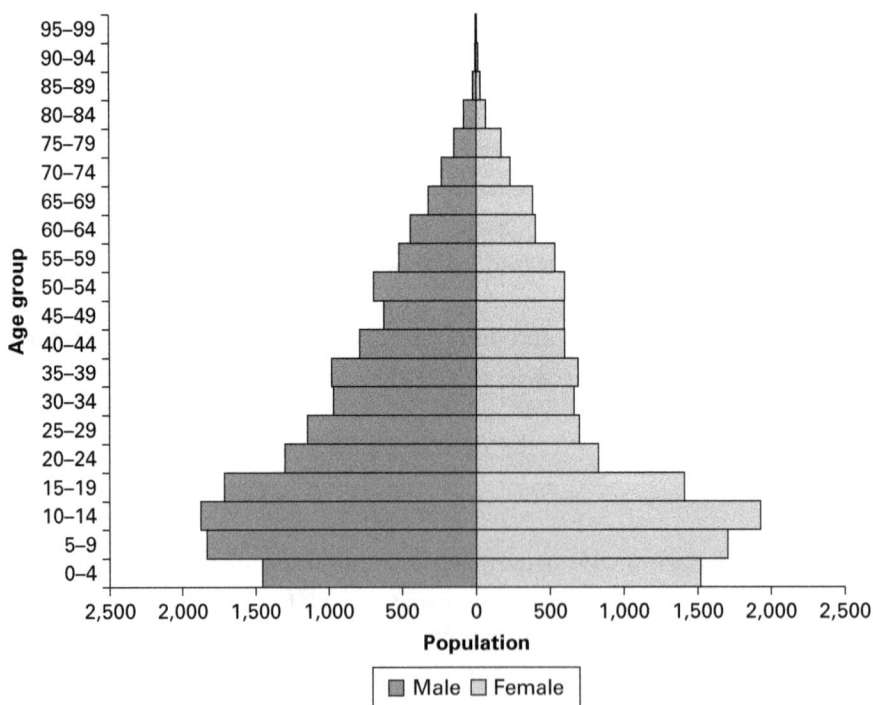

Source: Based on ADePT Gender using Nepal 2012b.

Figure 4.4: Population Pyramid in Countries with Gender Imbalance at Birth

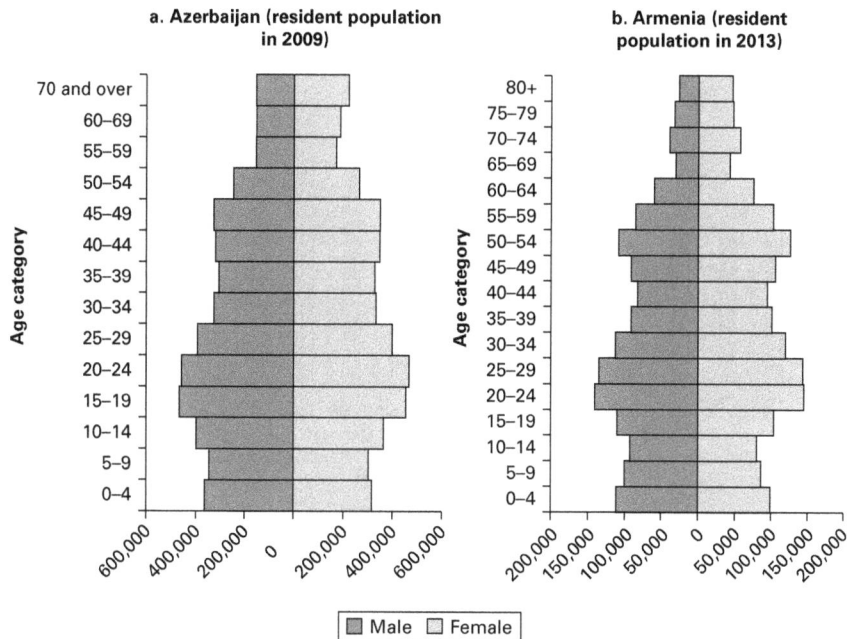

a. Azerbaijan (resident population in 2009)

b. Armenia (resident population in 2013)

☐ Male ☐ Female

Sources: South Caucasus Country Gender Assessment 2015; World Bank 2014.
Note: The Azerbaijan pyramid and the Armenia pyramid are in absolute numbers of persons.

world, after China and India. The gender asymmetry in the base of the pyramid hints at this problem.

In some countries, it is worthwhile to recalculate the population pyramids using other background characteristics. For example, if important internal waves of migration occur from rural to urban areas, where women are left behind, the pyramids should also be generated for urban and rural areas. Figure 4.5 shows the case of Kenya and the Russian Federation, where the same information that is shown in the population pyramid is plotted in a bar graph. In panel a, we see that more men than women are in urban areas, while the opposite is true in rural areas. However, the gender imbalance is not symmetric, suggesting that aside from an internal migration pattern of men from rural to urban areas, there might be migration waves of women outside the country or adult female mortality. In the Russian Federation, the pattern points to the adult mortality rate, which seems to be more acute in urban areas than in rural areas.

Figure 4.5: Sex Ratio by Age and Urban and Rural Areas for Kenya, 2005, and Russian Federation, 2006

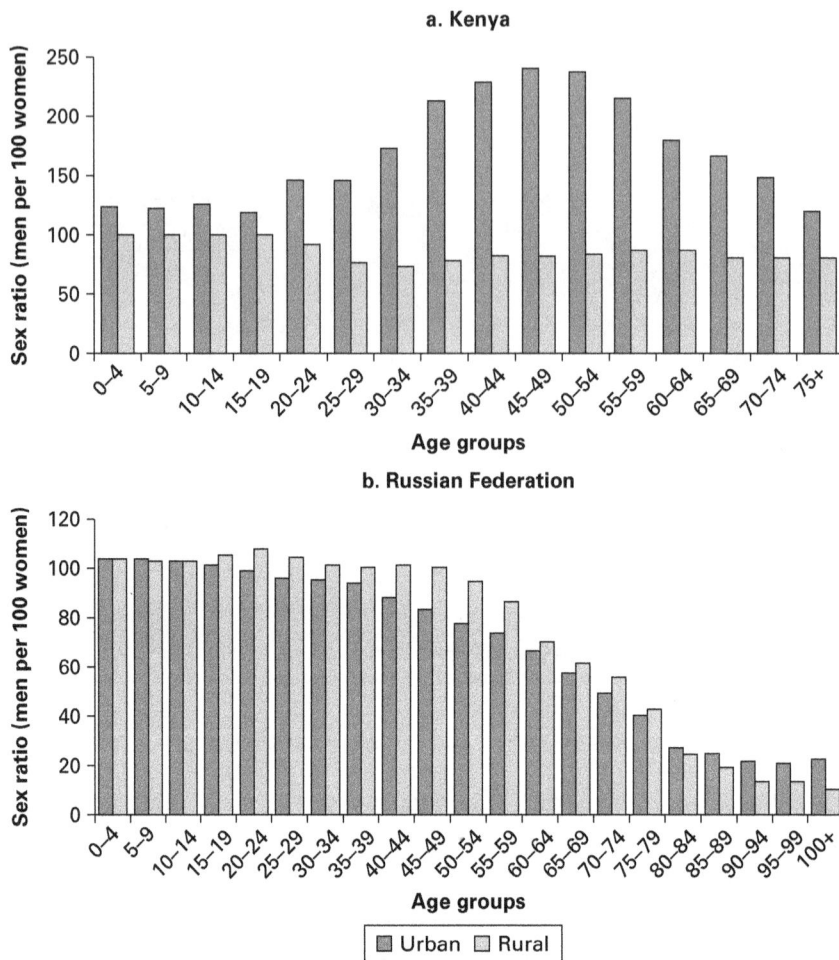

a. Kenya

b. Russian Federation

Urban ☐ Rural

Source: UN 2010.

Human Capital

Content

This section navigates the user through five ADePT tables (tables 2a–3b) that profile gender disparities in human capital: education, nutrition, and health. ADePT Gender tables 2a–2c show education outcomes, whereas ADePT tables 3a and 3b show health and nutrition outcomes. ADePT tables 2a–2c and 3a compare boys and girls, or men and women, whereas ADePT table 3b analyzes reproductive health outcomes for women of reproductive age. All outcomes are presented for the total country population and for select groups on the basis of household characteristics: gender of the household head, area of residence, poverty status, residence and poverty status combined, well-being quintile, and region of residence.

Concepts

We interpret human capital as the investment an individual receives or makes over the course of life in health, nutrition, and education. Investments in human capital have an intrinsic value, and a society that cares about equal opportunities for boys and girls and men and women should exhibit gender parity in human capital outcomes. This view is reflected in the Millennium Development Goals, which include gender parity targets. Most countries also have mandatory schooling laws that are gender blind, implying that countries value boys' and girls' education equally. For girls, better outcomes in health and education reinforce each other. Studies show that girls who are in school are more likely to be healthy—they are more likely to have a higher body mass index—and have a higher probability of finding wage work when compared with girls who are not in school. In contrast, education does not significantly change the outcomes for boys (World Bank 2012).

In addition, human capital is instrumental, as it determines both current and future productivity. Poor health outcomes cause health-related absences from the labor force and lower numbers of work hours and thus lower earnings (Case and Deaton 2003). Therefore, gender gaps in human capital accumulation generate and perpetuate wedges in labor market outcomes as reflected, for example, in the Human Opportunity Index (Molinas and others 2010). Children who are unhealthy have an increased probability of not growing into healthy adults; consequently, they cannot make meaningful economic contributions to the country. Low birth weights and childhood exposure to diseases have been linked to lower cognitive development, lower school attainment, less learning in adolescence, poorer maternal health, and even higher crime rates (Almond, Currie, and Hermann 2012; Case, Ferting, and Paxon 2005; Currie and others 2010; Currie and Tekin 2012).

Better-educated children will be more productive adults, which increases countries' economic opportunities and reduces poverty and inequality.

Finally, women's human capital also matters for household allocation of resources and affects the transmission of inequalities to future generations (Strauss and Thomas 1995; Thomas 1990). Healthier and better-educated women are more likely to make better choices for themselves and also for their offspring (Currie and Moretti 2003; Oreopoulos, Page, and Stevens 2006).

ADePT Gender lets the user choose health and nutrition indicators. In addition, ADePT Gender examines gender disparities in net and gross enrollment rates and in education attainment. The *net enrollment rate* (NER) is an indicator of access to education with respect to gender and other dimensions. Net enrollment rates are calculated as

$$Net\ enrollment\ rate_{eg} = \frac{\substack{population\ enrolled\ of\ gender\ g\ of\ the\ official \\ age\ group\ for\ the\ level\ of\ education}}{\substack{population\ of\ gender\ g\ of\ the\ official\ group\ for \\ the\ level\ of\ education}} \times 100.$$

The NER is not calculated for all education levels. Although theoretically possible and computationally feasible in ADePT Gender, tertiary education is left out since wide variations occur in the duration of programs at this level, which introduces difficulties in determining the denominator in the definition above.

The *gross enrollment rate* (GER) is also an indicator of access to education and shows the general level of participation in a given level of education. Unlike the NER, it does not count only children of official school age in the numerator. Hence, the GER is a complementary indicator, which denotes—in conjunction with the NER—the extent of overage and underage enrollment. Gross enrollment rates can exceed 100 percent and are calculated as

$$Gross\ enrollment\ rate_{eg} = \frac{\substack{population\ enrolled\ of\ gender\ g\ for\ the \\ level\ e\ of\ education}}{\substack{population\ of\ gender\ g\ of\ the\ official\ age\ group\ for\ the \\ level\ e\ of\ education}} \times 100.$$

Education attainment is measured as the percentage of the population—men or women—that has completed a certain level of education. Therefore, education attainment is calculated for only the adult working-age population.

Gender gaps in other education indicators can be examined using ADePT Education (described in box 4.1).

The past decades have seen much progress toward gender parity in education. Three main factors have been identified as increasing female enrollment in school: (a) higher returns to schooling in the labor market, (b) the removal of institutional constraints, and (c) higher household income (World Bank 2012). First, when returns to education in the labor market increase for women, parents' investments in girls' schooling also increase.

Box 4.1: Other ADePT Modules: Education and Health

ADePT Education

The ADePT Education module of the ADePT software—with its accompanying manual—produces output on education indicators and education inequality. It analyzes inequality in school participation, progression, and attainment for boys and girls. The output of ADePT Gender follows the same reasoning and structure, though it does not go into the same level of detail as ADePT Education. For example, ADePT Gender produces average gross and net enrollment rates by gender, but ADePT Education also produces such indicators as proportion out of school, gross and net intake rate, grade 1 students older than official grade 1 age, typology of those out of school, and so on. It also gives further disaggregation by gender and background characteristics (age, place of residence, gender, and quintile).

Aside from these core statistics, the software produces three additional sets of tables and graphs. The first group analyzes education inequality by computing standard inequality measures for years of schooling and earnings and for several slices of the population (gender crossed with age, place of residence, quintile). The two inequality measures are the concentration and the Theil indexes. Another group of tables examines household spending on education using household consumption data and goes into as much detail as possible with regard to type of expenditure. The third group of tables and graphs concentrates on youth and covers several employment outcomes and their interaction with education.

ADePT Health

ADePT Health is divided into two parts: health outcomes and health financing. The part on health outcomes can provide additional details, as this module covers more indicators than ADePT Gender and some of the tables are disaggregated by gender. A few of the tables also focus on maternal health. However, overall, this module is less suited to gender analysis than ADePT Education.

Users interested in going into more depth in these areas can easily switch between ADePT modules by clicking on the **Module** tab in the top bar.

Sources: Porta and others 2011; Wagstaff and others 2011.

Higher returns to education for women can result from better labor market opportunities, for instance, from the introduction of new technologies, outsourcing of production, and so forth (Jensen 2010; Oster and Millet 2010). Second, the removal of economic barriers to enrollment can be direct, reducing the cost of schooling (fees, uniforms, and books), or indirect, reducing the opportunity cost (wages that children could earn outside school or the value of household chores).

Households weigh the price of schooling and the opportunity cost of children. The balance might turn out to be different for boys and girls. Higher children's employment opportunities are associated with low school enrollment for boys (Edmonds, Pavcnik, and Topalova 2009). This is because boys are on average more likely than girls to engage in agricultural or other productive work. It has been estimated that the opportunity cost of education is about 10 times higher for boys than for girls (World Bank 2012). On the other hand, girls tend to have more responsibilities for household chores. Girls collect water, take care of younger siblings, and substitute for their mother in domestic activities. If domestic work is costly, households will be more likely to take girls out of school.

Higher household income reduces the need to rely on children's work. However, when households face economic shocks—because of a national economic crisis, a drought, or the unemployment of a breadwinner—a common coping mechanism is to reduce investments in education. Again, given that the opportunity cost and the returns to schooling are different for boys and girls, the shock might affect boys and girls differently. In middle-income countries, girls are more likely to drop out of school when household income experiences a shock. However, in high-income countries, boys with higher labor market opportunities are more likely to leave school (World Bank 2012). By the same token, safety nets that help households weather such shocks help keep children in school.

The same forces that affect the investment in children's education affect investments in health. It is worth noting that typically hardly any differences exist between boys' and girls' vaccination rates or nutrition outcomes. In addition, little or no association exists between excess mortality of girls and gender differences in vaccinations or access to nutrition or health care. The main factors explaining excess female mortality for infants and young girls is related to sanitation (World Bank 2012). Besides the social preferences for sons (discussed earlier) and households' unequal investment in boys and girls, there is a concern that health service providers discriminate in treatment, though hard evidence of such discrimination is difficult to come by (World Bank 2012).

Interpreting the Results

ADePT tables 2a–2c, 3a, and 3b show the mean value of the indicator specified in the column head for boys and girls (tables 2a, 2b, and 3a) or men and women (tables 2c and 3a), or reproductive-age women (3b) for the total of the country's population and for select groups defined by household characteristics—indicated in the table rows.

For example, table 4.5 reproduces ADePT table 2a using data from the 2010 Nepal Living Standards Survey. It shows that, overall, girls are more

Table 4.5: ADePT Gender Table 2a, Nepal 2010

Table 2a: Male and Female Net Enrollment Rates by Selected Household Characteristics: Primary and Secondary Education

	Primary		Secondary	
	Male	*Female*	*Male*	*Female*
Total	**81.2**	**84.2**	**4.1**	**4.1**
Gender of household head				
Male	79.5	83.1	4.1	3.3
Female	86.1	87.4	4.3	6.2
Area of residence				
Urban	82.2	84.7	9.0	9.2
Rural	81.0	84.1	3.0	3.0
Poverty status				
Poor	78.6	81.6	0.5	0.8
Nonpoor	82.8	86.0	5.5	5.6
Residence and poverty status				
Urban, poor	75.3	81.3	1.7	1.3
Urban, nonpoor	83.3	85.4	9.9	10.5
Rural, poor	78.8	81.6	0.4	0.7
Rural, nonpoor	82.6	86.2	4.1	4.1
Quintile of welfare aggregate				
Lowest quintile	79.1	80.5	0.0	0.8
2	79.3	84.3	1.3	0.4
3	80.8	82.8	3.1	2.1
4	82.7	86.2	5.0	7.3
Highest quintile	87.2	92.0	10.9	11.1
Region				
Eastern	83.2	87.0	4.2	4.2
Central	76.1	77.4	5.9	4.2
Western	82.1	87.1	4.6	4.8
Midwestern	86.0	86.2	0.7	3.9
Far western	83.9	92.3	1.9	2.6

Source: Based on ADePT Gender using Nepal 2012b.

likely than boys to enroll in primary school (84 percent versus 81 percent, respectively), but they are equally likely to enroll in secondary school (4.1 percent for both). The primary school advantage of girls persists when gender is crossed with other population groups (poverty, area of residence, and so forth). Figure 4.6 provides some reference values for primary and secondary enrollment rates by region of the world. Table 4.6 further shows the results on maternal health for Nepal in 2010. Although 80 percent of pregnant women had at least one prenatal care consultation during pregnancy, only 30 percent were assisted during the delivery. As table 4.7 shows, this percentage is extremely low when compared with the global average for developing countries but also with the 50 percent average rate for the Southern Asia region.

In general, gender imbalances in school enrollment vary with level of education. Despite the narrowing trend in gender education gaps, in most countries, boys are more likely than girls to be enrolled in primary education, and young women are more likely than boys to be enrolled in tertiary education—especially in countries with high rates of tertiary enrollment (World Bank 2012). However, important heterogeneity emerges both within and across countries, reflecting factors such as the gender of the household head, the level of household income, the labor market opportunities, and social norms, which can vary by region and between rural and urban areas.

In particular, higher income tends to increase the education enrollment and attainment of both boys and girls, and it often narrows gender education gaps or even reverses them in favor of girls. In addition, women tend to be more aware than men about the importance of investing in human capital, especially for female household members. Thus, in households where women have more control over resources, we observe larger investments in health and education resulting in higher gender parity in education and health. However, female-headed households typically have lower incomes, and this may have adverse effects on gender equality within the household as resources may be concentrated on boys, and girls might drop out of school to substitute for working mothers in household responsibilities.

Higher opportunity costs may also reduce investments in education in rural areas. Boys might be needed on the farm, whereas girls might be needed to care for younger siblings. Distance to school can increase the cost of education (in money, time, or both) and might contribute to favoring boys' enrollment over girls'. Also, lack of school infrastructure—such

Figure 4.6: Primary and Secondary Net Enrollment Rates, by Gender and Region, 1999 and 2007

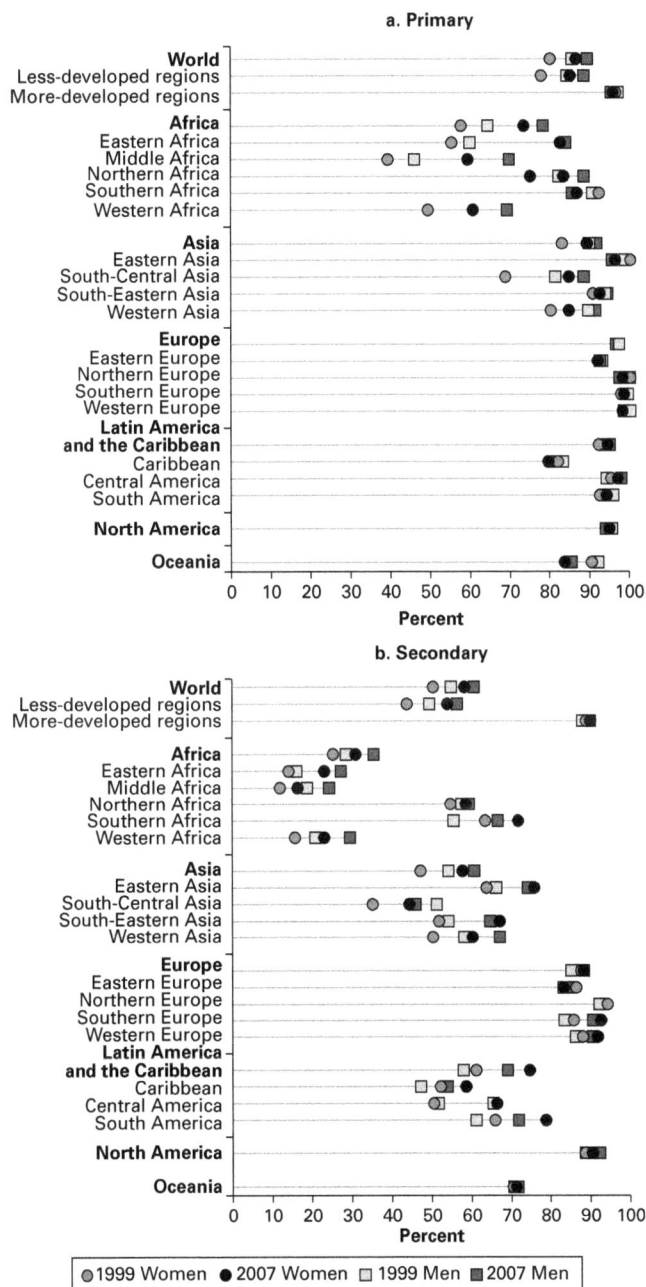

a. Primary

b. Secondary

● 1999 Women   ● 2007 Women   □ 1999 Men   ■ 2007 Men

Source: UN 2010, figures 3.8 and 3.13.
Note: Year is the latest available in the period of reference.

111

Table 4.6: ADePT Gender Table 3b, Nepal 2010

Table 3b: Maternal Health Outcomes for Women Ages 15–49 and Select Household Characteristics

	Delivery assistance	Prenatal control	Postnatal control
Total	**0.3**	**0.8**	**0.2**
Gender of household head			
Male	0.3	0.8	0.2
Female	0.4	0.8	0.2
Area of residence			
Urban	0.7	0.9	0.3
Rural	0.3	0.8	0.2
Poverty status			
Poor	0.2	0.6	0.1
Nonpoor	0.4	0.9	0.2
Residence and poverty status			
Urban, poor	0.3	0.8	0.1
Urban, nonpoor	0.8	0.9	0.3
Rural, poor	0.2	0.6	0.1
Rural, nonpoor	0.4	0.9	0.2
Quintile of welfare aggregate			
Lowest quintile	0.2	0.6	0.1
2	0.2	0.8	0.2
3	0.3	0.8	0.2
4	0.5	0.9	0.2
Highest quintile	0.7	1.0	0.4
Region			
Eastern	0.4	0.8	0.2
Central	0.3	0.8	0.2
Western	0.4	0.9	0.2
Midwestern	0.2	0.7	0.2
Far western	0.3	0.7	0.2

Source: Based on ADePT Gender using Nepal 2012b.

Table 4.7: Women Receiving Prenatal Care, Skilled Assistance at Birth, and Deliveries in Health Facilities, by Region, 1996 and 2000–08

	Percentage pregnant women receiving prenatal care (at least 1 visit)		Percentage deliveries with skilled assistance		Percentage deliveries in health facilities	
	1996	2000–08	1996	2000–08	1996	2000–08
Africa						
Northern Africa	65	80	66	82	57	78
Southern Africa	86	92	67	78	64	72
Eastern, Middle and Western Africa	66	79	42	53	37	48
Asia						
Eastern Asia	93	94	95	98	89	94
South-Eastern Asia	77	77	64	62	52	48

(continued)

Table 4.7: Women Receiving Prenatal Care, Skilled Assistance at Birth, and Deliveries in Health Facilities, by Region, 1996 and 2000–08 *(continued)*

	Percentage pregnant women receiving prenatal care (at least 1 visit)		Percentage deliveries with skilled assistance		Percentage deliveries in health facilities	
	1996	2000–08	1996	2000–08	1996	2000–08
Southern Asia	49	68	39	52	28	46
Central Asia	90	94	93	96	92	91
Western Asia	82	91	82	89	79	86
Latin America and the Caribbean						
Caribbean	95	96	88	92	86	79
Central America	75	90	70	82	62	76
South America	79	91	80	86	76	85
Oceania	**84**	**–**	**81**	**81**	**87**	**–**
Eastern Europe	**97**	**97**	**99**	**100**	**98**	**99**

Source: UN 2010, table 2.4.
Note: Year is the latest available in the period of reference.

as separate bathrooms for boys and girls—as well as sexual harassment might push girls and young women out of school. In general, the absolute and relative costs of education for girls and boys are the most relevant factor for determining gender educational level and parity. Policies to eliminate primary-level school fees and provide universal primary education were often associated with improving gender parity at the primary level (World Bank 2012).

When comparing and interpreting ADePT tables 2a and 2b, the user should remember that the net and gross enrollment rates provide different information. Both rates show education coverage for a certain level of education; however, the NER is constrained by age, whereas the GER is not. Thus, a positive difference between the GER and NER indicates incidence of underage and overage enrollment because of early or late entrants and grade repetition, respectively. If the GER exceeds 100 percent, additional information about the extent of repetition and late entrants is required to better interpret this indicator. The complement of the NER is usually thought to provide a measure of the proportion of children not enrolled at the specified level of education, but some of these children and youths could be enrolled at other levels.

Some possible explanations for observed gender differences between GER and NER include (a) girls can enroll later than boys or be the first to drop out in difficult times (World Bank 2012), and (b) if overage children are more likely to drop out of school, then boys might be more likely to be overage than girls, if they have to combine school with work. Boys and young men often exhibit higher repetition and dropout rates than their female counterparts at the primary level. However, whether the pressure to drop out is higher for boys or for girls depends on the country (UNESCO 2012, 43, 56).

The same explanations applied to schooling are relevant to gender gaps in boys' and girls' health and nutrition. Because of country efforts to vaccinate all children, vaccination rates tend to indicate full coverage of boys and girls. However, gender gaps might still be observed in some countries or for other outcomes, such as stunting, underweight, wasting, or vitamin deficiencies (such as vitamin A and salt iodization). Studies in South Asian countries using siblings who still live in the same household have found a higher percentage of boys who are fully immunized compared with girls (Singh 2012).

However, differences in human capital investments are not only a matter of boys and girls but also of the adult population. Given that adult education is rare, changes over time in adult education attainment are the result of education improvements in younger cohorts. However, other factors might be at play for adult health outcomes. Men and women might have different risks for certain diseases and factors, such as HIV or maternal health. As before, income, access to infrastructure, and access to information are key factors associated with preventive health care. For maternal health, access to prenatal care, skilled assistance at birth, and postnatal care are important factors that determine maternal mortality rates and children's health.

Health outcomes are often strongly associated with the availability of care, infrastructure, and similar factors. ADePT Education and ADePT Health are great resources that go beyond ADePT Gender (see box 4.1).

Economic Opportunities

Content

This section guides the user through 27 tables (ADePT tables 4–7) and seven figures that describe gender disparities in economic opportunities. ADePT tables 4 and ADePT figure 4 show the gender gap at the extensive margin—that is, in engagement in economic activities. ADePT tables 5 and 6 and ADePT figure 5 show gender gaps at the intensive margin, including type of employment and hours of work. ADePT tables 7a–7d show labor market wages. ADePT table 8 profiles gender differences in access to resources, and ADePT table 9 tabulates the main labor market outcomes for different groups of the population that could be linked to channels affecting economic opportunity: (a) number of children to capture family burden, (b) levels of education to capture investments in human capital, and (c) age to capture life-cycle channels, such as fertility and firm-specific and on-the-job human capital investments. Most of the tables are presented for the total working-age population, disaggregating for men and women. When describing employment, tables and figures represent most of the times men and women in wage employment. As before, further analysis is done for three vulnerable groups: rural and poor households, separately for male- and female-headed households.

Concepts

The indicators of economic opportunities profiled in the ADePT output are grouped into four categories. The first two refer to the extensive and intensive margin of participation in economic activities. The extensive margin simply measures participation, not taking into account the depth of the engagement. The intensive margin looks at depth by examining the type of employment and the number of hours worked. The third group is a measure of labor productivity—wages—and the fourth focuses on access to resources that might influence the observed labor market outcomes. This comprehensive set of outcomes is important given that the main message from the *WDR 2012: Gender Equality and Development* (World Bank 2012) is that gender gaps in productivity do not reflect that women are less productive farmers, entrepreneurs, or workers than men. Rather, gender differences in productivity and earnings are a result of differences in the type of economic activities that employ women (occupations and sectors) and women's limited access to resources.

Labor Market Participation

The working-age population can be employed, unemployed, or neither. A person is in the labor force if he or she is either employed or unemployed. A person not in the labor force is said to be out of the labor force or inactive. The size of the labor force (*LF*) is given by

$$LF = E + U,$$

where E is the number of employed persons, and U is the number of unemployed persons. Note that, as described in chapter 3, characterizing a person as employed does not take into account how many hours he or she works. Thus, this indicator does not say anything about the "intensity" of work. The labor force participation rate is defined as

$$LFP = \frac{E+U}{WAP} \times 100,$$

where LFP is the labor force participation rate, and WAP is the total working-age population of the country. If we want to construct the labor force participation of men or women, we need to adjust the formula in the following way:

$$LFP_g = \frac{E_g + U_g}{WAP_g} \times 100,$$

where g is the gender (male or female), LFP_g is the labor force participation rate of gender g, E_g is the number of employed persons of gender g, U_g is the number of unemployed persons of gender g, and WAP_g is the number of working-age persons of gender g.

The employment rate is defined as

$$Employment_g = \frac{E_g}{WAP_g} \times 100.$$

And the unemployment rate is

$$Unemployment_g = \frac{U_g}{LF_g} \times 100.$$

The above rates can be adjusted to represent a population group. In each case, it needs to make the subgroup the reference group. Take, for example, the labor force participation rate

$$LFP_{gx} = \frac{E_{gx} + U_{gx}}{WAP_{gx}} \times 100,$$

where x represents persons belonging to a certain group. The group can be defined either by individual or household characteristics.

A group of particular interest is the working poor, defined as employed persons who live in a household whose members are estimated to be below the nationally defined poverty line. The number of working poor can be calculated using the equation

$$Working\ poor = poverty\ rate \times labor\ force_{15},$$

where $labor\ force_{15}$ is the labor force ages 15 years and older. The key assumption behind using the labor force instead of employment numbers is that all, or nearly all, of the poor in the labor force are employed. This assumption is made because in countries with no social safety nets, poor individuals must work to maintain a subsistence level. Note that 15 years and older is typically used to define a country's standard working-age population. Some countries, however, apply other age limits. The nationally defined working-age population is what should be used here.

The working poverty rate is the proportion of working poor in total employment:

$$Working\ poverty\ rate = \frac{E_P}{E} \times 100,$$

where E_p is the number of employed persons living in a household with income below the poverty line, and E is the total number of employed persons. The version of the working poverty rate by gender is

$$Working\ poverty\ rate_g = \frac{E_{Pg}}{E_g} \times 100,$$

where we condition the expression on the gender of the employed population.

Another group of interest could be youths. Low labor force participation of young people should not be a concern if they are studying. However, a common problem is idleness. A young person is said to be *idle* if he or she is not in school or training, not employed, and not looking for job (World Bank 2014).[10] In other words, the concept of idleness serves to sort the percentage of out-of-labor force youths who are studying from those who are not.

Job/Employment Characteristics

The intensive margin is used to express the intensity of work. To measure the intensive margin, ADePT Gender provides two types of indicators: (a) the type of job, and (b) the number of hours worked as a measure of job engagement.

Systematic differences exist between men's jobs and women's jobs, whether across sectors, industries, occupations, job types, or firm types. The term *employment segregation* or *occupational segregation* refers to the unequal concentration of men and women in different jobs or occupations. Women are often more likely than men to work in agriculture and in many service sectors. Women are also overrepresented among unpaid workers and in the informal sectors. In many countries, better educated women seek out work in the public sector, which is viewed as socially acceptable. Women are more likely to be teachers, nurses, clerical workers, and sales and service employees. Men are more likely to work in construction and transport sectors. The clustering of women in particular groups is in part the reflection of the fact that some jobs are by nature less demanding with regard to hours and responsibilities and thus are friendlier to women who have significant family responsibilities. However, persisting social norms are another important factor.

The evidence suggests that various factors are at play that result in gender segregation and gender gaps in hours worked. One is economic structure. As countries develop, their economic structure changes and with it the types of jobs that are available (Gaddis and Klasen 2014; Mammen and Paxson 2000). Rural farm employment is replaced by city jobs, for instance, in factories or the service sector. This change of economic structure means more salaried and fewer informal jobs. These same patterns that are seen across countries are observed within a country by comparing low- and high-income households.

Beyond the economic structure, other factors influence occupational segregation and the number of hours worked. The *WDR* (World Bank 2012) argues that the four main factors are (a) gender differences in time-use patterns, (b) access to productive inputs, (c) the effects of markets and institutional failures, and (d) the constraints imposed by the choice in educational field (Flabbi 2011). Women are more likely to respond to market signals—higher wages—when other market and institutional failures are absent. For example, female labor force participation tends to grow faster when childcare services are in place or when labor participation (or the occupation) is seen as socially acceptable. More details on each of these factors can be found in World Bank (2012).

Earnings

Earnings are the main outcome by which to compare men's and women's performance in the labor market, either when running their own business or when working for others. A large part of the gender wage gap and the average productivity difference between male- and female-led firms is explained by occupational and industry segregation, as the jobs that are also more likely to be performed by women tend to be paid less. Furthermore, in a fairly large number of countries and occupations, segregation is universal, which prevents the analysis from finding a comparator group to even calculate a gender wage or productivity gap (Ñopo, Daza, and Ramos 2011).

Moreover, the difference in earnings can be masked by benefits; thus, as explained in chapter 3, earnings should include all types of remunerations. However, it is not always possible to have reliable data in earnings, and the analysis should use wages.[11] To control for differences in productivity and compensation on the job that are related to the number of hours worked, ADePT Gender compares the earnings per hour of work for men and women.

Interpreting the Results

Labor Market Participation

ADePT tables 4a–4d show three main indicators for economic participation—labor force participation rate, employment rate, and unemployment rate—for men and women by select individual and household characteristics. Each number represents the rate corresponding to the label indicated in the column head (for example, labor force participation rate) and for a population group that is determined by the combination of the column subhead (for example, men) and the row (for example, ages 15–24). The tables show the same breakdown used in previous tables, according to individual characteristics (table 4a), household characteristics (table 4b), or the combination of the two (tables 4c and 4d). ADePT figure 2 shows the percentage of women and men in each of three mutually exclusive labor statuses: employment, unemployment, and out-of-the labor force. Knowing the percentage of women in the employed or the unemployed population is highly important for policy makers. If a country is planning to introduce an unemployment benefit or raise labor taxes, for example, this information would indicate which group of the population would be most affected by the reform.

Globally, labor force participation is typically higher for men than for women. For example, in Panama in 2008, about 50 percent of women and 82 percent of men participated in the labor market (see table 4.8 showing ADePT table 4a). Factors affecting female and male participation relate to household-level decisions of labor supply and the division of tasks (see chapter 5 for a brief presentation of the household labor supply model). Map 4.1 provides a world map showing the wide variation of female labor force participation across countries Moreover, this indicator is highly correlated to development (measured by gross domestic product per capita) exhibiting a U-shaped function (see figure 4.7).[12]

The gender gap in unemployment rate can favor men or women, since opposing forces exist. On the one hand, women often face greater difficulties in finding a job than men. Women might have smaller networks and thus less access to information about job vacancies; they might be more selective in the jobs they apply for, so as to balance work and family; and they might face discrimination in the hiring process, resulting in higher unemployment rates and longer unemployment spells. On the other hand, women might become discouraged after a period of unemployment, abandon the job search sooner than men, and exit the labor force. If the latter effect is stronger than the former, women will have both lower unemployment rates and lower labor force participation rates than men.

As before, these factors could result in various outcomes for different sectors of the population. For example, better-educated women might have greater incentives to work, since the cost of staying at home (measured by the lost wage) is higher than for less educated women. However, if better-educated women marry better-educated men (assortative matching), their nonlabor income tends to be higher, and thus they also have more incentives to stay at home.[13] If the latter effect dominates, we would observe in ADePT table 4a that labor force participation decreases with the level of education. In the case of Panama, we observe that the first effect dominates the second, since female labor force participation increases with the level of education (table 4.9).

Table 4.8: ADePT Gender Table 4a, Panama 2008

Table 4a: Male and Female Labor Force Participation, Employment, and Unemployment Rates by Selected Individual Characteristics

	Labor force participation rate		Employment rate		Unemployment rate		Share of population out of the labor force	
	Male	*Female*	*Male*	*Female*	*Male*	*Female*	*Male*	*Female*
Total	**82.2**	**49.7**	**80.3**	**47.7**	**1.9**	**2.0**	**17.8**	**50.3**
Age								
15–24	59.3	31.4	56.1	28.5	3.2	2.9	40.7	68.6
25–34	93.1	58.2	91.5	55.7	1.6	2.5	6.9	41.8
35–44	96.2	63.6	95.1	61.2	1.1	2.3	3.8	36.4
45–54	92.4	59.3	91.2	58.3	1.2	1.1	7.6	40.7
55–64	76.9	35.8	75.4	35.8	1.5	0.0	23.1	64.2
Marital status								
Union	95.1	46.1	93.5	44.4	1.5	1.6	4.9	53.9
Married	90.8	49.8	89.8	48.7	1.0	1.2	9.2	50.2
Married separated	89.7	73.5	86.9	71.1	2.8	2.5	10.3	26.5
Union separated	89.5	66.9	88.6	63.6	0.9	3.3	10.5	33.1
Divorced	81.6	71.8	77.3	70.0	4.3	1.8	18.4	28.2
Widowed	83.7	44.8	83.7	43.4	0.0	1.4	16.3	55.2
Single	66.1	45.7	63.4	42.7	2.7	3.0	33.9	54.3
Education								
No education	85.2	39.2	84.2	38.9	1.0	0.3	14.8	60.8
Primary	78.5	36.9	77.0	35.4	1.6	1.5	21.5	63.1
Secondary	87.3	55.6	84.1	52.0	3.2	3.6	12.7	44.4
Post-secondary	85.9	72.7	84.0	70.0	1.9	2.7	14.1	27.3

Source: Based on ADePT Gender using Panama 2008.

Note: The working-age population is ages 15–64. Primary and secondary refer to completed levels.

Map 4.1: Female Labor Force Participation around the World

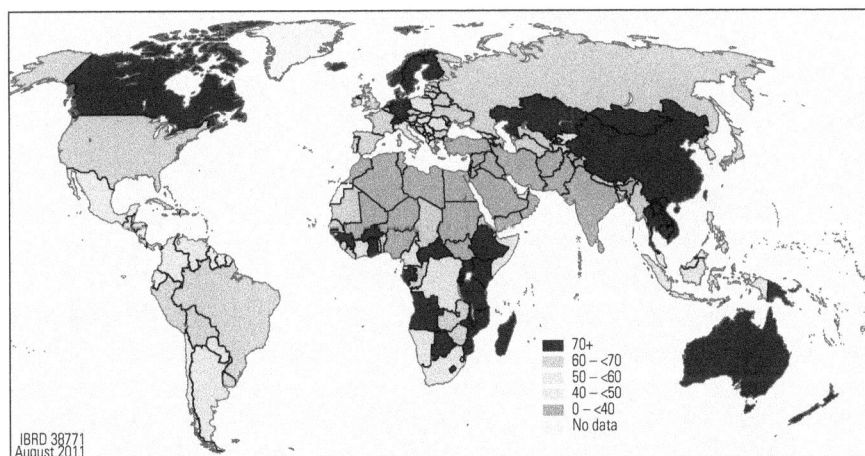

Source: World Bank 2012.

Figure 4.7: U-Shape Relationship between Female Labor Force Participation and GDP, 1990 and 2010

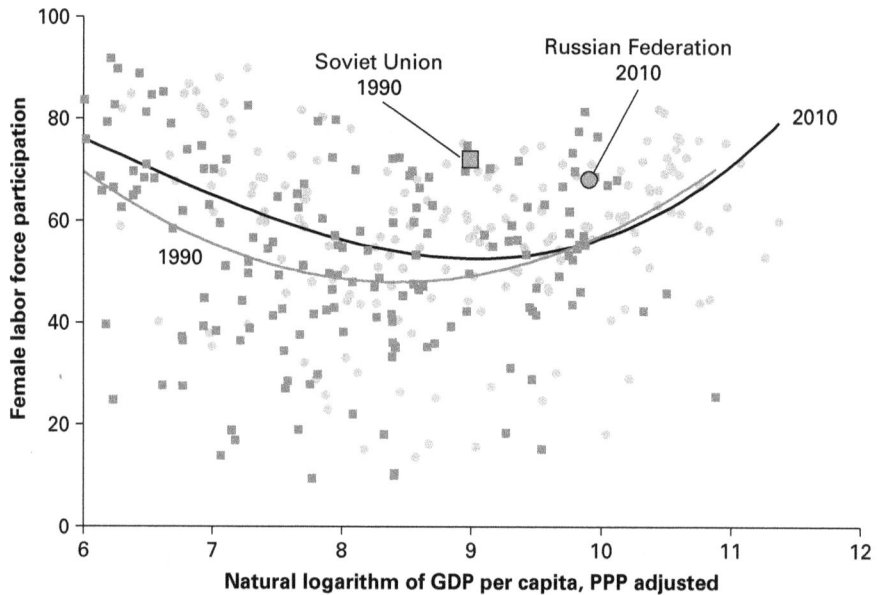

Source: Gamberoni, Munoz Boudet, and Posadas 2014.
Note: GDP = gross domestic product; PPP = purchasing power parity.

Alternatively, women in poor households may be more likely to work outside the home to supplement household income or to do unpaid work (working in the household or on the farm). If this hypothesis were true, ADePT table 4b should show that female labor force participation rates decrease when we move from the bottom to the top quintile of the welfare aggregate. Our example of Panama does not reflect this case. Female labor force participation for the bottom quintile is 36 percent, but it rises to 65 percent at the top of the welfare distribution.

Obviously, these factors do not operate in isolation. Both education and household income level matter, as do many other factors. ADePT tables 4a–4e show only partial effects, which ought to be complemented with further regression analysis and in-depth research to understand the contribution of each factor. Part III of this manual describes how to further analyze gender gaps in labor market outcomes to estimate the contribution of different variables to gender gaps in the labor market. In addition, the

Table 4.9: ADePT Gender Table 4b, Panama 2008

Table 4b: Male and Female Labor Force Participation, Employment, and Unemployment Rates by Selected Household Characteristics

	Labor force participation rate		Employment rate		Unemployment rate		Share of population out of the labor force	
	Male	Female	Male	Female	Male	Female	Male	Female
Total	**82.2**	**49.7**	**80.3**	**47.7**	**1.9**	**2.0**	**17.8**	**50.3**
Gender of household head								
Male	83.8	45.6	82.1	43.7	1.7	1.9	16.2	54.4
Female	75.8	58.5	73.2	56.2	2.6	2.3	24.2	41.5
Area of residence								
Urban	81.0	54.4	78.7	51.9	2.3	2.5	19.0	45.6
Rural	84.6	39.2	83.5	38.2	1.1	1.0	15.4	60.8
Poverty status								
Poor	82.7	36.8	81.2	35.1	1.5	1.7	17.3	63.2
Nonpoor	82.0	54.4	80.0	52.2	2.0	2.2	18.0	45.6
Residence and poverty status								
Urban, poor	77.0	37.7	74.4	34.0	2.6	3.7	23.0	62.3
Urban, nonpoor	81.6	57.3	79.4	54.9	2.2	2.3	18.4	42.7
Rural, poor	85.5	36.3	84.6	35.8	0.9	0.5	14.5	63.7
Rural, nonpoor	83.5	42.6	82.3	41.1	1.2	1.5	16.5	57.4
Quintile of welfare aggregate								
Lowest quintile	83.7	36.3	82.3	35.0	1.3	1.2	16.3	63.7
2	81.0	39.7	79.1	38.0	1.8	1.7	19.0	60.3
3	80.6	48.0	78.2	45.7	2.4	2.3	19.4	52.0
4	82.7	53.0	80.5	50.4	2.2	2.6	17.3	47.0
Highest quintile	83.1	64.7	81.5	62.6	1.5	2.1	16.9	35.3
Region								
Western	82.1	44.3	80.6	43.3	1.4	1.0	17.9	55.7
Eastern	85.6	58.4	85.4	58.1	0.2	0.2	14.4	41.6
Metropolitan	81.4	53.0	79.2	50.3	2.2	2.7	18.6	47.0
Central	84.4	43.2	83.0	42.1	1.4	1.1	15.6	56.8

Source: Based on ADePT Gender using Panama 2008.
Note: The working-age population is ages 15–64.

ADePT Labor and ADePT ILO modules provide useful resources to further understand the functioning of the labor market and some of the gender gaps. The main feature of ADePT Labor is that it combines labor markets and poverty angles by looking at the labor income of the household. In addition, ADePT ILO produces International Labour Organization labor market indicators that can be computed using household surveys.

Job Characteristics

ADePT Gender figure 5 (figure 4.8) shows the percentage of women in different types of jobs defined by the type of work (wage work, self-employment,

Figure 4.8: ADePT Gender Figure 5a, Panama, 2008
Percentage of Women in Each Employment Type

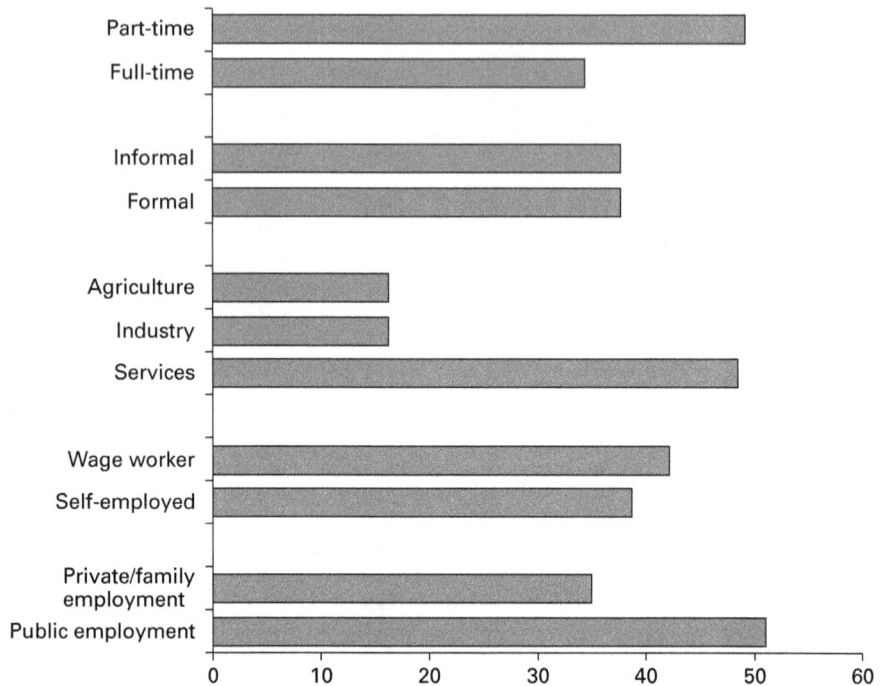

Source: Based on ADePT Gender using Panama 2008.

and so on), the sector, the type of firm ownership (public or private), the formality status, the full-time status, the occupation, and the industry. Generally, women are more likely to be part-time workers and to have service or public sector jobs. Women are often clustered in certain industries—such as health, education, and hotels and restaurants—and in certain occupations related to administrative tasks. For example, in Panama in 2008, 51 percent of public sector workers were female, and only 35 percent of private sector jobs were held by women.

ADePT tables 5a (table 4.10) and 5b show the distribution of employment by job characteristics for men and women separately. All the numbers in the two tables are read in blocks of rows. The first block shows the distribution of the population that is employed, unemployed, and out of the labor force. The following blocks show the distribution of the employed population by specific job characteristics as indicated by the block subtitle

Table 4.10: ADePT Gender Table 5a, Panama 2008

*Table 5a: Male and Female Employment by Selected Employment
Characteristics: Total, Rural, and Poor Households*

	Total		Rural		Poor	
	Male	*Female*	*Male*	*Female*	*Male*	*Female*
Total			100.0	100.0		
Employed	80.3	47.7	83.5	38.2	81.2	35.1
Unemployed	1.9	2.0	1.1	1.0	1.5	1.7
Out of labor force	17.8	50.3	15.4	60.8	17.3	63.2
Public sector employment						
Private/family employment	88.8	80.0	94.0	88.6	96.4	94.4
Public employment	11.2	20.0	6.0	11.4	3.6	5.6
Full-time status						
Part-time	17.4	28.0	25.4	47.7	27.1	52.2
Full-time	82.6	72.0	74.6	52.3	72.9	47.8
Formal status						
Informal	52.2	50.0	72.7	78.2	73.1	84.2
Formal	47.8	50.0	27.3	21.8	26.9	15.8
Broad sector						
Agriculture	22.8	7.2	55.5	25.8	54.3	27.5
Industry	24.5	8.6	18.2	14.1	19.3	14.2
Services	52.7	84.2	26.3	60.2	26.4	58.4
Work category						
Wage work	79.3	81.5	75.7	63.4	77.7	64.2
Self-employed	20.7	18.5	24.3	36.6	22.3	35.8

Source: Based on ADePT Gender using Panama 2008.
Note: The working-age population is age 15–64. Private employment includes family employment.

(for example, part time or full time). The last two columns present results for two vulnerable populations—rural areas and the poor. For example, in Panama, about half of employed men and women are informal workers. However, this percentage rises considerably if the analysis is restricted to men and women living in poor households, where 73 percent of employed poor men and 84 percent of employed poor women are informal workers. Table 4.11 provides some reference values of the distribution for women and men by type of work.

This information is complemented with four additional graphs that show women's participation along the welfare distribution in agricultural and non-agricultural employment (ADePT figures 5b and 5c) and in wage work versus self-employment (ADePT figures 4c and 4d). Nonagricultural jobs are typically more productive, and hence better remunerated, than agricultural jobs. Moreover, individuals from the upper end of the welfare distribution are more likely to have benefited from secondary or tertiary education that allows

Table 4.11: Distribution of Women and Men by Type of Work

	Women				Men			
	Wage and salaried workers (%)	Employers (%)	Own-account workers (%)	Contributing family workers (%)	Wage and salaried workers (%)	Employers (%)	Own-account workers (%)	Contributing family workers (%)
Africa								
Northern Africa (3)	46	2	19	34	58	8	22	11
Southern Africa (3)	76	3	17	4	82	7	9	2
Eastern and Western Africa (6)	20	1	47	32	24	1	56	18
Asia								
Eastern Asia (3)	86	2	7	5	80	7	13	<1
South-Eastern Asia (6)	52	2	23	23	52	4	34	9
Southern Asia (5)	30	1	22	46	44	3	40	12
Western Asia (6)	80	1	6	12	79	5	13	2
CIS in Asia (4)	45	1	39	15	50	3	39	7
Latin America and the Caribbean								
Caribbean (5)	80	2	16	2	67	3	27	1
Central America (6)	64	3	25	7	64	6	24	6
South America (9)	62	3	28	6	62	6	28	3
More developed regions								
Eastern Europe (8)	84	2	10	4	78	4	16	1
Northern Europe (5)	93	2	4	1	84	5	10	<1
Southern Europe (9)	81	3	10	6	74	6	17	2
Western Europe (4)	89	3	6	3	84	7	8	1
Other more developed regions (4)	88	2	7	2	83	5	11	1

Source: UN 2010.
Note: Parenthetical numerals indicate the number of countries. CIS = Commonwealth of Independent States.

them to access employment opportunities outside agriculture. Thus, we would expect that the share of agricultural employment declines as we move along the welfare distribution. Figure 4.9 illustrates this pattern for Panama.

Regarding the measures of work intensity, ADePT tables 5c and 5d show the average number of hours worked (in the specified reference period; see chapter 3) for different groups of the population indicated in the column heads and for different types of employment indicated in the rows. In general, it is observed that men work on average more hours than women. For example, in Panama, the average man works 189 hours per month (45 hours per week), compared to 161 hours for the average woman (38 hours per week).[14]

It is often argued that women choose informal jobs because they are more flexible than formal ones. In Panama, women in informal jobs work

Figure 4.9: ADePT Gender Figures 5b and 5c, Panama 2008

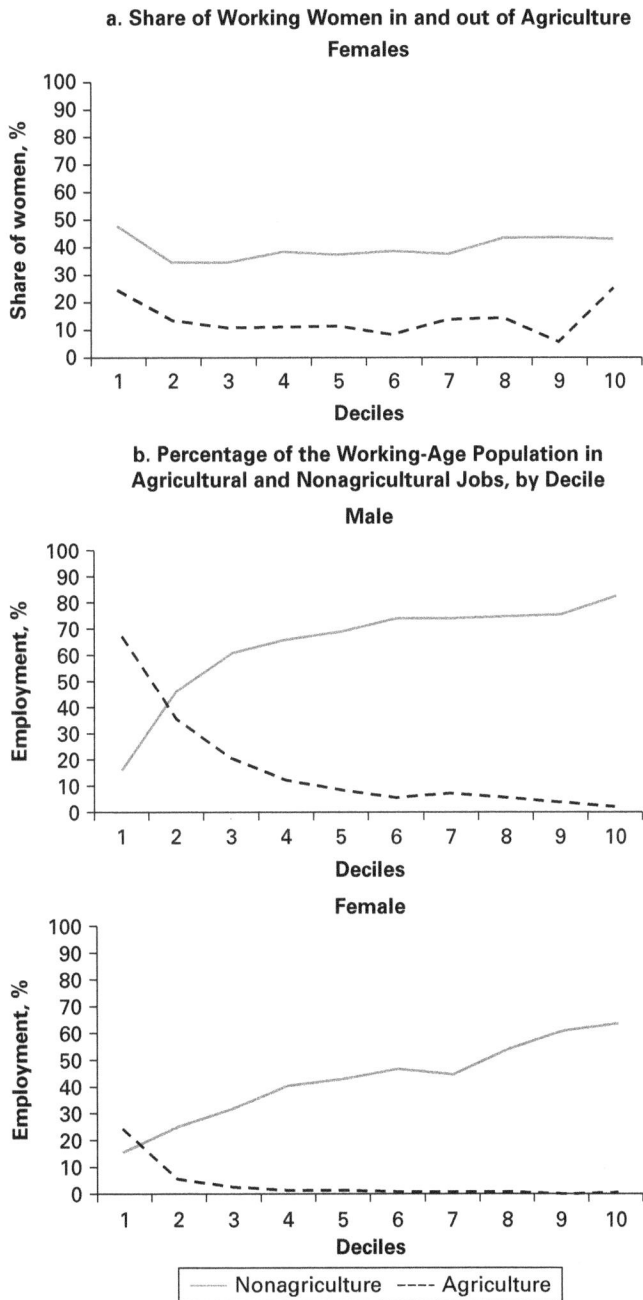

a. Share of Working Women in and out of Agriculture

Females

b. Percentage of the Working-Age Population in Agricultural and Nonagricultural Jobs, by Decile

Male

Female

Nonagriculture ---- Agriculture

Source: Based on ADePT Gender using Panama 2008.
Note: The working-age population is ages 15–64.

127

fewer hours per week than the average woman. Also, women in part-time jobs typically work much less than the threshold of 35 hours per week. In Panama, they work fewer than 20 hours per week. It is also found that many women prefer public sector jobs because of their stability, relatively higher pay, and lower time demands. However, in Panama, men and women employed in the public sector report working slightly more hours than men and women employed in the private sector (see table 4.12, which corresponds to ADePT table 6a).

Earnings

ADePT tables 5e–5h show monthly earnings by gender and type of job. The user needs to ensure that the variables populated in the **Hours** and **Earnings** fields have the same periodicity (see chapter 3 for more details). ADePT tables 5e and 5f show mean earnings, while ADePT tables 5g and 5h show median earnings. Tables 5e and 5g present the statistics for different types of jobs, while tables 5f and 5h show them for industry and occupation. All statistics are interpreted as in ADePT tables 5a and 5b. They show the

Table 4.12: ADePT Gender Table 6a, Panama 2008

Table 6a: Male and Female Mean Monthly Hours Worked by Selected Employment Characteristics: Total, Rural, and Poor Households

	Total		Rural		Poor	
	Male	*Female*	*Male*	*Female*	*Male*	*Female*
Total	**188.9**	**160.9**	**179.2**	**139.0**	**176.2**	**132.1**
Public sector employment						
Private/family employment	188.4	160.0	177.9	136.4	175.8	131.1
Public employment	192.7	164.0	197.1	157.2	186.9	147.8
Full-time status						
Part-time	83.2	71.6	84.5	66.3	83.1	67.0
Full-time	211.0	195.4	211.3	204.8	210.9	202.9
Formal status						
Informal	176.9	141.8	168.0	126.9	165.3	121.1
Formal	200.4	178.7	204.2	177.7	201.5	185.5
Broad sector						
Agriculture	168.2	97.8	166.4	95.2	162.3	91.8
Industry	190.5	155.3	192.7	128.6	192.4	145.3
Services	195.7	166.2	193.0	158.5	189.4	146.5
Work category						
Wage work	195.1	170.8	198.1	161.3	196.4	155.7
Self-employed	179.8	134.9	178.8	142.8	179.9	131.5

Source: Based on ADePT Gender using Panama 2008.
Note: The working-age population is ages 15–64.

statistic for a group of the population that is defined by the combination of the column's heads and subheads and the row titles. For example, the top left cell of ADePT table 7a (see table 4.13) contains the mean earnings for all employed men.

More vulnerable jobs are usually associated with larger gender earnings gaps. If women lack access to better paid formal jobs, they will also have problems accessing well-paid informal jobs. Instead, some men who choose informal jobs most likely had the option of taking formal jobs but preferred to remain in the informal sector. In addition, the interpretation of ADePT tables 5e–5h needs to be linked to the previous findings. For example, a larger percentage of women in vulnerable jobs could face restricted access to good job opportunities,[15] and thus higher gender earnings gaps should be expected. Missing data on wages are particularly common for women. Further understanding of these issues can be gained from regression analysis (see chapters 5 and 6) and by looking at access to productive resources and repeating the analysis for population subgroups, as discussed next.

Table 4.13: ADePT Gender Table 7a, Panama 2008

Table 7a: Male and Female Mean Monthly Earnings by Selected Employment Characteristics

	Total		Rural		Poor	
	Male	*Female*	*Male*	*Female*	*Male*	*Female*
Total	**529.3**	**454.8**	**311.4**	**210.1**	**233.3**	**153.1**
Public sector employment						
Private/family employment	482.9	387.0	287.3	151.7	223.5	135.7
Public employment	859.7	694.1	622.2	527.1	448.8	359.7
Full-time status						
Part-time	259.0	179.5	147.1	86.1	115.5	73.5
Full-time	579.4	545.8	355.7	291.0	267.8	215.5
Formal status						
Informal	349.0	211.7	229.1	106.3	162.9	97.2
Formal	690.1	652.8	472.0	453.3	374.6	351.4
Broad sector						
Agriculture	218.8	109.9	192.3	93.0	142.7	54.8
Industry	479.1	350.0	383.6	63.1	300.7	84.6
Services	652.0	476.0	452.2	260.7	322.4	183.8
Work category						
Wage work	630.0	519.3	449.9	302.1	348.0	217.6
Self-employed	414.1	212.7	318.5	83.3	205.8	68.1

Source: Based on ADePT Gender using Panama 2008.
Note: The working-age population is ages 15–64.

Disaggregating Economic Outcomes–By Life-Cycle Stage and Education

Economic outcomes, particularly for women, are strongly influenced by education and family responsibilities. ADePT tables 9b–9d show economic outcomes by broad age group (suffix A, for age)—which is meant to reflect (a woman's) life-cycle stage—the number children in the household (suffix C for children), and the level of education (suffix E for education). ADePT table 9b shows labor force participation and employment rates (extensive margin), ADePT table 9c presents numbers of hours (intensive margin), and ADePT table 9d earnings. The interpretation of the tables is otherwise the same as in the corresponding ADePT tables 5a—5c.

Figure 4.10 shows labor force participation rates for men and women of different ages in selected countries. For example, in Japan, women substantially decrease their engagement in the labor market when they have young children, but they return later on. In Chile, female labor force participation is generally much lower, but a much smaller dip occurs for women in their 30s, suggesting that some women work and others stay out of the labor market all their life. In Tunisia, there is evidence of cohort

Figure 4.10: Female Labor Force Participation over the Life Cycle

(a) Japan

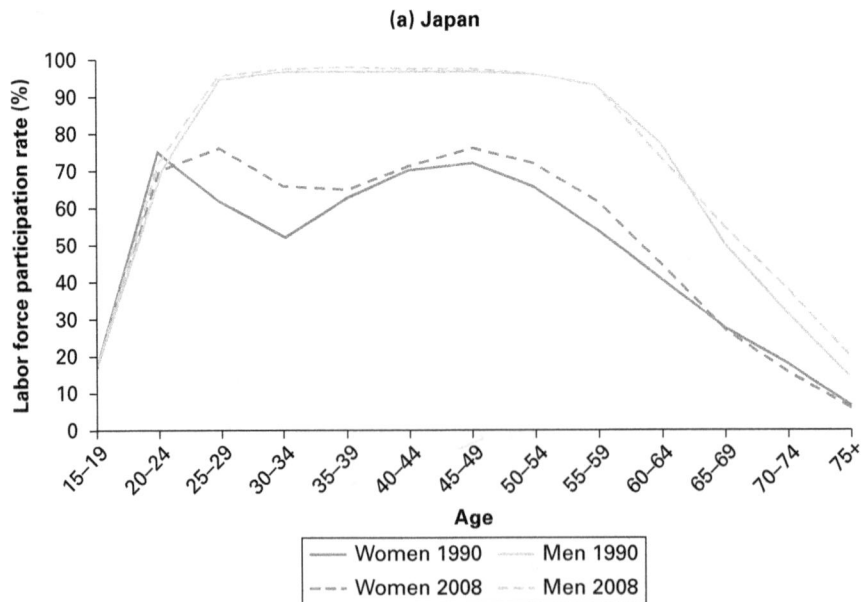

(continued)

130

Figure 4.10: Female Labor Force Participation over the Life Cycle *(continued)*

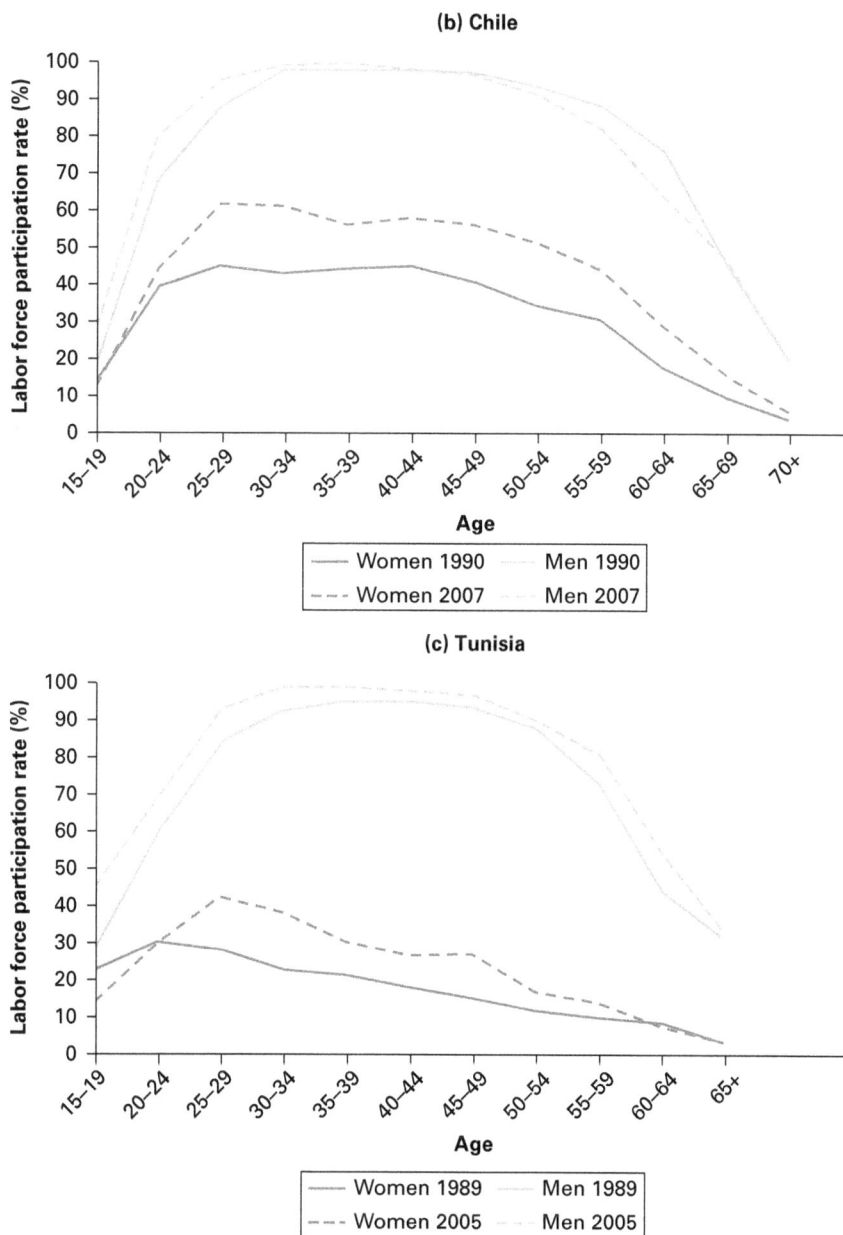

(b) Chile

(c) Tunisia

Source: UN 2010.
Note: Year is the latest available in the period of reference.

effects—comparatively few women work, but younger cohorts are more likely to participate in the labor market than older cohorts.

Access to Resources

Finally, ADePT table 8a explores whether men and women have differential rates of access to household assets and whether they use them differently (World Bank 2012). Table 4.14 illustrates the logic of table 8a, using the example of credit use, an important financial asset.

The first column of ADePT table 8a shows the percentage of households owning these assets for the population subgroups defined by the household characteristics indicated in the rows. For example, in Panama, 10 percent of rural households and 19 percent of urban households reported having a loan. In the columns farther to the left of ADePT table 8a, we see the within-household gender differences in access, defined here by who has the primary responsibility for the loan. In particular, the second to fourth columns show the percentage of households in which (a) only men, (b) only women, or (c) both men and women have the primary responsibility for the loan (out of all households with loans). For instance, in 69 percent of the households with loans in rural Panama, the primary responsibility for the loan rests with male household members, whereas in only 23 percent it rests only with females, and in 7 percent the responsibility was joint.

Country Context: Voice, Agency, and Participation

Content

This section describes nine tables (ADePT tables 10–11h) that profile voice and agency outcomes. The tables are grouped according to the five dimensions of voice and agency presented in the *World Development Report* (World Bank 2012). ADePT tables 10, 11a, and 11b focus on the dimension *decision making over family formation*, ADePT table 11 on *freedom of movement*, and so on. ADePT tables 10, 11a, and 11b require specific variables, whereas ADePT tables 11d–11h leave flexibility to explore other dimensions for which data are available in the survey. As before, all tables show outcomes for all of the population (tables 11a, 11c, 11e, and 11g) and for selected subgroups (tables 11b, 11d, 11f, and 11h). Examples in this section are based on the Living Standards Management Survey for

Table 4.14: ADePT Gender Table 8a, Panama 2008

Table 8a: Household Access to Economic Resources and Intrahousehold Access by Selected Household Characteristics

	Primary credit borrowers				HH uses credit	
	Primary credit borrowers	Only men	Only women	Both	No	Yes
Total	**100.0**	**55.0**	**34.3**	**10.7**	**83.7**	**16.3**
Household head's sex						
Male	100.0	66.8	23.2	10.0	83.8	16.2
Female	100.0	20.6	66.6	12.8	83.5	16.5
Area of residence						
Urban	100.0	51.2	37.2	11.7	80.6	19.4
Rural	100.0	69.4	23.4	7.2	90.0	10.0
Poverty status						
Poor	100.0	70.2	25.5	4.2	93.8	6.2
Nonpoor	100.0	52.5	35.7	11.8	80.7	19.3
Residence and poverty						
Urban, poor	100.0	71.0	29.0	0.0	91.1	8.9
Urban, nonpoor	100.0	49.2	38.0	12.8	79.2	20.8
Rural, poor	100.0	69.4	21.7	8.9	95.1	4.9
Rural, nonpoor	100.0	69.4	24.1	6.5	85.7	14.3
Quintiles of welfare aggregate						
Lowest quintile	100.0	75.8	21.4	2.8	96.5	3.5
2	100.0	68.7	23.5	7.8	88.9	11.1
3	100.0	59.4	30.9	9.7	83.7	16.3
4	100.0	54.4	34.6	10.9	79.9	20.1
Highest quintile	100.0	41.7	44.1	14.2	78.1	21.9
Region						
Región Occidental	100.0	54.1	33.4	12.4	84.7	15.3
Región Oriental	100.0	84.0	13.1	2.9	91.3	8.7
Región Metropolitana	100.0	53.2	36.4	10.4	82.3	17.7
Región Central	100.0	59.8	29.3	10.8	86.2	13.8

Source: Based on ADePT Gender using Panama 2008.
Note: HH = household. The working-age population is ages 15–64.

Panama (2008) and the Living Standards Survey for Nepal (2012b), but Demographic and Health Surveys (DHS) can also be used, as they typically include a wealth of information in this area (see chapter 3 and appendix C).

Concepts

Women's agency matters in its own right, but evidence is emerging that it also matters for economic development (Narayan 2005; World Bank 2012). This section focuses on selected proxies of agency for which data are commonly available. Given that this area of research is new—at least among economists—most of the findings show associations, but they have not been proved to be causal. Agency outcomes are boosted by economic growth and affected by markets and formal and informal institutions (World Bank 2012). For example, social norms shape women's agency.

Available indicators of *decision making over family formation* tend to be less controversial than for other dimensions but fail to provide a complete description of this dimension. ADePT Gender measures the age at first marriage and the age at first birth and gives the option of adding variables chosen by the user, as surveys vary considerably in the available information on this topic. For example, variables that could be informative in some cases and are usually included in DHS are the percentage distribution by months since the preceding birth, the median number of months since the preceding birth, and knowledge/use of contraception methods. Box 4.2 lists the relevant indicators that can be constructed using DHS data.

There is less agreement on how to measure the other dimension of agency, and access to data on the relevant indicators is more limited, at least at the household or individual level. Chapter 6 discusses the progress made to collect better data and analyze more directly and accurately all measures of agency. Given the scarcity of indicators and the variability in availability across surveys, ADePT Gender does not request any specific variable. The rest of the report further discusses the other dimensions of agency using the DHS as a reference.

The main indicators used to capture outcomes related to *control over resources* are related to decision making over income, property rights, or management of individual or household assets. The DHS has a set of questions on decision making regarding income and expenditures, and a few questions on asset ownership (see appendix B). In general, women with more education and from wealthy households are more likely to have more decision-making power and more access to and ownership of resources.

Travel records are usually used as a proxy of the *ability to move freely* (see appendix B). Better infrastructure, good roads, and safe public transportation promote this dimension of agency (World Bank 2012). In addition, social norms are of great importance for women to have control of their mobility. *Freedom from violence* is particularly relevant for women in poor households and women without bargaining power.

Box 4.2: Demographic and Health Survey Indicators on Contraception

The diagnostic on contraception covers all women between ages 15 and 49 for the lifetime of the woman interviewed (or since she was age 15).

Knowledge of contraception: Percentage of women who know of any, a modern, or a traditional contraceptive method. The numerator for any of these indicators is the number of women who say they know of a (specific) contraceptive method (or methods). *Any method* refers to the number of women who say they know of at least one method. The denominator is all women ages 15–49.

Use of contraception: Percentage of women who have ever used any, a modern, or a traditional contraceptive method. The numerator for any of these indicators is the number of women who say they used the (specific) contraceptive method (or methods). *Any method* refers to the number of women who say they used at least one of the methods. The denominator is all women ages 15–49.

Current use of contraception: Percentage of women who currently use any, a modern, or a traditional contraceptive method. The indicators are calculated as those above, and the period of reference is defined by the respondent. One indicator is more widespread—the contraceptive prevalence rate (CPR), defined as

$$CPR = \frac{\begin{array}{c}\textit{Number of currently married women} \\ \textit{who use any method of contraception}\end{array}}{\textit{Number of currently married women}} \times 100.$$

Need for family planning: Percentage of currently married women with (a) an unmet need for family planning, (b) a met need for family planning, or (c) total demand for family planning.

All of the above indicators can be computed in ADePT Gender using the open fields, since they are simply averages of dummy variables.

Source: Rutstein and Rojas 2006.

The last dimension of agency—*ability to have voice in society*—is easily measured at macro levels and often comes from administrative data. However, many household surveys and surveys conducted to evaluate programs ask respondents about their involvement in community networks and public life. Understanding women's participation in public life is important, since women's voice has been found to be positively associated with women's ability to transform societies (World Bank 2012).

Women can influence the social, economic, and political environment by participating in informal associations and through collective actions. However, their collective success starts with their ability to have individual agency.

More important, women's agency matters, since it shapes their children's future. Children who experience or witness violence are more likely to perpetrate crimes and are less likely to be productive workers when adults (Currie and Tekin 2012; World Bank 2012). In addition, social norms are formed at home, and children's perceptions—those of both boys and girls—of what is acceptable (and what is not) are often shaped at home and early in life (Farré and Vella 2007; Fernández, Fogli, and Olivetti 2004).

Interpreting the Results

ADePT table 10 shows the median age at first marriage and age at first birth for select household characteristics. Across countries, we find that different dimensions of agency are highly correlated to each other (Klugman and others 2014). Figure 4.11 presents results for three of the four dimensions that can be analyzed with simple cross tabulations of microdata.

Figure 4.11: Share of Women Who Experience Overlapping Agency Deprivations in Three Domains (Percentage)

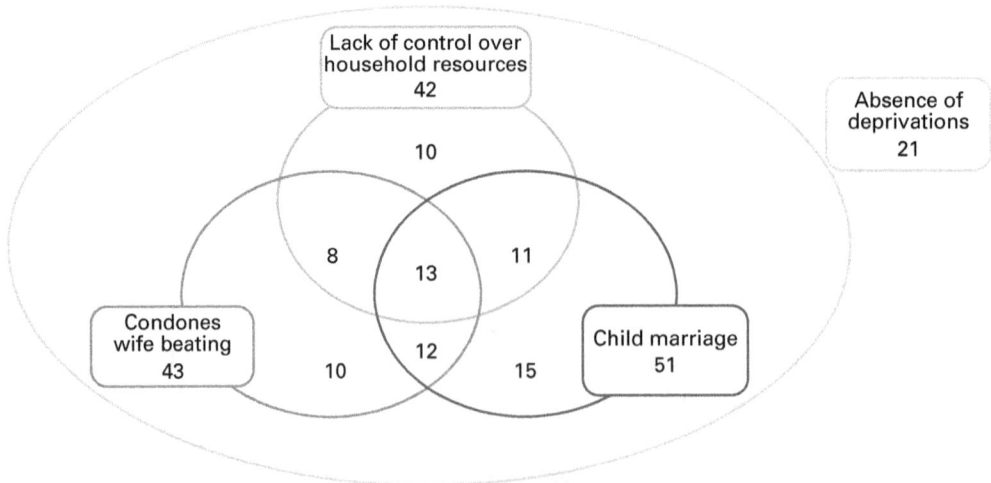

Source: Klugman and others 2014, based on Demographic and Health Surveys for 54 countries using the latest data available, 2001–12.

Within a country, women in general—but particularly women with less education or in poor households—often marry and have children at a young age. For example, in the case of Nepal in 2010–11 (table 4.15, corresponding to ADePT table 10), women in the bottom quintile were more likely to be married younger than women in the top quintile (Nepal 2012b). To give an idea of variation across countries, figure 4.12 reproduces a graph from the United Nations (2010) showing the mean age of marriage in countries where women marry at a very young age. The same report offers additional statistics, such as the proportion of girls ages 15–20 in marriages or consensual unions, which can be used to compare the country's situation with the rest of the world.

Table 4.15: ADePT Gender Table 10, Nepal 2010–11
Table 10: Mean age at first marriage and first birth among females by selected household characteristics

	Age at first marriage	Age at first birth
Total	**17.3**	**19.3**
Household head's sex		
Male	17.4	19.4
Female	17.2	19.2
Area of residence		
Urban	18.5	19.7
Rural	17.1	19.2
Poverty status		
Poor	16.6	19.3
Nonpoor	17.7	19.4
Residence and poverty		
Urban, poor	16.4	18.0
Urban, nonpoor	18.7	19.8
Rural, poor	16.6	19.3
Rural, nonpoor	17.3	19.2
Quintiles of welfare aggregate		
Lowest quintile	16.5	19.2
2	16.8	19.3
3	17.2	19.2
4	17.5	19.1
Highest quintile	18.5	19.8
Regions		
Eastern	17.9	19.9
Central	17.3	19.3
Western	17.5	19.3
Midwestern	16.9	18.8
Far western	16.8	18.9

Source: Based on ADePT Gender using the Nepal 2012b.
Note: Working women ages 15–64.

Figure 4.12: Mean Age at Marriage for Women and Men and the Difference in Years, Countries Where Women Marry on Average at Age 20 or Earlier, 2002–06

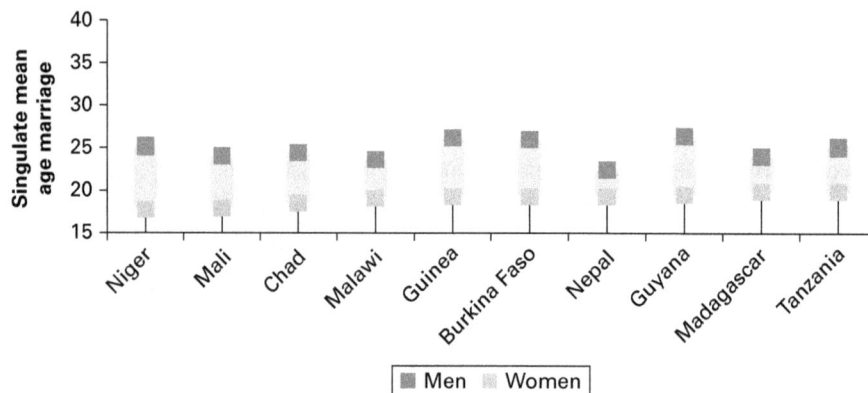

Source: UN 2010.
Note: Year is the latest available in the period of reference.

Table 4.16: ADePT Gender Table 11g, Nepal 2010–11

Table 11g: Mean Outcomes Related to Control over Resources by Selected Individual Characteristics

	School	Number of children	Health of children	Food	Major purchase	Assets	Loans	Use of loans	Migration	Remittances
Age										
15–24	0.7	0.8	0.8	0.7	0.7	0.6	0.7	0.7	0.6	0.8
25–34	0.8	0.8	0.8	0.8	0.8	0.7	0.7	0.7	0.7	0.9
35–44	0.8	0.8	0.8	0.8	0.8	0.7	0.7	0.7	0.7	0.9
45–54	0.7	0.7	0.8	0.8	0.7	0.7	0.7	0.7	0.7	0.8
55–64	0.7	0.5	0.7	0.8	0.7	0.7	0.7	0.7	0.7	0.7
65+	0.6	0.7	0.7	0.7	0.7	0.7	0.7	0.7	0.6	0.7
Marital status										
Never married	0.6	—	0.9	1.0	0.9	0.9	0.7	0.5	1.0	1.0
Married	0.7	0.8	0.8	0.8	0.7	0.7	0.7	0.7	0.7	0.8
Widowed	0.8	0.7	0.9	0.9	0.9	0.9	0.9	0.9	0.8	0.8
Divorced	—	—	1.0	1.0	1.0	1.0	1.0	1.0	—	1.0
Education										
No education	0.7	0.7	0.8	0.8	0.7	0.7	0.7	0.7	0.7	0.8
Primary	0.8	0.8	0.9	0.8	0.8	0.7	0.7	0.7	0.7	0.8
Secondary	0.8	0.8	0.9	0.8	0.8	0.6	0.7	0.8	0.9	0.9
Postsecondary	0.8	0.9	0.8	0.9	0.9	0.8	0.7	0.7	0.7	0.8
Employment status										
Employed	0.7	0.8	0.8	0.8	0.8	0.7	0.7	0.7	0.7	0.8
Unemployed	0.8	0.9	0.9	1.0	0.9	1.0	0.8	0.7	1.0	1.0
Out of labor force	0.7	0.8	0.8	0.8	0.8	0.7	0.7	0.7	0.7	0.8

Source: Based on ADePT Gender using Nepal 2012a.
Note: — = No observations to produce the estimate.

ADePT tables 11a–11h present average values of the variables that are proxies for each of the four dimensions of agency: (a) control over family formation, (b) freedom of movement, (c) freedom from domestic violence, and (d) control over resources. As with all the tables in ADePT Gender diagnostics, there is one table in which the information is also disaggregated for selected individual characteristics (ADePT tables 11a and 11g) and household characteristics (ADePT tables 10, 11b, and 11h). Table 4.16 reproduces the results from ADePT Gender for Nepal 2010–11. It shows the average percentage of women who participate in decision making ranging from small decisions—such as household purchases of food—to important decisions—such as getting a loan and how to spend it. One feature worth highlighting is that in Nepal, women's involvement in decision making is fairly constant by wealth of household. This result is somewhat atypical, as in most countries, women in poor households participate less in any decision. Figure 4.13 reproduces results from the 2012 *WDR*.

Figure 4.13: Women's Control over Household Decisions

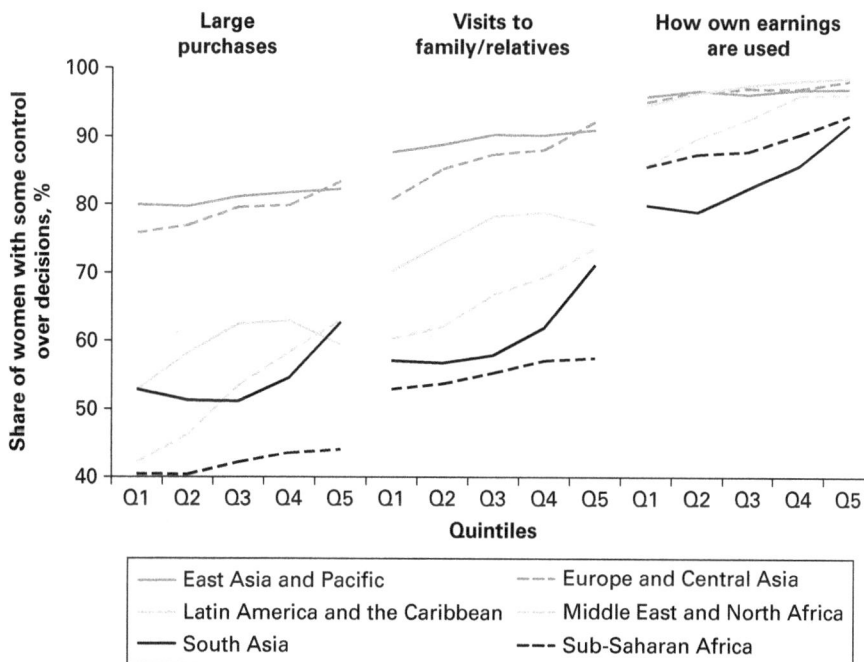

Source: World Bank 2012.

Notes

1. For more details on the core gender indicators, the reader can consult IHSN (2015).
2. Estimates might not be precise enough when the data are too noisy (that is, significant dispersion in the values of the observations) or because not enough observations exist for the type of statistic the analyst is trying to estimate.
3. If another survey is used to illustrate particular results, it will be clarified in the appropriate table or graph.
4. *Stopping behavior* is the term used to describe a situation where parents who gave birth to a boy—most of the time the first birth—would stop having additional children. This behavior results in low fertility rates and missing women at birth. This was the case in the Republic of Korea in the 1980s and is currently prevalent in Armenia.
5. For a visualization of the typology, see Buvinic, Das Gupta, and Casabonne (2009, 350).
6. The interpretation of the results relies on not having biases coming from missing data. If data are missing, and as briefly discussed in chapter 3, the user needs to evaluate whether the missing observations could alter the interpretation of the results.
7. See appendix C for a discussion of the steps needed to evaluate whether a difference in indicators is statistically significant.
8. This, however, depends on the country. In many parts of Sub-Saharan Africa, female-headed households have lower poverty rates than male-headed households. Such findings may be due to the use of non-comparable or inconsistent measures of living standards or benchmarks for judging deprivation, most likely for how adjustments are made for household size and composition, as well as economies of scale in consumption (Milazzo and van de Walle 2015). For example, in some countries, only women with adequate economic positions can afford not to remarry; thus, they head households after the marital dissolution.
9. The complete ADePT output for Panama 2008 and Nepal 2011 can be found on the ADePT website, under the tab for "Gender," at http://go.worldbank.org/0GA4FDMQY0.
10. This concept is also known as NEET (not in education, employment, or training).

11. One of the reasons why people find it difficult to report earnings is that they do not know their exact job benefits or how to value them.
12. This does not imply that individual countries follow a U-shaped trajectory over time (Gaddis and Klasen 2014).
13. This is called an income effect.
14. The common practice for moving from hours worked per month to hours worked per week is to divide by 4.2, since many months exceed four weeks.
15. Good jobs could be defined as being formal, having higher wages, having higher career progress opportunities, stability, and so forth.

References

Almond, Douglas, Janet Currie, and Mariesa Hermann. 2012. "From Infant to Mother: Early Disease Environment and Future Maternal Health." *Labour Economics* 19 (4): 475–83.

Angel-Urdinola, Diego F., and Victor Macias. 2008. "FYR Macedonia Labour Market Profile 2004–2007: A Policy Note." World Bank, Washington, DC.

Buvinic, Mayra, and Geeta Rao Gupta. 1997. "Female-Headed Households and Female-Maintained Families: Are They Worth Targeting to Reduce Poverty in Developing Countries?" *Economic Development and Cultural Change* 45 (2): 259–80.

Buvinic, Mayra, Monica Das Gupta, and Ursula Casabonne. 2009. "Gender, Poverty and Demography: An Overview." *World Bank Economic Review* 23 (3): 347–69.

Case, Anne, and Angus Deaton. 2003. "Consumption, Health, Gender, and Poverty." Policy Research Working Paper 3020, World Bank, Washington, DC.

Case, Anne, Angela Ferting, and Christina Paxon. 2005. "The Lasting Impact of Childhood Health and Circumstance." *Journal of Health Economics* 24 (2): 365–89.

Currie, Janet, and Enrico Moretti. 2003. "Mother's Education and the Intergenerational Transmission of Human Capital: Evidence from College Openings." *Quarterly Journal of Economics* 118 (4): 1–22.

Currie, Janet, Mark Stabile, Phongsack Manivong, and Leslie L. Roos. 2010. "Child Health and Young Adult Outcomes." *Journal of Human Resources* 45 (3): 517–48.

Currie, Janet, and Erdal Tekin. 2012. "Understanding the Cycle: Childhood Maltreatment and Future Crime." *Journal of Human Resources* 47 (2): 509–49.

Edmonds, Erik, Nina Pavcnik, and Petia Topalova. 2009. "Child Labor and Schooling in a Globalizing World: Evidence from Urban India." *Journal of the European Economics Association Papers and Proceedings* 7 (2–3): 498–507.

Farré, Lídia, and Francis Vella. 2007. "The Intergeneration Transmission of Gender Role Attitudes and Its Implications for Female Labor Force Participation." IZA Discussion Paper 2802, Institute for the Study of Labor, Bonn.

Fernández, Raquel, Alessandra Fogli, and Claudia Olivetti. 2004. "Mothers and Sons: Preference Formation and Female Labor Force Dynamics." *Quarterly Journal of Economics* 119 (4): 1249–99.

Flabbi, Luca. 2011. "Gender Differentials in Education, Career Choices and Labor Market Outcomes on a Sample of OECD Countries." Background paper for *World Development Report 2012*.

Gaddis, Isis, and Stephan Klasen. 2014. "Economic Development, Structural Change, and Women's Labor Force Participation." *Journal of Population Economics* 27 (3): 639–81.

Gamberoni, Elisa, Ana Maria Munoz Boudet, and Josefina Posadas. 2014. *Russian Federation Gender Assessment.* Report ACS7863. Washington, DC: World Bank.

Gamberoni, Elisa, and Josefina Posadas. 2012. "Gender Gaps in Labor Market Outcomes: Participation, Unemployment, and Wage Gaps in FYR Macedonia." Mimeo, World Bank, Washington, DC.

IHSN (International Household Survey Network). 2015. "How Well Are Gender Issues Covered in Household Surveys and Censuses? An Analysis Using the IHSN–World Bank Gender Data Navigator." http://ihsn.org/HOME/sites/default/files/resources/Gender_Issues_July-2015.pdf.

Jensen, Robert. 2010. "The (Perceived) Returns to Education and the Demand for Schooling." *Quarterly Journal of Economics* 125 (2): 515–48.

Klasen, Stephan, and Claudia Wink. 2003. "'Missing Women': Revisiting the Debate." *Feminist Economics* 9 (2–3): 263–99.

Klugman, Jeni, Lucia Hanmer, Sarah Twigg, Tazeen Hasan, Jennifer McCleary-Sills, and Julieth Santamaria. 2014. *Voice and Agency: Empowering Women and Girls for Shared Prosperity.* Washington, DC: World Bank.

Mammen, Kristin, and Christina Paxson. 2000. "Women's Work and Economic Development." *Journal of Economic Perspective* 14 (4): 141–64.

Milazzo, Annamaria, and Dominique van de Walle. 2015. "Women Left Behind? Poverty and Headship in Africa." Policy Research Working Paper 7331, World Bank, Washington, DC.

Molinas, José, Ricardo Paes de Barros, Jaime Saavedra, and Marcelo Giugale. 2010. "Do Children Have a Chance? The 2010 Human Opportunity Index Report for Latin America and the Caribbean." World Bank, Washington DC.

Narayan, Deepa. 2005. *Measuring Empowerment: Cross Disciplinary Perspectives.* Washington, DC: World Bank.

Nepal, Government of. 2012a. "Nepal Demographic and Health Survey 2011." Population Division, Ministry of Health and Population, Kathmandu.

———. 2012b. "Nepal: Living Standards Survey 2010–2011, Third Round." Central Bureau of Statistics, National Planning Commission Secretariat, Kathmandu. http://microdata.worldbank.org/index.php/catalog/1000.

Ñopo, Hugo R., Nancy Daza, and Johanna Ramos. 2011. "Gender Earnings Gaps in the World." IZA Discussion Paper 5736, Institute for the Study of Labor, Bonn.

Oreopoulos, Philip, Marianne E. Page, and Ann Huff Stevens. 2006. "The Intergenerational Effects of Compulsory Schooling." *Journal of Labor Economics* 24 (4): 729–60.

Oster, Emily, and M. Bryce Millett. 2010. "Do Call Centers Promote School Enrollment? Evidence from India." NBER Working Paper 15922, National Bureau of Economic Research, Cambridge, MA.

Panama, Government of. 2008. "Encuesta de Niveles de Vida 2008" ("Living Standards Survey 2008"). Ministerio de Economia y Finanzas, Panama City. http://microdata.worldbank.org/index.php/catalog/70.

Porta, Emilio, Gustavo Arcia, Kevin Macdonald, Sergiy Radyakin, and Michael Lokshin. 2011. *Assessing Sector Performance and Inequality in Education.* Washington, DC: World Bank.

Rutstein, Shea Oscar, and Guillermo Rojas. 2006. "Guide to DHS Statistics." Demographic and Health Surveys, ORC Macro, Calverton, MD.

Singh, Ashish. 2012. "Gender Based Within-Household Inequality in Immunization Status of Children: Some Evidence from South Asian Countries." Working paper, Indira Gandhi Institute of Development Research, Mumbai.

Strauss, John, and Duncan Thomas. 1995. "Human Resources: Empirical Modeling of Household and Family Decisions." In *Handbook of Development Economics*, vol. 3, edited by Hollis Chenery and T. N. Srinivasan, 1883–2023. Amsterdam and New York: North-Holland.

Thomas, Duncan. 1990. "Intra-Household Resource Allocation: An Inferential Approach." *Journal of Human Resources* 25 (4): 635–64.

UN (United Nations). 2010. *The World's Women 2010: Trends and Statistics.* New York: UN. http://unstats.un.org/unsd/demographic/products /Worldswomen/WW_full%20report_color.pdf.

UNESCO (United Nations Educational, Scientific, and Cultural Organization). 2012. *World Atlas of Gender Equality in Education.* Paris: UNESCO.

UNFPA (United Nations Population Fund). 2011. "Population Dynamics in the Least Developed Countries: Challenges and Opportunities for Development and Poverty Reduction." New York. https://www.unfpa .org/sites/default/files/pub-pdf/CP51265.pdf.

Wagstaff, Adam, Marcel Bilger, Zurab Sajaia, and Michael Lokshin. 2011. *Health Equity and Financial Protection: Streamlined Analysis with ADePT Software.* Washington, DC: World Bank. https://openknowledge .worldbank.org/handle/10986/2306.

World Bank. 2012. *World Development Report 2012: Gender Equality and Development.* Washington, DC: World Bank. https://openknowledge .worldbank.org/handle/10986/4391.

———. 2014. "South Caucasus Country Gender Assessment 2015." World Bank, Washington, DC.

Chapter 5

Technical Notes for the
Country Gender Diagnostic

This chapter provides guidance and a brief overview of topics that serve as background when interpreting the tables and figures presented in chapter 4. The framework of the *World Development Report 2012: Gender Equality and Development* (World Bank 2012)—discussed in chapter 1—places households at the center, since they make choices on the basis of preferences, incentives (which come from the markets), and constraints (which arise from both formal and informal institutions). This chapter provides an overview of two household models, which will help the user better frame the results from the tables and figures of the country gender profile.

This manual relies on the concepts and models of classical economics, particularly, the household labor supply model and the intrahousehold decision model. However, other schools of thought also support the approach taken by ADePT Gender. The most salient is the feminist school of thought that has run parallel to the classical economics for a long time. This approach has been less quantitative but equally rigorous and highly influential at the intersection of gender and development. Moreover, in recent decades, advances in economics and other social sciences have narrowed the distance between these two schools of thought by developing (quantitative) theoretical models and trying to quantify the concepts of these other social sciences.

It is beyond the objective of this manual to summarize the wealth of knowledge produced over so many years by the social sciences, by the feminist and economics schools of thought and their interlinks.

Users interested in knowing more can consult England (2003), which discusses how the two schools of thought have become closer with the development of bargaining and endogenous taste models in economics and by care models in feminist economics. Moreover, if England were to write her paper today, more recent models offered by behavioral economics would help further narrow the distance between these schools of thought. Users interested in learning more about neoclassical economics can consult Blau, Ferber, and Winkler (2006).

The first section of this chapter describes in a very simple manner the household labor supply model. This neoclassical economics model, which has been at the core of family economics for a long time, relies on strong assumptions but produces results that replicate many outcomes observed in reality. The second section describes the intrahousehold allocation models, also called bargaining models. These models are richer in the sense that they relax some of the strong assumptions of the household labor supply model and assume that individuals do not live in isolation but in a family that is subject to constraints and has its own rules. Thus, it sometimes makes sense to focus on the behavior of the household. At the same time, the reader should bear in mind that, in economics, a theory is not to be judged by its resemblance to reality but rather by the extent to which it enables us to grasp the salient features of reality.

Household Labor Supply Model

As stated previously, households are at the center of the framework used to design ADePT Gender tables and graphs. Families make decisions on how many children to have, when to have them, and how much to invest in their sons' and daughters' health and education. These decisions are shaped by household members' preferences, incentives coming from the market, and constraints from formal and informal institutions. The household labor supply model was developed several decades ago and is still relevant for understanding the mechanisms through which market incentives and institutional constraints are transmitted to households.[1]

Since the seminal work of Gary Becker (1965, 1974) and Jacob Mincer (1962) on family decisions on labor allocation between the household and the market, economists and social scientists have developed and used many models. Despite its limitations, the unitary model is still useful for predicting certain patterns of a family's division of labor. For example, household labor supply models have contributed to explaining observed facts, such as women's increasing labor force participation, declining fertility rates, and increasing investments in children's education, especially for girls.

The household labor supply model is based on three main assumptions. First, household well-being depends on goods that are produced at home using market goods and household members' time. For example, food needs to be bought at the market and requires some preparation, furniture needs to be bought and later arranged at home and maintained, and children need care. As a result, time can be allocated among three competing tasks: (a) market work outside the home, (b) production of household goods (using market goods as inputs), and (c) leisure. Second, most households have more than one adult; thus, decisions about the time allocation for these three competing activities are made jointly.[2] In some cases, we can further assume that the productivity of household members varies with the task. For example, women might be more productive in producing household goods, and men might be more productive in market work. Third, the models can be extended to incorporate a time dimension. For example, the time spent at home can be substituted by time in the market (substitution of time between activities in and out of the household), time spent working for pay today can be substituted by leisure tomorrow (substitution of time between activities over the life cycle).

Labor Supply Model with Household Production

This section shows a simple model in which people can use their time for two tasks: (a) working for pay outside the home and (b) working in household production of goods. Time spent in household production includes time spent on chores or leisure.[3] In reality, people spend time on several activities. Table 5.1 shows the average number of hours that men and women spent on different activities, based on survey data from the Lao People's Democratic Republic (Lao PDR 2008). Although no differences occur in the number of hours spent sleeping (or these differences are not significant; see appendix C), significant gender differences exist in time spent in household production and leisure. Women spend almost one hour more per day than men in childcare and eldercare, and about half an hour less per day on leisure activities. They also spend slightly less time than men in market activities, but this is a highly country specific result.[4]

Table 5.1: Daily Hours Spent in Household Work, Paid Work, and Leisure for Men and Women

	Hours spent sleeping		Hours spent on childcare/eldercare		Hours spent on leisure		Hours spent on market activities	
	Male	Female	Male	Female	Male	Female	Male	Female
Total	**8.8**	**8.7**	**0.2**	**0.9**	**4.4**	**3.8**	**1.5**	**1.3**
Gender of household head								
Male	8.8	8.7	0.2	0.9	4.4	3.8	1.5	1.2
Female	8.9	8.7	0.1	0.6	4.7	4.4	2.4	2.5
Area of residence								
Urban	8.7	8.4	0.2	0.8	4.7	4.2	3.2	2.8
Rural	8.9	8.8	0.2	0.9	4.3	3.7	0.9	0.7
Poverty status								
Poor	9.0	8.8	0.3	1.1	4.5	3.5	0.7	0.7
Nonpoor	8.8	8.7	0.2	0.8	4.4	3.9	1.7	1.5
Residence and poverty status								
Urban, poor	8.9	8.3	0.3	0.9	4.6	4.0	2.8	3.3
Urban, nonpoor	8.6	8.4	0.2	0.8	4.7	4.2	3.2	2.7
Rural, poor	9.0	8.8	0.3	1.2	4.4	3.4	0.3	0.2
Rural, nonpoor	8.9	8.8	0.2	0.9	4.3	3.8	1.0	0.9
Quintile of welfare aggregate								
Lowest quintile	9.0	8.8	0.3	1.1	4.4	3.5	0.7	0.7
2	8.8	8.7	0.2	1.0	4.4	3.9	1.0	0.7
3	8.8	8.7	0.2	0.9	4.4	3.8	1.4	1.2
4	8.8	8.7	0.2	0.8	4.5	3.9	1.6	1.4
Highest quintile	8.7	8.5	0.2	0.7	4.4	4.1	2.6	2.3
Region								
Vientiane	8.7	8.3	0.1	0.7	5.1	4.4	3.5	3.6
North	8.7	8.5	0.3	0.9	4.4	3.6	0.9	0.7
Central	8.9	8.8	0.2	1.0	4.2	3.7	1.7	1.3
South	9.0	9.0	0.1	0.9	4.4	4.1	0.9	0.8

Source: Authors' calculations based on Lao PDR 2008 using ADePT Gender, adapted table 3a.
Note: Includes all men and women, ages 15–64.

Gender differences in the use of time are particularly high for vulnerable groups. Whereas women at the bottom of the welfare distribution spend more than one hour per day in childcare and eldercare, women at the top spend half an hour less than women at the bottom in these activities. As a result, women at the top of the welfare distribution can have more leisure time, which closes the gender gap in leisure time. The time allocation is also affected by social norms and women's opportunity cost. Women in female-headed households spend less time on childcare and eldercare than women in male-headed households. The same result is observed for the Vientiane region. This difference may be attributed to the fact that women in female-headed households and in the Vientiane region are more likely to work (not shown), or these women have more voice and agency because of different social pressures or household dynamics.

These facts can be partially explained by the household labor supply model. The model assumes that the household behaves as a single unit; thus, for ease of exposition, it can be regarded as if it has only one decision maker. Consider a household with a single female adult and two children below the working age. The adult is the sole decision maker and takes into account the well-being of all family members, giving the same importance to each of them. She has 24 hours per day to devote to work outside the home, household work, and leisure. Allowing for 8 hours of sleeping, she needs to decide how to allocate the remaining 16 hours between paid work and household production to maximize the household well-being subject to the time constraint. The problem the decision maker faces is graphically represented in figure 5.1.

The space depicted in figure 5.1, panel a, is money and hours, over which a budget constraint and a utility (or well-being) function can be defined. The y-axis indicates money that can be used to purchase goods that derive well-being, and the x-axis represents time that can be used for household work, which generates well-being through consumption of goods produced at home, or for work for pay, which serves to buy goods in the market—which in turn might or might not require additional time at home. The x-axis

Figure 5.1: Household Time Allocation Problem

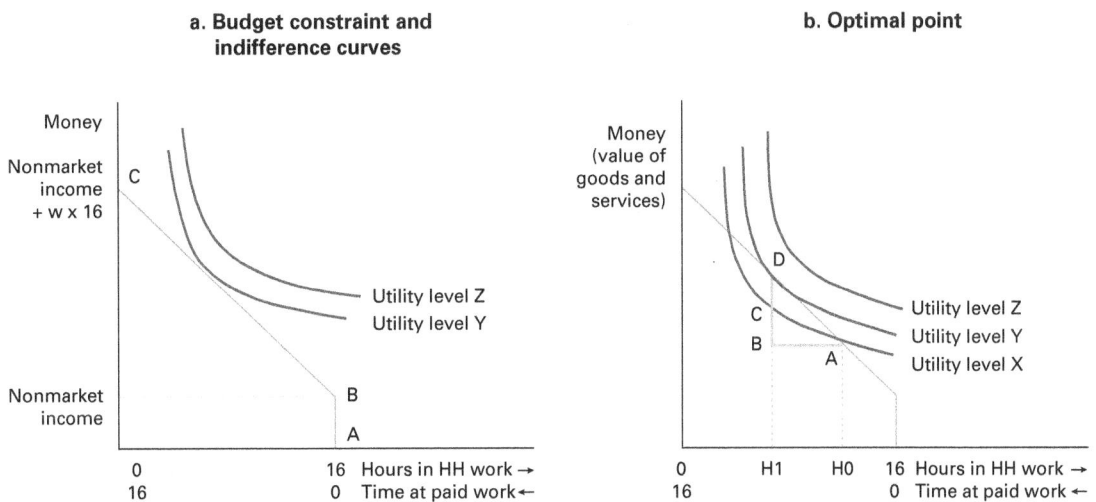

a. Budget constraint and indifference curves

b. Optimal point

Note: HH = household.

149

thus indicates hours spent in household and market work, as hours of household work increase moving right, the hours of paid work decrease (this is indicated with two arrows associated with the axis name). The maximum possible value of hours is 16. The line that connects points A, B, and C represents the possible combinations of time and money for the household.[5] Without any work, the household has some money from nonlabor activities that can be spent on goods that generate well-being (the vertical segment from A to B). As the adult reallocates time away from leisure toward paid work, disposable money increases by an amount equal to the wage earned in that time. If all available hours are spent on paid work, the decision maker would have earned the hourly wage times 16 hours of work. Point C indicates the total earnings plus the nonlabor income. The well-being (or utility) is represented by indifference curves (that is, curves that present combinations of leisure and work that produce the same level of well-being), and the farther right the indifference curve is in the diagram, the higher the well-being of the household.

The optimization problem is solved at point D in figure 5.1, panel b. At point D, the household achieves the maximum level of utility that is feasible with the available time and wage. A point like A will not maximize the utility of the household, since higher indifference curves can be achieved by substituting hours in household work for paid work (from A to B). This substitution improves the household well-being, since more money is gained (from B to D) than what was necessary to maintain the same level of well-being (from B to C).

Next, assume the household has more than one decision maker and thus more than one person generating income. The allocation of time is clearly affected by the power of each person in the couple, differences in utility functions between husband and wife, and social norms or customs. However, part of the decision responds to economic incentives, for example, how much men and women are paid for one hour of work in the market.

Couples often find it beneficial to specialize, to some extent, in both household and market work. Often, one person will assume the main responsibility of working outside the home, while the other person focuses on household production. Two economic justifications make this outcome optimal. First, it makes more sense for the person who can earn more money outside the home to spend more hours in the labor market (see figure 5.2, panel a). Second, labor specialization might lead to economies of scale. It might be more productive for one person to work only in the labor market

Figure 5.2: Budget Constraints in Households with One Female Adult and One Male Adult

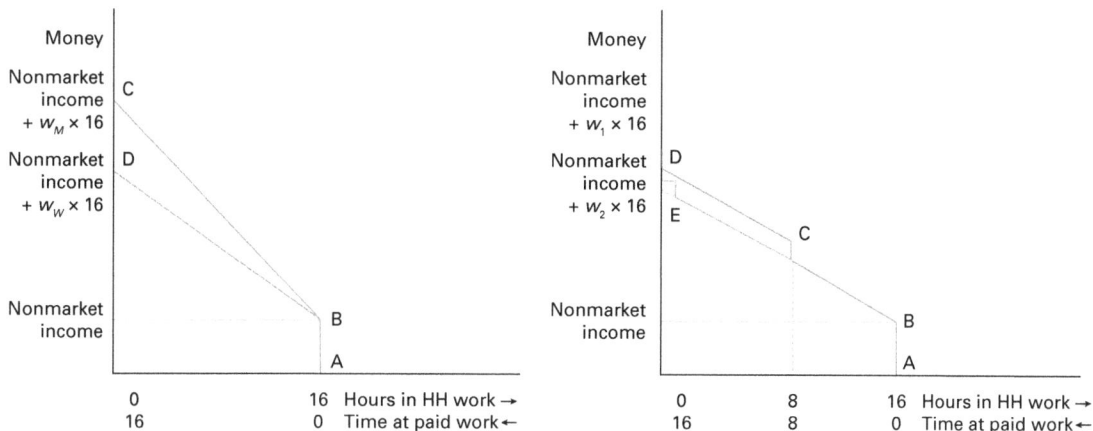

Note: HH = household.

and the other only at home, than if each of them split their time between the two activities.[6] Figure 5.2, panel b, shows this as a kink at eight hours of work, based on the assumption that the wage jumps when a person, either male or female, works eight hours.

Empirically, it has been found that as wives' wages increase relative to their husbands' wages, it is more likely that women spend more time outside the household working, and men increase the time they spend on household work (Hersch and Stratton 1994). Clearly, noneconomic factors influence not only women's participation in paid work but also the labor division of household chores. This is partly due to the positive association between female bargaining power in the household and female economic empowerment (of which wages may be a determinant). In addition, higher female wages give rise to substitutions within the household. As women earn money outside the household, they can outsource the production of certain household goods—for example, women can buy ready-to-wear clothes instead of fabric to make clothes at home. At the same time, changes in the relative price of household production goods will generate substitutions between hours in household work and hours in paid work. The changes in relative prices are often driven by new technologies. The invention of the washing machine was found to have liberated time for women, which was later used for income-generating activities (Greenwood, Seshardri, and Yorukoglu 2005). Other technological developments, such as electricity, were found to have similar effects (Dinkelman 2011; van de Walle and others 2013). A study on increased access to water found that women's freed-up time did not result in greater off-farm work, but that children's health and education improved—so the extra time was most likely spent caring for children (Koolwal and van de Walle 2013). Although rudimentary, the description of the household labor supply model is intended to remind ADePT Gender users about the trade-offs among the competing activities behind the data. Although the summary tables cannot show all the factors behind the results, users need to keep them in mind when interpreting the tables and graphs, and when they propose additional analysis beyond ADePT Gender.

Intrahousehold Allocation Model

The household labor supply model assumes that the household behaves as a single unit, with one well-being function. However, it is now widely accepted that households do not behave as a single entity but rather as a group of persons with individual preferences. The *unitary model* for household decisions has been rejected by the empirical evidence from a substantial body of research (for example, Attanasio and Lechene 2002; Duflo 2003; Lundberg, Pollak, and Wales 1997; Schultz 1990; Thomas 1990; Ward-Batts 2008; and many others). This led to the development of the so-called collective models, in which each household member maximizes his or her own utility or well-being. These models assume that household members care about one another, but because they have different preferences, they might disagree. Within this group, *cooperative models* can be differentiated from *noncooperative models*, with the main distinction being whether an optimum outcome[7] is achieved (Lundberg and Pollak 1993, 2003; Manser and Brown 1980; McElroy and Horney 1981).

Under the assumptions of collective models, outcomes usually differ from the unitary model solutions and individual optimal choices. The differences arise from changes in the household budget constraint and in relative prices that influence the "power" of each member's household decision making, which is influenced by the endowments (both in the form of human capital and productive resources), the social norms, and the legal environment. Finally, the outcomes that are affected by household decisions are of a different kind, as described in chapter 1.

The predictions of all these models have been subject to empirical tests. For the unitary model, most of the studies tested the income-pooling hypothesis, which implies that the effect of a transfer of income on household behavior is independent of the recipient's identity (husband or wife). The first generation of these studies investigated whether a correlation existed between the origin of household income (typically, what fraction comes from the wife) and the way it is spent. Using data from Brazil, Thomas (1990) finds that the relative share of nonlabor income from the wife has a very significant effect on the health status of the children. However, this finding was challenged, arguing that this phenomenon can be driven by unobserved differences, preferences, and income composition. For example, women who have higher nonlabor income because they saved in the past or they received larger inheritances may also be more likely to spend more on their children's health and education. The unitary model and the income-pooling hypothesis were also rejected using tests based on exogenous variation in income. Lundberg, Pollak, and Wales (1997) studied the impact of the April 1977 reform of the United Kingdom's child public support system. Before that time, families with children received a child allowance paid together with their wage. That relationship effectively meant that the child benefits were paid to the higher earner, primarily the father. After April 1977, the old scheme was dropped in favor of a nontaxable child benefit, which is paid directly to the mother. This reallocation of income within the household can be reasonably treated as exogenous to the affected households. Moreover, the child benefit was a sizable transfer (equal to 8 percent of male earnings for a two-child household). The authors focus attention on the ratio of expenditures on children's clothing and women's clothing, both relative to men's clothing. Their findings are unequivocal—both ratios rose significantly after the reform.

Another strong rejection is provided by Duflo (2003), who analyzed a reform of the South African social pension program for the elderly that extended benefits to a large, previously not covered, black population. Because of the eligibility criteria, the coverage was not universal—in some households, only one of the grandparents receives the benefit. Duflo uses a difference-in-differences approach[8] based on the demographics of the household to control for selection in eligibility. She shows that the recipient's gender is of considerable importance for the effect transfers have on children's health—a payment to the grandfather has no significant effect, whereas the same amount paid to the grandmother results in a huge improvement in the health status of girls in the family.

As for the empirical evidence that rejects the income-pooling prediction mounted, collective models were developed. One of these models' predictions is that outcomes depend on the "power" or "distribution factors" of spouses, since they influence the household decisions (Bourguignon and Chiappori 1992; Chiappori 1988). These models predict that a transfer to women might have a different effect than a transfer to men, and that the differential effect depends on the "power" the recipient has in household decisions (Attanasio and Lechene 2002). Later, Bourguignon, Browning, and Chiappori (2009) translated this argument into a testable prediction. If the collective setting is correct, all distribution factors should operate in a similar way and thus their respective effects on various aspects of household behavior, or equivalently into what the experts in this subfield call the property of the "z-conditional demands." Empirically, this means that once the effect of distribution factors is controlled for—which is what z-conditional demands do—they should have no effect on household decision making.

Thus, the key questions become what influences the "distribution factors" or "power" within the household, and how they can be measured. It is with these two questions in mind, along with an awareness of power's role in outcomes, that tables on voice and agency should be interpreted and included in an analysis.

Notes

1. This section draws on the presentation of the household labor supply model in Blau, Ferber, and Winkler (2006); Blundell and Macurdy (1999); and Ehrenberg and Smith (2009).
2. Or decisions are made by a head of household who takes into account the well-being of each household member, giving all of them equal importance.
3. Leisure is another consumption good.
4. Other countries' time patterns can be found in World Bank (2012), chapter 5, 217–22.
5. This is equivalent to a budget constraint in the simple consumption maximization problem.

6. For example, because they become faster at doing the job, because they save in transportation costs to the workplace, and so on.
7. This optimum outcome is called a Pareto outcome, based on the extensive research of Vilfredo Pareto.
8. A difference-in-differences approach is an econometric method used to estimate causal relationships.

References

Attanasio, Orazio, and Valérie Lechene. 2002. "Tests of Income Pooling in Household Decisions." *Review of Economic Dynamics* 5 (4): 720–48.

Becker, Gary. 1965. "A Theory of the Allocation of Time." *Economic Journal* 75 (2999): 493–517.

———. 1974. "A Theory of Marriage." In *Economics of the Family: Marriage, Children, and Human Capital*, edited by Theodore W. Schultz, 299–351. Chicago: University of Chicago Press.

Blau, Francine D., Marianne A. Ferber, and Anne E. Winkler. 2006. *The Economics of Women, Men, and Work.* 5th ed. Upper Saddle River, NJ: Pearson/Prentice Hall.

Blundell, Richard, and Thomas Macurdy. 1999. "Labor Supply: A Review of Alternative Approaches." In *Handbook of Labor Economics*, vol. 3, edited by Orley Ashenfelter and David Card, 1559–1695. Amsterdam: Elsevier.

Bourguignon, François, Martin Browning, and Pierre-André Chiappori. 2009. "Efficient Intra-Household Allocations and Distribution Factors: Implications and Identification." *Review of Economic Studies* 76 (2): 503–28.

Bourguignon, François, and Pierre-André Chiappori. 1992. "Collective Models of Household Behavior: An Introduction." *European Economic Review* 36 (2–3): 355–64.

Chiappori, Pierre-André. 1988. "Rational Household Labor Supply." *Econometrica* 56 (1): 63–90.

Dinkelman, Taryn. 2011. "The Effects of Rural Electrification on Employment: New Evidence from South Africa." *American Economic Review* 101 (7): 3078–108.

Duflo, Esther. 2003. "Grandmothers and Granddaughters: Old-Age Pensions and Intrahousehold Allocation in South Africa." *World Bank Economic Review* 17 (1): 1–25.

Ehrenberg, Ronald G., and Robert S. Smith. 2009. *Modern Labor Economics*. 10th ed. Boston: Pearson/Addison-Wesley.

England, Paula. 2003. "Separative and Soluble Selves: Dichotomous Thinking in Economics." In *Feminist Economics Today: Beyond Economic Man*, edited by Marianne A. Ferber and Julie A. Nelson, 33–59. Chicago: University of Chicago Press.

Greenwood, Jeremy, Ananth Seshardri, and Mehmet Yorukoglu. 2005. "Engines of Liberation." *Review of Economic Studies* 72 (1): 109–33.

Hersch, Joni, and Leslie S. Stratton. 1994. "Housework, Wages, and the Division of Household Time for Employed Spouses." *American Economic Review* 84 (2): 120–25.

Koolwal, Gayatri, and Dominique van de Walle. 2013. "Access to Water, Women's Work, and Child Outcomes." *Economic Development and Cultural Change* 61 (2): 369–405.

Lao PDR, Government of. 2008. "Household Survey 2008." Department of Statistics, Ministry of Planning and Investment, Vientiane.

Lundberg, Shelly J., and Robert A. Pollak. 1993. "Separate Spheres Bargaining and the Marriage Market." *Journal of Political Economy* 101 (6): 988–1010.

———. 2003. "Efficiency in Marriage." *Review of Economics of the Household* 1 (3): 153–67.

Lundberg, Shelly J., Robert A. Pollak, and Terence J. Wales, 1997. "Do Husbands and Wives Pool Their Resources? Evidence from the United Kingdom Child Benefit." *Journal of Human Resources* 32 (3): 463–80.

Manser, Marilyn, and Murray Brown. 1980. "Marriage and Household Decision-Making: A Bargaining Analysis." *International Economic Review* 21 (1): 31–44.

McElroy, Marjorie B., and Mary Jean Horney. 1981. "Nash-Bargained Household Decisions: Toward a Generalization of the Theory of Demand." *International Economic Review* 22 (2): 333–49.

Mincer, Jacob. 1962. "Labor Force Participation of Married Women: A Study of Labor Supply." In *Aspects of Labor Economics*, edited by H. Gregg Lewis, 63–105. Princeton, NJ: Princeton University Press.

Schultz, T. Paul. 1990. "Testing the Neoclassical Model of Family Labor Supply and Fertility." *Journal of Human Resources* 25 (4): 599–634.

Thomas, Duncan. 1990. "Intra-Household Resource Allocation: An Inferential Approach." *Journal of Human Resources* 25 (4): 635–64.

van de Walle, Dominique, Martin Ravallion, Vibhuti Mendiratta, and Gayatri Koolwal. 2013. "Long-Term Impacts of Household Electrification in Rural India." Policy Research Working Paper 6527, World Bank, Washington, DC.

Ward-Batts, Jennifer. 2008. "Out of the Wallet and into the Purse: Using Micro Data to Test Income Pooling." *Journal of Human Resources* 43 (2): 325–51.

World Bank. 2012. *World Development Report 2012: Gender Equality and Development*. Washington, DC: World Bank. https://openknowledge .worldbank.org/handle/10986/4391.

PART III

Analyzing Gender in Labor Markets

Part III of the ADePT Gender manual goes into more depth on gaps in economic opportunities, particularly gaps in employment and earnings, and occupational segregation. In this section, ADePT Gender aims to work with tools that have long been used in country analyses of labor market inequalities and also introduces a few of the more recent methods for studying the intersection of gender and labor economics.

Chapter 6 provides guidance on how to produce and interpret the tables and graphs to further analyze gender gaps in the labor market. Using the household survey from Nepal in 2010–11 and Panama in 2008, the chapter discusses select tables and graphs to show the user how to interpret them. Mirroring the organization of part II, chapter 7 provides technical notes for understanding the theories behind the empirical analysis.

This organization aims to help different audiences quickly access the necessary inputs and interpret outputs. The user familiar with quantitative analysis and gender issues may need to consult only chapter 6, whereas the user less familiar with quantitative analysis or the economic angle of gender issues can also consult chapter 7.

How to Interpret the Results of Labor Market Analysis

This chapter discusses how to interpret the results from the tables and graphs of ADePT Gender of the labor market analysis. The description of the tables and graphs is directed toward practitioners with a basic knowledge of econometrics and statistics in the context of labor markets. To complement the guidance of this chapter, chapter 7 includes a brief discussion of key topics of econometrics and labor markets for those who need to acquire or review them, including references for those with an appetite for more material.

The chapter relies on techniques that have been used extensively by researchers and policy makers to explain gender gaps in employment and earnings. The first section covers the output that provides measures of earnings inequality: overall, within gender, and between men and women. These measures of inequality offer context for the analysis of gender. We know that gender imbalances are present everywhere, but are they more or less important than other inequalities that exist for vulnerable and minority groups? How large is the gap in pay between men and women? Does the pay gap depend on the type of employment? Are these results consistent with the evolution of other outcomes as those described in part II? These are some of the questions that these groups of tables and graphs aim to shed light on.

The second section tries to help the user understand the different factors that influence the gender gap in pay. Following the wealth of literature in this area, ADePT Gender focuses on reduced-form approaches that provide an estimate of the potential (net) effect of a bundle of factors. That is done using decomposition techniques that separate "composition" and "wage structure" effects—that is, factors coming from observable differences in labor market skills of men and women and all the other residual factors. The main question that decomposition methodologies seek to answer is the extent of the gender gap in pay there would be if women received the same pay for their skills as men. Or conversely, how large the gender gap would be if women had the same labor market skills as men. Thus, decomposition methodologies help the user understand how much of the gender gap in pay can be "solved" or narrowed by helping women access education and employment in certain sectors and occupations to match men. Instead, the wage structure effect is a blurred measure of any other issue that translates into differences in wages between men and women. These differences could range from unobserved skills, such as ability to work in teams, to more complex issues, such as discrimination, which would require a change in society's mentality.

All of the analysis is conducted using logs of wages per hour as the main variable to be explained. This chapter and the next might loosely refer to wages without clarifying that the variable being analyzed is the natural logarithm of the hourly wage. It is standard to use logs, because they are linked to the formal model of investment in human capital, and because they provide a parsimonious specification that fits data from different countries extremely well. Also, this chapter uses wages and earnings interchangeably, though it was noted in chapter 3 that they correspond to different components of labor income.

Earnings Inequality

Content

This section describes four tables (ADePT tables 12a–12d) and three graphs (ADePT figures 12a–12c) with measures of earnings inequality.[1] All the measures are presented separately for wage workers and self-employed workers. To understand gender inequality, it is necessary to first understand the overall wage structure prevalent in the labor market.[2] Gender differences in employment and pay can be affected by how dispersed or compressed the distribution of earnings is and the supply and demand of low- and high-skilled workers in the labor market, which in turns affects the price of skills. For example, the gender wage gap is more likely to be larger in economies with high returns to education and a disproportionately large group of working women with little education.

The *overall earnings inequality* measures distributional aspects of earnings, computed using all employed men and women. The term *within-gender earnings inequality* refers to differences in earnings, but for men and women separately. ADePT tables 12a–12d and ADePT figure 12b show several measures of earnings inequality—both overall and within gender. Notice that in this module of ADePT, inequality measures are computed using earnings as opposed to household or per capita income. Many of these measures can also be computed for income or other welfare aggregates in the ADePT Poverty and inequality module, and a few of them for household labor income in the ADePT Labor module.

In this ADePT Gender module, all measures are computed separately for wage workers and the self-employed. As discussed in chapter 3, earnings for the two groups are calculated using different survey questions—even modules[3]—leaving room for different types of measurement errors that might invalidate the comparison. In addition, the sample of wage workers and self-employed can differ in the observable and unobservable characteristics; thus, gender biases can show up if men and women are sorted differently into these two types of occupations. ADePT table 12a reports the three most used inequality measures in labor economics: (a) the log wage differential between the 90th and 10th percentiles, (b) the log wage differential between the 90th and 50th percentiles, and (c) the log wage differential between the 50th and 10th percentiles. Looking into more detail at the whole distribution of earnings, ADePT table 12b reports the share of total earnings captured by each welfare decile (see table 6.2). ADePT table 12c goes into further details on inequality measures that labor economics borrows from the poverty and inequality field. It reports inequality measures from the Theil index, the Atkinson index, and the generalized entropy inequality index. These indicators are included for sensibility analysis. Accompanying these tables, ADePT figure 12a plots the earnings distribution for men and women, wage earners, and the self-employed separately.

The term *gender gap in earnings*—or simply gender gap in pay—refers to the differences in earnings between men and women. ADePT table 12d shows the "raw gap" in earnings computed at different points of the earnings distribution, whereas ADePT figures 12b and 12c compare the earnings distributions of men and women. The term *raw gap* is usually used to denote the differences in pay by simply comparing men's earnings and women's earnings (average or other statistics), before conditioning in other variables that could serve to explain it.

Concepts

Overall and Within-Gender Earnings Inequality

The analysis of the wage structure of labor markets focuses on understanding the wages associated with different jobs. Understanding the wage structure of the labor market is important for several reasons. From a gender perspective, it is useful to understand how large gender inequality is compared with other inequalities in the labor market. For example, is the gender gap in pay as large as the difference in pay between low-skilled and high-skilled workers? Is the gender gap in pay as important as the racial or ethnic gap in pay? Moreover, understanding the overall earnings inequality is crucial for poverty and income inequality, as labor income is the poor's main source of income.

Labor economists are usually interested in understanding the difference in pay between low-skilled and high-skilled workers. With that purpose in mind, it is assumed that workers with the lowest earnings (bottom of the distribution density function of earnings) are low skilled and workers with the highest earnings (top of the distribution density function of earnings) are high skilled. This is probably the most common measure used in studies of labor markets and of gender wage gaps (Autor, Katz, and Kearny 2008; Blau and Kahn 1997; Katz and Autor 1999; Katz and Murphy 1992; Mulligan and Rubinstein 2008). Others, however, prefer to work directly with the ratio of earnings between different education levels, such as the ratio of wages between college and high school workers. If the user is also interested in comparing countries with very different education attainments, the ratio of wages in the 90th to 10th percentiles of the cumulative density distribution curve might be better suited to show the relative wage differences.

The ratio of wages in the 90th and the 10th percentiles of the earnings distribution curve, mathematically, is

$$90p/10p = \log w_{90p} - \log w_{10p},$$

where $\log w_{90p}$ is the natural logarithm of the wage that leaves 90 percent of employed workers below that cutoff after sorting all workers according to hourly rate of pay. Similarly, $\log w_{10p}$ is the wage that leaves 10 percent of employed workers below that level of earnings. Other ratios can be computed in the same vein. For example, the ratio 90p/50p and 50p/10p inform whether the distribution of earnings is symmetric around the median. As expected, they are mathematically defined as

$$90p/50p = \log w_{90p} - \log w_{50p},$$
$$50p/10p = \log w_{50p} - \log w_{10p}.$$

The main advantage of these measures—based on ratios of logs of wages taken at different points in the distribution curve—is that computing and interpreting them is straightforward. However, they use information only from a few points (or percentiles) of the distribution curve and miss its other characteristics. To complete the description of the distribution curve of earnings, ADePT table 12c shows additional inequality measures borrowed from the field of poverty and inequality. Working with these measures is important for sensibility analysis, as they capture different features of the distribution's functions. Moreover, users might be interested in comparing labor income and total income inequality, in which case it is necessary to have the same measures. Furthermore, these measures are associated with the theory of welfare, which has a long tradition in economics. These measures are explained in more detail by Foster and others (2013), and this section presents only a quick description of each of them. In all cases, ADePT Gender focuses on inequality of outcomes. The user interested in inequality of opportunities can use other available tools, such as the World Bank's Human Opportunity Index.

The *coefficient of variation* is a measure of the distribution curve's dispersion that is normalized by its mean to allow—among other reasons—comparisons over time or across countries. The normalization removes the scale of the variable. Mathematically,

$$CV = \frac{\left[\sum_{i=1}^{N} (w_i - \mu_w)^2 / N \right]}{\mu_w},$$

where w_i represents the earnings of individual i, μ_w is the sample mean of wages, and N is the total number of employed persons in the sample.

The Gini *coefficient* is one of the most popular inequality indicators. Its objective is to summarize in one number the information coming from the *Lorenz curve* (see figure 6.1). This curve shows the percentage of total income that belongs to the poorest p percent of the population. If the income were perfectly even in distribution, the Lorenz curve would be equivalent to a 45-degree line—or the *line of equality*. The farther away the Lorenz curve is from the line of equality, the more pervasive the inequality. In the case of earnings (in contrast with income), the adjusted Lorenz curve shows the percentage of total earnings that belongs to the poorest p percent of the population. Comparing the Lorenz curves generated with total income with those coming from earnings allows us to examine the contribution of nonlabor income to inequality.

The Gini coefficient measures the area between the Lorenz curve and the line of equality. It can be expressed as a function of the Lorenz curve,[4]

$$\text{Gini} = \frac{A}{A+B'},$$

$$\text{Gini} = \frac{\left(\frac{1}{2} - B\right)}{\frac{1}{2}},$$

$$\text{Gini} = 1 - 2.\,B,$$

$$\text{Gini} = 1 - 2\int_0^1 L(p).\,dp,$$

where p stands for the lowest p percent of the working population, and $L(p)$ refers to the share of total earnings received by the lowest p percent of the working population—that is, the Lorenz curve. The Gini coefficient takes values between 0 and 1: the larger the Gini, the more severe the inequality. There are two extreme cases. When earnings are evenly distributed among the entire working population, the Lorenz curve coincides with the line of equality, the area A equals 0; hence, the Gini coefficient is 0. When only one individual has access to all earnings of the group, the Lorenz curve is 0 for all $p < 100$, the area B is 0, and the Gini coefficient is 1, its maximum value.

Figure 6.1: Lorenz Curve

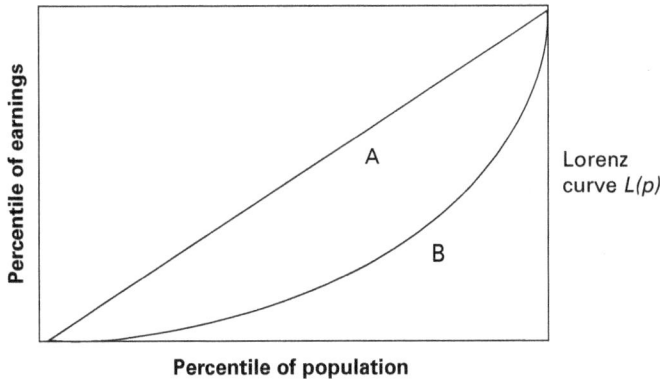

Behind each of the following inequality measures are implicit value judg-ments. The Atkinson index has the advantage of making these judgments explicit. Assume a social welfare function,

$$W(w) = W(w_1, w_2, w_3, w_4, \ldots w_N),$$

where this function depends on the earnings of each person in the population—that is, its independent variable is $N \times 1$ vector of earnings for a given population of size N, w_i represents the income of individual i, and μ_w is the mean wage under this distribution of earnings. Next, consider a certain level of wage w^* such that

$$W(w_1, w_2, w_3, \ldots, w_N) = W(w^*, w^*, w^*, \ldots, w^*).$$

Under this earnings distribution, every individual would earn the same, w_*, and the society will achieve an equivalent level of social welfare to that under the current distribution of earnings. Then, the Atkinson index is

$$A(w) = \frac{\mu_w - w^*}{\mu_w}.$$

It measures the fraction of the average earnings that a social planner would be willing to give up to get an even distribution of earnings.

In practice, the specific value of $A(w)$ depends on the specification of $W(w)$. Atkinson (1970) proposes the following functional form:

$$W(w) = \frac{1}{N} \sum_{i=1}^{N} \frac{yw_i^{(1-\varepsilon)}}{(1-\varepsilon)}.$$

The great advantage of this functional form is that it is possible to summarize the value judgment in the parameter ε, known as *inequality aversion*. Note that when ε equals 0, $W(w)$ corresponds to μ_w, the average income of the population. This is the case in which the social planner cares about only the "size of the pie." Mathematically, for $\varepsilon = 0$

$$W(w) = \sum_{i=1}^{N} \frac{w_i}{N}.$$

Alternatively, when the inequality aversion ε approaches infinity ($\varepsilon \rightarrow \infty$), it turns into the Rawlsian welfare function

$$W(w) = \min\{w_1, w_2, w_3, w_4, ..., w_N\} = w_{poorest}.$$

In this case, the lower the ratio $w_{poorest}/\mu_w$, the higher the earnings inequality. In practice, researchers use values of ε that fall between these two extremes, such as $\varepsilon = 0.5$, $\varepsilon = 1$, and $\varepsilon = 2$.

In a similar vein, the *generalized entropy index of inequality* and *Theil index* have their origins in the theory of information (Cowell 2000). The formula is

$$E(c) = \frac{1}{N.c(c-1)} \cdot \left[\sum_{i=1}^{N} \left(\frac{w_i}{\mu_w} \right)^c - 1 \right].$$

One if the main advantages of this index is that it allows us to focus on the inequality in different components of the distribution by choosing the value of c. The larger the value of c, the larger the weight given to changes in the right tail of the distribution. It is possible to show that when $c \rightarrow 1$, the entropy index converges to the Theil index.[5]

Adjusting these indexes to labor market analysis is not fully possible, since differences in earnings are necessary to maintain the incentives for individuals to invest in education. However, the Atkinson index can be used as a signal of the reallocation of skills and jobs that should happen to achieve greater equality in the labor market. This way of thinking about the differences gets closer to the concept of equality of opportunity.

Even if ADePT Gender users' ultimate goal is to understand the underlying factors that contribute to the gender gap in pay, analyzing the within-gender inequality is important, since it is a way to gather information about the economy's wage structure. All the measures described above are thus computed for men and women separately.

Gender Earnings Inequality

ADePT Gender computes the differences in wages between men and women at different points along the earnings distribution curve. The mean *gender pay gap* is computed as the differences between the log wage of men and women. This gender pay gap is usually referred to as the *raw* gender pay gap, because it does not take into account any factor that could explain the differences in wages between men and women. The gender pay gap is usually presented as the percentage difference. Mathematically,

$$\overline{GWG} = \ln(\overline{w_M}) - \ln(\overline{w_F}),$$

where $\overline{GWG}$ is the raw average gender wage gap; $\ln(\overline{w_M})$ is the natural logarithm of the mean male (hourly) wage; and $\ln(\overline{w_F})$ is the natural logarithm of the mean female (hourly) wage. This is an approximation of the following:

$$\overline{GWG} = -\frac{w_M - w_F}{w_F}.$$

Analysts use the average wage of women, men, or total employed as a reference point, and the calculation has subtle differences that have implications for the interpretation. The different formulas are presented in box 6.1.

The gender gap in pay can be estimated at other points of the earnings distribution in the following way:

$$GWGp = \ln(w_{Mp}) - \ln(w_{Fp}),$$

where GWG_p is the raw gender wage gap measured at the *pth* percentile; $\ln(w_{Mp})$ is the natural logarithm of the male (hourly) wage evaluated at the *pth* percentile of the male earnings distribution curve; and $\ln(w_{Fp})$ is the

Box 6.1: Interpreting Different Measures of the Gender Gap in Pay for the Whole Distribution of Earnings

The following are some of the most widely used metrics of the gender gap in pay:

$$\overline{G}_{1a} = \frac{\overline{w_M} - \overline{w_F}}{\overline{w_M}},$$

$$\overline{G}_{1b} = \frac{\overline{w_M} - \overline{w_F}}{\overline{w_F}},$$

$$\overline{G}_{1c} = \frac{\overline{w_M} - \overline{w_F}}{\overline{w}},$$

$$\overline{G}_2 = \ln(\overline{w_M}) - \ln(\overline{w_F}), \quad \overline{G}_3 = \overline{\ln(w_M)} - \overline{\ln(w_F)},$$

where the upper bar indicates the (arithmetic) mean. Even when all these metrics are used interchangeably with the same objective—to measure the gender gap in pay—they may yield different values.

The first two metrics indicate the difference between men's and women's average wages as a percentage of the "reference group," which can be either men ($\overline{G}_{1a}$) or women ($\overline{G}_{1b}$). The third metric uses the average of all employed workers.

Since most of the time the analyst works with logs of wages, the gender gap in pay can be approximated by $\overline{G}_2$, which is a good approximation of $\overline{G}_{1b}$, if the difference between $\overline{w_M}$ and $\overline{w_F}$ is "small." The reason is that the logarithm function passes through the point $(0, 1)$, with a local slope of 1. Thus, for $x = 1$ or a small deviation, it holds that $y = \ln(x) \approx x - 1$. If we say that $x = \frac{\overline{w_M}}{\overline{w_F}}$, then

$$\overline{G}_2 = \ln\left(\frac{\overline{w_M}}{\overline{w_F}}\right) \approx \frac{\overline{w_M}}{\overline{w_F}} - 1 = \frac{\overline{w_M} - \overline{w_F}}{\overline{w_F}} = \overline{G}_{1b}.$$

In general, when $\overline{w_M} > \overline{w_F}$, $\overline{GWG}_{1b} \approx \overline{GWG}_2 \geq \overline{GWG}_{1a}$. All metrics can be interpreted as the percentage difference between the average wages for men and women, regardless of which gender is used as the reference.

Another measure is the difference between the means of the log wages as opposed to the log of mean wages. On the basis of the properties of natural logarithms, this measure is equivalent to the difference of the logs of the geometric—as opposed to the arithmetic—means of the wages:

$$\overline{G}_3 = \frac{1}{n}\sum_{i=1}^{n}\ln(w_{Mi}) - \frac{1}{s}\sum_{j=1}^{s}\ln(w_{Fj}) = \ln\left[\left(\prod_{i=1}^{n}w_{Mi}\right)^{1/n}\right] - \ln\left[\left(\prod_{j=1}^{s}w_{Fj}\right)^{1/s}\right].$$

To some extent, it is possible to establish a relationship between the values of $\overline{G}_2$ and $\overline{G}_3$. Notice that the arithmetic mean is always greater than the geometric mean, except when all wages are the same. The difference between the two increases with the level of wage inequality.

natural logarithm of the female (hourly) wage evaluated at *pth* percentile of the female earnings distribution curve.[6]

Interpreting the Results

This section presents concrete examples using data from the 2008 Panama living standards household survey to show how to interpret the tables and graphs produced by ADePT Gender. It first discusses how to interpret most of the output related to the overall and the within-gender earnings inequality. Later, we address measures of gender gap in pay, including data limitations, such as the issue that women are more likely to have missing data on earnings.

Overall and Within-Gender Inequality

ADePT tables 12a–12c present different measures of overall and within-gender earnings inequality. ADePT table 12a presents three different ratios of earnings at different percentiles: 90p/10p, 90p/50p, and 50p/10p (see table 6.1). The three measures can be interpreted in the same way as the log point difference of two wages—for example, w_{90p} and w_{10p}—for all wage workers. This difference

Table 6.1: ADePT Gender Table 12c, Panama 2008

Table 12c: Male and Female Earnings Shares and Ratios: Wage Workers and Self-Employed

	Wage worker			Self-employed		
	Total	Male	Female	Total	Male	Female
Decile						
1	0.9	1.2	0.5	3.1	3.5	1.9
2	2.5	3.2	1.3	3.5	3.8	2.3
3	3.8	4.7	2.1	5.2	5.1	5.7
4	5.6	6.2	4.5	5.4	5.5	5.2
5	6.4	6.9	5.4	7.1	7.5	5.7
6	8.9	9.5	7.7	8.0	8.8	5.3
7	9.4	10.2	8.1	9.5	9.6	9.3
8	11.8	10.7	13.6	14.2	14.3	14.0
9	16.3	14.7	19.2	18.7	18.8	18.5
10	34.4	32.6	37.6	25.1	23.3	32.0
Earnings ratio						
p90/p10	6.9	5.4	9.4	62.4	46.7	57.6
p90/p50	2.6	2.5	2.7	5.8	4.7	6.9
p50/10	2.7	2.1	3.4	10.8	10.0	8.4

Source: Based on ADePT Gender using Panama 2008.
Note: p = percentile.

can also be interpreted as the growth rate—for example, wage workers in the 90th percentile earn almost twice as much as wage workers in the bottom percentile of the earnings distribution. Note that when comparing the measures of all workers and those by gender, the dispersion of women's earnings is larger than that of men's, probably resulting from more women earning very little relative to men. This factor can be further corroborated with more specific analyses, which are described in the coming sections of this chapter. The measures of inequality borrowed from the poverty field are shown in ADePT table 12b (table 6.2). Within-gender inequality is always higher for women than for men, regardless of the chosen measure.[7] Notice also that inequality is higher among the self-employed than among the wage workers.

Measures featuring the whole distribution of earnings can be found in ADePT table 12c and figure 12b.[8] As can be seen at first glance, the distribution of earnings for the self-employed is more dispersed than the one for wage workers, and even more so for women than for men (see figure 6.2). These results are consistent with those from ADePT table 12c that indicate that the dispersion is 10 times larger among the self-employed than among wage workers; the 90p/10p ratio is 2 times larger for the self-employed than for wage workers (table 6.1).

Table 6.2: ADePT Gender Table 12b, Panama 2008

Table 12b: Male and Female Earnings Inequality Indexes (Detailed): Wage Workers and Self-Employed

Work category	Total	Male	Female
Wage worker			
Gini coefficient	0.434	0.423	0.448
Coefficient of variation	1.208	1.235	1.142
A(½)	0.165	0.158	0.174
A(−1)	0.570	0.517	0.619
A(0)	0.298	0.277	0.323
GE(0)	0.353	0.324	0.391
GE(1)	0.388	0.382	0.391
GE(2)	0.781	0.798	0.723
Self-employed			
Gini coefficient	0.664	0.632	0.723
Coefficient of variation	2.438	2.256	3.016
A(½)	0.382	0.346	0.453
A(−1)	0.924	0.907	0.931
A(0)	0.656	0.611	0.716
GE(0)	1.069	0.944	1.259
GE(1)	0.907	0.805	1.172
GE(2)	2.458	2.096	3.795

Source: Based on ADePT Gender using Panama 2008.
Note: A = Atkinson index; GE = General Entropy index.

Figure 6.2: ADePT Gender Figure 12b, Panama 2008

Figure 12b: Male and Female Earnings Distributions: Wage Earners and Self-Employed

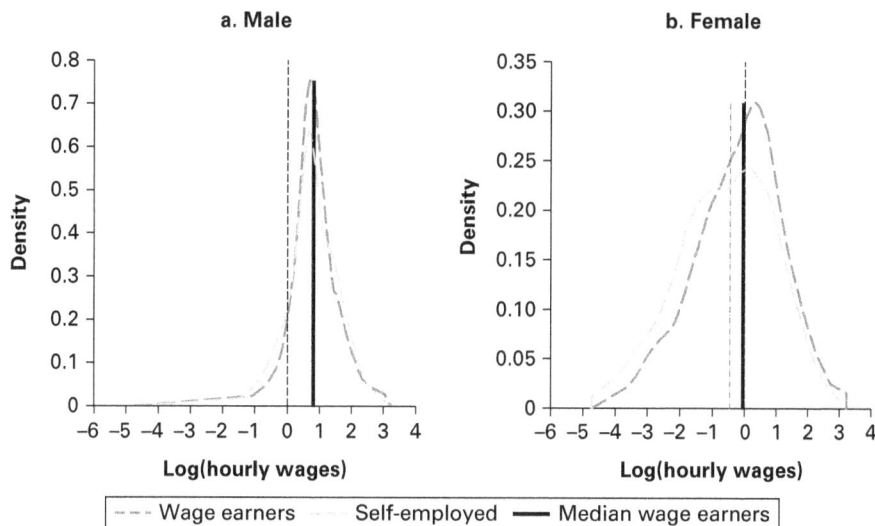

a. Male   b. Female

--- Wage earners   Self-employed   ━━ Median wage earners

Source: Based on ADePT Gender using Panama 2008.

Complementing these two graphs, ADePT table 12c (table 6.1) shows how much workers in each population decile—determined by sorting households according to the welfare aggregate measure selected by the user—contribute to the total earnings of a certain employed population. Note that by construction, the sum of each column equals 100, reflecting the total earnings of the group indicated in the column (that is, female wage earners). For example, in Panama in 2008, employed men in the bottom 10th wealth decile got only 5 percent of their total earnings from wage employment. The contribution of workers to earnings increases as the decile becomes wealthier. Their contribution after the eighth decile is more than 10 percent, larger than the percentage of the population.

Gender Gap in Pay

This section discusses how to interpret the tables and graphs that compare women's and men's earnings. ADePT table 12d presents the most common measures of the gender gap in pay. They include the average (or mean) gender gap in pay and the percentile that the median female earning represents in the male earnings cumulative distribution curve. It is useful to look at the gender gap in pay evaluated at different points of the earnings distribution, but these are provided later when presenting the Juhn-Murphy-Pierce decomposition. Each of the measures is computed separately for wage workers and the self-employed.

Table 6.3 shows the measures for the example illustrated throughout the book. In Panama in 2008, employed women in wage jobs earned 7 percent less than employed men. For an idea of the magnitude of the gap in the local context, the next measure evaluates the percentile in the male distribution at which the median wage of women lands. The median wage of women is equivalent to moving 12 percentiles down from the midpoint of the male distribution.

The same concept is plotted with more detail in ADePT figure 12c (figure 6.3), which captures where women stand in the male earnings distribution. In the graph, the x-axis represents the percentile of earnings for men, and the y-axis represents the percentile of earnings for men or women. Hence, the 45-degree line represents male percentiles—or line of gender equality in pay—and the curve represents female percentiles in the men's earnings distribution. When the women's curve is above the 45-degree line, the gender wage gap favors men; when the women's curve is below the 45-degree line, women earn more than men. If the curve crosses the 45-degree line from left to right, low-skilled women earn less than low-skilled men, and high-skilled women earn more than high-skilled men. The distance of the curve to the 45-degree line offers an idea of the size of the gap—the farther away the curve is from the diagonal line, the larger the size of the gap. For example, if we take the wage of the 20th percentile of men's earnings distribution, the curve indicates that a woman with that same wage is in the 31st percentile of the women's earnings distribution curve. In general, the farther the curve is from the 45-degree line, the larger the gender wage gap.

Table 6.3: ADePT Gender Table 12d, Panama 2008

Table 12d: Male-Female Gap in Earnings: Wage Workers and Self-Employed

	Mean gender earnings gap (in %)	Percentile of women's median in men's distribution
Work category		
Wage worker	6.6	38.3

Source: Based on ADePT Gender using Panama 2008.
Note: The mean gender earnings gap is the difference of the mean log female earnings and the mean log male earnings.

Figure 6.3: ADePT Gender Figure 12c, Panama 2008

Figure 12c: Male-Female Earnings Concentration Curves: Wage Earners and Self-Employed

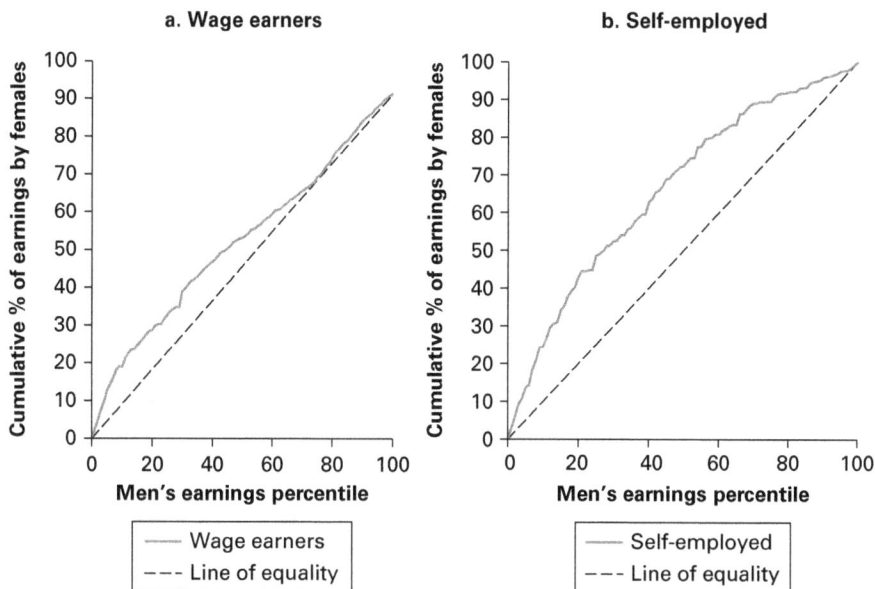

a. Wage earners   b. Self-employed

Source: Based on ADePT Gender using Panama 2008.

To shed additional light on how to measure the distribution of earnings, ADePT table 16a also shows the gender gap in pay computed at different percentiles of the earnings distribution of men and women. For example, in ADePT table 16a for Panama 2008, women in the 10th percentile of women's wage distribution earn 28 percent less than men in the 10th percentile of the men's distribution.

Earnings Decompositions

Contents

ADePT Gender produces 16 tables (ADePT tables 13a to 17d) and 8 graphs (ADePT figures 13a to 17b) with different earnings decompositions by gender. All the decompositions are done using two specifications: the human capital model and the full model (see box 6.2 for explanations of these models). ADePT Gender generates estimates for three types of

Box 6.2: ADePT Gender Model Specifications for Earnings Equations

Human capital specification—This specification includes education and experience variables and controls for place of residence.

Education—Education can be included in the regression model in three ways: (a) using number of years of completed education, (b) using a set of dummy variables for levels of completed education, or (c) using a combination of the two previous specifications, including years of completed education and dummies for the levels of education. The choice of education variables clearly depends on the available information, as well as on the country context. Generally, researchers use both years of education and dummy variables to indicate completion of education levels, since level of completion can have an additional payoff.[a] The ideal combination of the two sets of variables differs from country to country, depending on the prevalent distribution of education. One possible specification could be to add secondary, vocational, and college. However, for certain African countries, it might be reasonable to use secondary and postsecondary or to use only vocational and college for a middle-income country.

Experience—ADePT Gender uses age as a proxy for potential experience. Potential experience is defined as *age − years of education − age of entrance to school*. However, given that users might decide to compare countries that have different ages of school entrance, ADePT Gender uses age. Age and potential experience can be thought of as a similar variable—given that the education variables are also included in the regression estimation—but they differ on its interpretation.

Place of residence—ADePT Gender controls for place of residence with urban dummies and region of residence dummies.

Full model specification—This specification includes all the variables from the human capital specification plus industry and occupation dummies.

Occupation—Occupation is usually included as a set of dummy variables. The general recommendation is to include them as one-digit International Standard Classification of Occupations (ISCO) classifications (see chapter 3 for more details). However, on occasion, some analyses use two- and three-digit dummies when they have a large number of observations. For ADePT Gender, the omitted category is the lowest number in the occupation classification, which, if the user follows the ISCO classification, is agriculture. Users following other classifications should avoid having an "other" category for omitted occupations, which could make interpretation difficult.

Industry—Similar to occupation, the most common approach for industry is to include dummies at the one-digit International Standard Industrial Classification (ISIC) level. The same rules for the omitted category apply.

Other specifications—Other authors have used other specifications, depending on the richness of their data. Variables can be classified in two types: (a) those that directly

(continued)

Box 6.2: ADePT Gender Model Specifications for Earnings Equations
(continued)

affect productivity (as explained by theories) and (b) those that are good proxies for a household's responsibilities. The first group (those that affect productivity) includes controls for union affiliation and size of firm (that is, number of employees). Regarding household duties, the typical controls are marital status and number and age of children. ADePT Gender does not include any of these variables because they are not widely available or—as in the case of household responsibilities—must be interpreted with caution, as they might be endogenous to the model. The user always has the option to add them.

Source: Based on Blau and Kahn 1997.
Notes: a. The additional payoff of having completed a certain level of education can be explained by different factors. First, the government or large enterprises might have policies about hiring employees with a certain level of education. The most common example for middle- and high-income countries is the secondary degree. Companies like Walmart hire employees with a secondary degree. Second, signaling theories applied to labor markets can be tested using completed levels of education (Bedard 2001).

decompositions methodologies that are the most commonly used and with the easiest interpretation. The two parametric decompositions are the Oaxaca-Blinder, which decomposes earnings at the mean of the earnings distribution curve, and the Juhn-Murphy-Pierce, which decomposes earnings at different percentiles of the earnings distribution curve. Finally, ADePT Gender also presents the results of one of the nonparametric decompositions—the Ñopo decomposition—that have been applied to several developing countries (World Bank 2012).

Decompositions must be used with caution, and users should avoid drawing overly ambitious conclusions from them. It is important to understand the models' underlying assumptions as well as to remember that decompositions are partial equilibrium approaches and do not measure causal relations. Decompositions do not deepen our understanding of the *mechanisms* underlying the relationships between factors and outcomes; rather, they signal potential mechanisms at play to engage in further analysis. For example, if the decomposition indicates that differences in occupational affiliation account for a large fraction of the gender wage gap, one should explore in more detail why and how men and women choose their fields of study and occupations and whether discrimination exists in accessing certain occupations or jobs. Decompositions are an excellent tool for tracking progress and assessing the magnitude of the problem.

All decomposition methodologies use the Mincer earnings equation as the starting point. That means that this reduced-form analysis relies on the assumptions of the human capital model described in chapter 5 and other econometric assumptions of the earnings equation. Users who are unfamiliar with the Mincer earnings equation can find an introduction to it in chapter 7. Box 6.2 describes the variables used for the earnings equations by ADePT Gender. In addition, for both the Oaxaca-Blinder and the Juhn-Murphy-Pierce decompositions, the results are also presented correcting for nonrandom selection of women into the labor force. Nonrandom selection of women is a very important problem in measuring the gender pay gap. Chapter 7 also includes a description of the nature of the problem and econometricians' proposed solutions.

These econometric models were not developed in isolation. They were the empirical response to the economic theories of discrimination that were proposed in the 1960s and 1970s. Although still included in all undergraduate textbooks, these theories have become increasingly obsolete, as more sophisticated theoretical and empirical models have emerged. Nevertheless, a brief summary of these concepts and theories can be found in chapter 7 to give users who are not that familiar with economics further context and understanding on why and how the Oaxaca-Blinder decomposition originated.

Concepts

Decomposition methods are applied to several diverse topics. In particular, decompositions are widely used in the area of gender gaps in pay. Decompositions can be grouped in several ways according to different characteristics: (a) parametric versus nonparametric, (b) mean versus other moments of the earnings distribution (for example, variance or quantiles), (c) uncorrected versus corrected for nonrandom selection of women in the labor force, and (d) over groups (for example, men and women) versus over time. This section reviews the methods used by ADePT Gender and provides some discussion of the advantages and disadvantages of these methods compared with others. The user interested in knowing more or in working with more sophisticated methods can consult Fortin, Lemieux, and Firpo (2011).

Assume that there are only two types of workers—men and women. Male workers' average wage is $\overline{w_M}$, and female workers' average wage is $\overline{w_F}$.

The simplest way to measure gender inequality is to compute the difference in wages, usually called the *raw gender wage gap*:

$$\Delta \overline{w} = \overline{w_M} - \overline{w_F}. \tag{6.1}$$

This definition of inequality is informative but subject to flaws, as many factors beyond discrimination can influence the raw gender gap in wages, some of which result from choices and others from constraints. Perhaps the most critical is the difference in labor market skills. Those with professional degrees earn more; if one of the two groups has more members with professional degrees, the raw gender wage gap would capture a "pure inequality" or discrimination effect as well as the returns to having a professional degree. If more women have professional degrees than men, the raw gender gap would underestimate the pure gender inequality or discrimination effect. Instead, if more men than women have professional degrees, then the raw gender gap would overestimate a discrimination effect.

Therefore, a good measure of gender inequality in pay should take into account differences in characteristics that affect labor productivity. The adjustment is conducted by constructing counterfactual earnings of how much members of a group would earn if they shared one another's characteristics.

The seminal papers by Oaxaca (1973) and Blinder (1973) developed decomposition methods in labor economics. The linear regression is the basic building block of the Oaxaca-Blinder decomposition. This methodology explains differences in *mean* outcomes. As a result of the dramatic increase in wage inequality that has taken place in the United States since the late 1970s, decomposition methods have been further improved with the objective of analyzing distributional parameters other than the mean, such as the variance or the quantiles of the outcome distribution. Tools from the program evaluation literature have also been applied to extend the Oaxaca-Blinder setup. Contributions in this domain have been to clarify the assumptions underlying the Oaxaca-Blinder framework, to introduce alternative estimators for elements of the decomposition, and to formally derive formal statistical properties of decomposition terms. Table 6.4 summarizes the main decomposition methodologies and their advantages and disadvantages.

Oaxaca and Blinder

The papers by Oaxaca (1973) and Blinder (1973) are among the most heavily cited in labor economics as well as in other fields of economics. The basic

Table 6.4: Most Commonly Used Decomposition Methodologies

Decomposition methodology	In ADePT Gender	Description	Advantages	Disadvantages
Oaxaca (1973) and Blinder (1973)	Yes	Decomposes the gender gap in pay in a composition and wage structure effect measured at the mean	Allows estimating the effect of each variable; simple to compute and interpret	May hide different results for other groups that are not represented by the mean; attention needs to be paid to interpretation depending on how the baseline category is defined
Juhn, Murphy, and Pierce (1991, 1993)	Yes	Decomposes the gender gap in pay in a composition and wage structure effect measured at the different percentiles or for the variance	Provides an idea of the variation of the composition and wage structure effect at different points of the distribution	Does not allow estimating the effect of each variable
DiNardo, Fortin, and Lemieux (1996)	No	Decomposes the gender gap in pay in a series of marginal distributions	Allows the analyst to examine the whole distribution of wages	Is complex to estimate and requires a large number of observations for the semiparametric estimation, and results are path dependent;[a] works better with categorical variables, ideally binary variables; does not allow for selection correction
Ñopo (2008)	Yes	Estimates the effect from the lack of overlapping support (for both men and women) and a composition and wage structure effect	Estimates the results after controlling for lack of overlapping support; relatively easy to interpret	Requires a large number of observations for the semiparametric estimation, and results are path dependent; Does not allow for selection correction
Fortin, Lemieux, and Firpo (2011)	No	Estimates the composition and wage structure effect for any statistics, including the percentiles	Allows the analyst to examine the whole distribution of wages and to estimate the contribution of each covariate	Is complex to estimate and requires a large number of observations for the semiparametric estimation; does not allow for selection correction

Note: a. Path dependent means that the results vary with the order in which the marginal distributions are estimated.

assumption of the Oaxaca-Blinder decomposition is that earnings (measured with the logarithm of the hourly rate of pay) can be estimated by a linear regression that yields

$$\overline{\ln w_M} = \widehat{\alpha}^M + \widehat{\rho}^M S_M + \widehat{\beta}_1^M X_M + \widehat{\beta}_2^M X_M^2,$$
$$\overline{\ln w_F} = \widehat{\alpha}^F + \widehat{\rho}^F S_F + \widehat{\beta}_1^F X_F + \widehat{\beta}_2^F X_F^2, \tag{6.2}$$

where $\overline{\ln w_M}$ is the average of the log of hourly rate of men, S_M is average number of years of schooling of men, X_M is the average years of experience, and the coefficients estimated in the linear regression are $\widehat{\alpha}^M$ for the constant, and $\widehat{\rho}^{M}$ and $\widehat{\beta}_1^{M}$ for each of the corresponding variables. The separate regression for women is indicated with the subscript F or superscript F. The estimated average gender wage gap, $\widehat{\Delta}_O^{\mu}$, can be written as

$$\widehat{\Delta}_O^{\mu} = \overline{\ln w_M} - \overline{\ln w_F},$$

$$\widehat{\Delta}_O^{\mu} = \underbrace{\left(\widehat{\alpha}^{M} - \widehat{\alpha}^{F}\right) + \overline{S_F}\left(\widehat{\rho}^{M} - \widehat{\rho}^{F}\right)}_{\widehat{\Delta}_S^{\mu}\,(\text{Unexplained})} + \underbrace{\widehat{\rho}^{M}\left(\overline{S_M} - \overline{S_F}\right)}_{\widehat{\Delta}_X^{\mu}\,(\text{Explained})}. \qquad (6.3)$$

For expositional purposes, the contribution of experience and its squared value—X variable in equation (6.2)—are dropped; however, it can be easily added by repeating the terms for education but applying them to experience. The components of equation (6.3) are as follows:

- $\widehat{\Delta}_O^{U}$, the *overall* or *raw* gender wage gap;
- $\widehat{\Delta}_X^{\mu}$, the *composition* effect, also called the *explained* component or part; and
- $\widehat{\Delta}_S^{\mu}$, the *wage structure*, which includes the average differences between men and women, also called the *unexplained* component.

The results from the decomposition are usually presented following these three components: $\widehat{\Delta}_O^{\mu} = \widehat{\Delta}_S^{\mu} + \widehat{\Delta}_X^{\mu}$, or in full detail—usually called *detailed decomposition*—where the contribution of each covariate or variable is shown.

The intuition behind the Oaxaca-Blinder decomposition can be explained using a graph with a simplified version of the Mincer equation. Assume that earnings depend solely on the number of years of education: workers with more years of education earn more. Women are paid less than men when neither of them have any education, and women also have lower payoffs for each additional year of education than men. Assume men have on average more years of education than women, $\left(\overline{S_F} < \overline{S_M}\right)$. The raw gender wage gap is $\left(\overline{w_M} - \overline{w_F}\right)$. However, it has two components: one related to the differential treatment of women with respect to men (unexplained or wage structure component) and the other related to the gender difference in years of schooling (explained or composition component). If women were paid like men, they would earn w_F^{*}; under discrimination toward women, this is usually larger than $\overline{w_F}$ and smaller than $\overline{w_M}$. Therefore, $\left(w_F^{*} - \overline{w_F}\right)$ is the wage structure effect, and $\left(\overline{w_M} - w_F^{*}\right)$ is the composition effect due to differences in labor market skills. Moreover, the wage structure effect can be divided into its two components: one coming from differences in the returns to schooling $\overline{S_F}\left(\hat{\rho}^M - \hat{\rho}^F\right)$ and the other coming from "everything else"—that is, the constant $(\alpha_M - \alpha_F)$. A very useful graphical representation of the Oaxaca and Blinder decomposition can be found in Borjas (2005).[9]

The accuracy of the discrimination measurement from the Oaxaca-Blinder decomposition depends on the validity of the estimation of the wage equations. If variables that are omitted bias the estimation of the coefficients of the included variables, and for which differences exist between men and women, the estimated wage structure (unexplained) effect will be biased. For example, consider the case in which the analyst leaves the experience variable out of the wage equation. Assume that men and women have the same number of years of education, but women accumulate fewer years of experience because of employment interruptions for child rearing. A wage gap exists between men and women, and it would be incorrect to assume that the entire wage gap is due to discrimination. In reality, it is partly explained by differences in other unmeasured skills, such as experience.[10]

Thus, one of the disadvantages of measuring discrimination—usually identified with the unexplained component—using decomposition techniques is that it can always be argued that part of the discrimination effect is actually capturing the gender difference in some unobserved (that is, excluded in the regression) labor market skills. Even when working with rich datasets, there will always be some other unobserved characteristic—such as ability, effort, motivation, or responsibility—that can be used to argue that differences between men's skills and women's skills exist. As a result, modern labor economics more often refers to this factor as the wage structure component as opposed to a discrimination effect.

In response to this criticism, it can be argued that any other gender difference in unobserved variables is due to the influence of formal and informal institutions on men and women. If women exert less effort at a job than men, it could be due to the fact that they are rewarded less or have too many other responsibilities in the household. In other words, some other factors are responsible for the difference. Very likely, the reality lies somewhere in the middle of these two points of view.

In summary, the Oaxaca-Blinder decomposition can be a powerful tool for understanding the factors behind gender inequality. Analysts must be careful about how they interpret the unexplained coefficient—depending on the set of included variables in the Mincer wage equation—and they must be familiar with the country's cultural and social norms so as to understand the possible gender differences in the omitted unobserved variables. It is critical to correctly interpret the unexplained component.

Switching Reference Groups and Pooled Decomposition

So far, the discussion has focused on using men as a reference group by adding and subtracting $\hat{\rho}^M \overline{S_F}$ to obtain the rearrangement in equation (6.3). This approach amounts to interpreting the "explained" component as the value of the difference in skills (or endowments as more generally discussed in the introduction) between men and women, as valuated by the men's earnings equation; and the "unexplained" component as the difference between how the men's and women's earnings equations value the average skills of women. Two points are worth noting. First, women can also be used as a reference group—which would yield equation (6.4) with some adjustment in the interpretation of the results—to mirror what has been discussed so far using men as the reference point. Oaxaca (1973) refers to this as the "index number problem"—the decomposition is sensitive to the group chosen as a reference.

$$\hat{\Delta}_O^\mu = \underbrace{\left(\hat{\alpha}^M - \hat{\alpha}^F\right) + \overline{S_M}\left(\hat{\rho}^M - \hat{\rho}^F\right)}_{\hat{\Delta}_S^\mu \text{ (Unexplained)}} + \underbrace{\hat{\rho}^F\left(\overline{S_M} - \overline{S_F}\right)}_{\hat{\Delta}_X^\mu \text{ (Explained)}}. \tag{6.4}$$

Second, some may implicitly assume that discrimination goes only one way (targeting women if men are the reference, and vice versa). A more general version of the decomposition assumes that underevaluation of one group is likely to go hand in hand with overevaluation of the other. To address this assumption, and to separate the effects of positive and negative discrimination in the unexplained component, a "nondiscriminatory" vector of parameters (composed of $\hat{\alpha}^*$ and $\hat{\rho}^*$) could be introduced as the reference point. This vector of parameters will lie in the middle of the male and female reference point.

$$\hat{\Delta}_O^\mu = \underbrace{\left(\hat{\alpha}^M - \hat{\alpha}^*\right) + \overline{S_M}\left(\hat{\rho}^M - \hat{\rho}^*\right) + \left(\hat{\alpha}^* - \hat{\alpha}^F\right) + \overline{S_M}\left(\hat{\rho}^* - \hat{\rho}^F\right)}_{\hat{\Delta}_S^\mu \text{ (Unexplained)}} + \underbrace{\hat{\rho}^*\left(\overline{S_M} - \overline{S_F}\right)}_{\hat{\Delta}_X^\mu \text{ (Explained)}}. \tag{6.5}$$

Different methodologies have been proposed to estimate such nondis-criminatory reference points. Possible solutions include using an average of the group-specific coefficients (simple or weighted by population size) or the coefficients from a pooled regression over both groups—Oaxaca-Ransom decomposition, also called a pooled decomposition (Oaxaca and Ransom 1994). This approach is a way to overcome the "index number problem" and to focus on positive and negative discrimination.

Detailed Decomposition

Because the linear regression is the basic building block of the Oaxaca-Blinder decomposition, each of its components is in fact a sum over the effects of individual variables. If instead of limiting the discussion to educa-tion, we include all variables in the Mincer earnings equation, an equivalent full version of equation (6.5) is

$$
\hat{\Delta}_O^\mu = \left(\hat{\alpha}^M - \hat{\alpha}^F\right) + \overline{S_F}\left(\hat{\rho}^M - \hat{\rho}^F\right) + \overline{X_F}\left(\hat{\beta}_1^M - \hat{\beta}_1^F\right) + \overline{X_F^2}\left(\hat{\beta}_2^M - \hat{\beta}_2^F\right) +
$$
$$
\hat{\rho}^M\left(\overline{S_M} - \overline{S_F}\right) + \hat{\beta}_1^M\left(\overline{X_M} - \overline{X_F}\right) + \hat{\beta}_2^M\left(\overline{X_M^2} - \overline{X_F^2}\right).
$$

(6.6)

The main advantage of the detailed decomposition is that it allows us to further identify each factor's contribution to the gender gap. However, users must keep two caveats in mind. First, it can be shown that the unexplained component of the decomposition is sensitive to arbitrary scaling decisions if the variables do not have natural zero points (that is, are not so-called ratio variables, for which the level "zero" is a meaningful value and indicates absence of the property being measured). In this case, simply rescaling the variable affects the relative magnitude of the part of the unexplained com-ponent captured in the constants and the part due to the coefficients of the variable in question.[11]

Second, the unexplained portion of the detailed decomposition is also sensitive to the choice of the excluded category when the regressions include dummy variables to capture the effect of categorical predictors. This arbitrary choice is again reflected in a trade-off between the compo-nents, as changes in the base category alter the (slope) coefficients, which determine the wage structure effect. The solution to the problem—proposed by Gardeazabal and Ugidos (2004) and Yun (2005)—is to restrict the coefficients of the single categories to summing to zero, that is, to express coefficients as deviations from the overall mean. This approach is equal to averaging the results obtained from a series of decompositions in which categories are excluded one by one (Yun 2005). However, this solution would cover the differences in means across countries if working with cross-country data.

Threefold Decomposition

Equation (6.5) is not the only possible decomposition that separates the role of observable characteristics from that of returns to labor market skills. An alternative decomposition, yielding three terms instead of two, can be written as

$$\hat{\Delta}_O^\mu = \underbrace{\left(\hat{\alpha}^M - \hat{\alpha}^F\right) + \overline{S_F}\left(\hat{\rho}^M - \hat{\rho}^F\right)}_{\hat{\Delta}_C^\mu \text{(Coefficients)}} + \underbrace{\hat{\rho}^F\left(\overline{S_M} - \overline{S_F}\right)}_{\hat{\Delta}_E^\mu \text{(Endowments)}} + \underbrace{\left(\overline{S_M} - \overline{S_F}\right)\left(\hat{\rho}^M - \hat{\rho}^F\right)}_{\hat{\Delta}_I^\mu \text{(Interaction)}}. \quad (6.7)$$

The effect of different predictors, the "endowments" component E, can be viewed as the expected change in the mean raw gender wage gap if they had men's characteristics; the effect of a different coefficient, C, can be seen as the expected change of the gender wage gap if women had unchanged characteristics but were paid as men. The last addendum is an interaction term that captures the differences in mean characteristics, and coefficients exist simultaneously. On the one hand, the interpretation of this version of the decomposition might be, in a way, more convenient, given that in both the endowments and coefficients components, the reference group is the same (in this case, women). On the other hand to equate the right-hand side and left-hand side, the interaction term must be added, and its interpretation in economic terms is not straightforward, as noted in Blinder (1973).

Oaxaca-Blinder with Selection Correction

It is possible to incorporate a selection correction in the Oaxaca-Blinder decomposition by modifying the underlying regressions accordingly. The selection correction is needed when the analyst has reasons to believe that women who work are different from women who do not work, with regard to their unobservable skills. As a result, the wages of working women are not good predictors of the potential wages of nonworking women, if they were employed. In other words, working women are not a random selection of all women of working age. The correction was introduced by Heckman (1974) and later applied to the Oaxaca-Blinder decomposition. Simply, the parameters of the earnings equations can be estimated through a Heckit[12] procedure for both groups (or more commonly, for only women, since men's labor force participation is usually high, random, or both). The basis of the decomposition will then be the Heckman-corrected equivalent of equation (6.3), which includes a regressor, the Mills ratio:[13]

$$\hat{\Delta}_O^\mu = \overline{\ln w_M} - \overline{\ln w_F}$$
$$= \left[\hat{\alpha}^M + \hat{\rho}^M \overline{S_M} + \hat{\beta}_1^M \overline{X_M} + \hat{\beta}_2^M \overline{X_M^2} + \hat{\lambda}_M \gamma_M \right] \tag{6.8}$$
$$- \left[\hat{\alpha}^F + \hat{\rho}^F \overline{S_F} + \hat{\beta}_1^F \overline{X_F} + \hat{\beta}_2^F \overline{X_F^2} + \hat{\lambda}_F \gamma_F \right].$$

As Neuman and Oaxaca (2004) note, it is not immediately obvious how the added Mills ratio should be regarded in the overall decomposition scheme. They discuss several alternative ways of allocating it to the decomposition terms: as a component of the explained part, as a component of the unexplained part, or as a stand-alone term. However, a common way to work around this issue is simply to net out the "selection" term from the left-hand side, thus leaving the familiar decomposition terms on the right-hand side:

$$\hat{\Delta}_O^\mu - \left[\hat{\lambda}_M \gamma_M - \hat{\lambda}_F \gamma_F \right] = \left(\hat{\alpha}^M - \hat{\alpha}^F \right) + \overline{S_M} \left(\hat{\rho}^M - \hat{\rho}^F \right) + \hat{\rho}^F \left(\overline{S_M} - \overline{S_F} \right), \tag{6.9}$$

where S is the adjusted difference in outcomes. The resulting decomposition is not conceptually different from the nonselection-corrected version seen above; however, one needs to use some care in interpreting it. What we are left with on the right-hand side are the "true" (that is, random sample) population parameters that describe the effect of regressors on the underlying, uncensored dependent variable. Accordingly, the left-hand side is no longer equal to the observed difference overall gender wage gap, but to the selection-corrected difference—the difference that would be observed if our selected sample were indeed a random draw from the population. The interpretation of the explained and unexplained terms is the usual (and comes with the usual caveats), but the quantity being decomposed now incorporates the effect of selection (that is, it is bigger if there is a larger positive selection into the labor force for women than for men, as it is usually the case).

Several decomposition methodologies seek to shed light on aspects that are left out of the Oaxaca-Blinder decomposition framework. Below are some of these extensions, which are part of the ADePT Gender output. We first discuss issues they are designed to tackle and then outline the expression of the decomposition, highlighting the differences with respect to Oaxaca-Blinder.

Juhn, Murphy, and Pierce

The value that the Juhn-Murphy-Pierce methodology adds to the Oaxaca-Blinder decomposition discussed above is that it allows the analyst to separate the effect of skills (or endowments) from the effect of changes in returns to observable characteristics and the effect of unobservable characteristics. The methodology takes the name of the authors who introduced it in 1991 when analyzing reduction in the wage gap between blacks and whites in the United States (Juhn, Murphy, and Pierce 1991) and changes in wage inequality over time in the United States (Juhn, Murphy, and Pierce 1993). From a methodological point of view, it represents a step up toward methodologies that move away from the mean by looking at the overall distribution of a variable. From a conceptual point of view, it allows one to measure the price of skills that the analyst cannot observe. Moreover, this methodology has also been applied to perform double decompositions—or the change over time of the wage decomposition across groups, such as men and women or blacks and whites—providing an additional advancement with respect to the seminal Oaxaca-Blinder work.

For simplicity, this subsection works with a reduced version of the earnings equation introduced above that includes only the constant and the education variable. The notation is compacted too, where X_{gi} indicates both the constant and the only regressor (denotes a matrix), and β^g indicates both β_0^g and ρ_1^g (denotes a vector):

$$\ln w_{gi} = \beta_0^g + \rho_1^g S_{gi} + \varepsilon_{gi} = \beta^g X_{gi} + \varepsilon_{gi}, \tag{6.10}$$

where $g = M, F$, that is male and female. The error term in the equation has no role in the Oaxaca-Blinder framework, since wage regressions are estimated by least squares and then averaged over the sample, which implies that residuals equal zero (it is an algebraic property of ordinary least squares). But the error term can be further exploited, as it has information about the unobserved skills. Take a group of workers who have the same education and experience. If observable characteristics were their only determinant of productivity, they

187

Figure 6.4: Illustration of Unobserved Skills

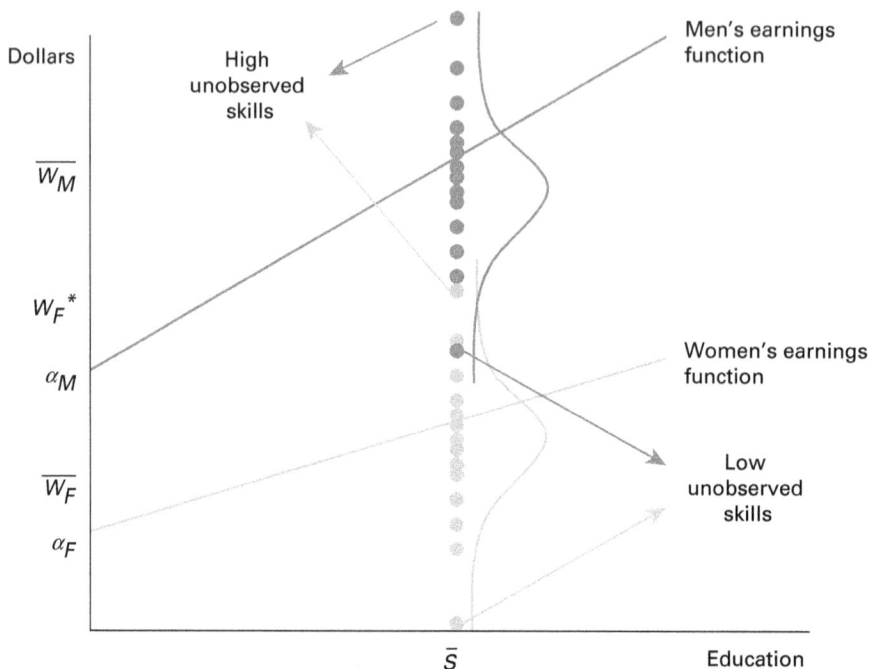

would all earn the same wage per hour. However, that is not the reality. It can be said that those workers with higher wages—all other things constant—have better unobserved labor market skills. The unobserved skills can then be thought of as the position in the distribution of the residuals of the earnings equation, or the percentile in the distribution. Figure 6.4 illustrates the logic: take level of education $\bar{S}$—the expected return for that level of education is reflected by the line that shows the mean fitted equation for men and women. Men with high unobserved skills will earn more that the value of the mean.

Similar to the Oaxaca-Blinder decomposition, the next step is to work out the resulting summary statistics of the regressions to express the raw wage gap in terms of separate components. Appendix D includes the transformation step by step. The Juhn-Murphy-Pierce decomposition accomplishes this by summarizing observed and counterfactual wages at each percentile and then arranging the gender differences among the terms specified above in the following way:

$$w_{Mp} - w_{Fp} = \left[w_{Mp}^{X} - w_{Fp}^{X} \right] + \left[\left(w_{Mp}^{obs} - w_{Fp}^{obs} \right) - \left(w_{Mp}^{X} - w_{Fp}^{X} \right) \right]$$
$$+ \left[\left(w_{Mp}^{unobs} - w_{Fp}^{unobs} \right) - \left(w_{Mp}^{obs} - w_{Fp}^{obs} \right) \right], \tag{6.11}$$

$$\hat{\Delta}_O^{\mu} = \hat{\Delta}_{\chi obs}^{\mu} + \hat{\Delta}_{\chi unobs}^{\mu} + \hat{\Delta}_S^{\mu}, \qquad (6.12)$$

where $\hat{\Delta}_{\chi p}^{\mu} = \left[w_{Mp}^{\chi} - w_{Fp}^{\chi} \right]$ is the part of the raw wage gap at percentile p due to gender differences in observed characteristics, in this case education (the "endowments" effect); $\hat{\Delta}_{Rp}^{\mu} = \left[\left(w_{Mp}^{obs} - w_{Fp}^{obs} \right) - \left(w_{Mp}^{\chi} - w_{Fp}^{\chi} \right) \right]$ is the part of the raw wage gap at percentile p due to gender differences in the returns to education (the "prices" effect); and $\hat{\Delta}_{Rp}^{\mu} = \left[\left(w_{Mp}^{unobs} - w_{Fp}^{unobs} \right) - \left(w_{Mp}^{obs} - w_{Fp}^{obs} \right) \right]$ is the part of the raw wage gap at percentile p due to unobserved characteristics, as well as their returns (the "unobservables" effect). Thus, the innovation of the Juhn-Murphy-Pierce decomposition with respect to the basic Oaxaca-Blinder setting is the ability to measure gender gaps at different positions in the distribution of residuals—or percentiles—and the explicit separation of the effect of unobservable characteristics and their "prices" from the effect of whatever we can observe—in this example, education and its returns.

As described in the next section, ADePT Gender computes the decomposition at the 5th, 10th, 25th, 50th, 75th, 90th, and 95th percentiles.

Ñopo

Another more recent trend in the literature on decompositions uses methodologies from program evaluation to generate the counterfactuals. This approach has generated some controversy among academics who believe the spirit of program evaluation cannot be applied to analyses of gender or race. Some purists argue that the core principle of program evaluation relies on the fact that a program can be delivered to a treatment and a control group. However, when analyzing gender differences, we cannot deliver the program "male" to a woman; in other words, no intervention can convert a woman into a man from a labor market perspective. Thus, differences that cannot be addressed will always remain between the two groups.

In this strand of literature, Ñopo (2008) identified that a potential bias can arise when using the Oaxaca-Blinder decomposition if *no common support* exists in the distribution of the observable individual characteristics— the support of a random variable being the set of values that has a positive probability of being observed. In simpler terms, estimates of differences between the returns to schooling might be biased if there are no examples of men having levels of education as low as women or no women having levels of education as high as men. The reason is that the comparison of the returns to education of men and women will be based on an implicit assumption: the linear estimators of returns to education are also valid for the out-of-support individual characteristics for which they were estimated. The empirical evidence suggests that such an assumption of a common support tends to overestimate the component of the gap attributable to differences in the prices of the skills.

Figure 6.5 illustrates the possible bias arising from the lack of common support in the Oaxaca-Blinder linear decomposition. The light gray points on the x-axis indicate the levels of education observed for women and are used to estimate the returns for women; the dark gray points indicate the levels of education observed for men and are used to estimate men's returns. Because the observed samples do not have women with high levels of education, the predicted return for high levels of education for women is underestimated,

Figure 6.5: Illustration of Bias from a Lack of Common Support

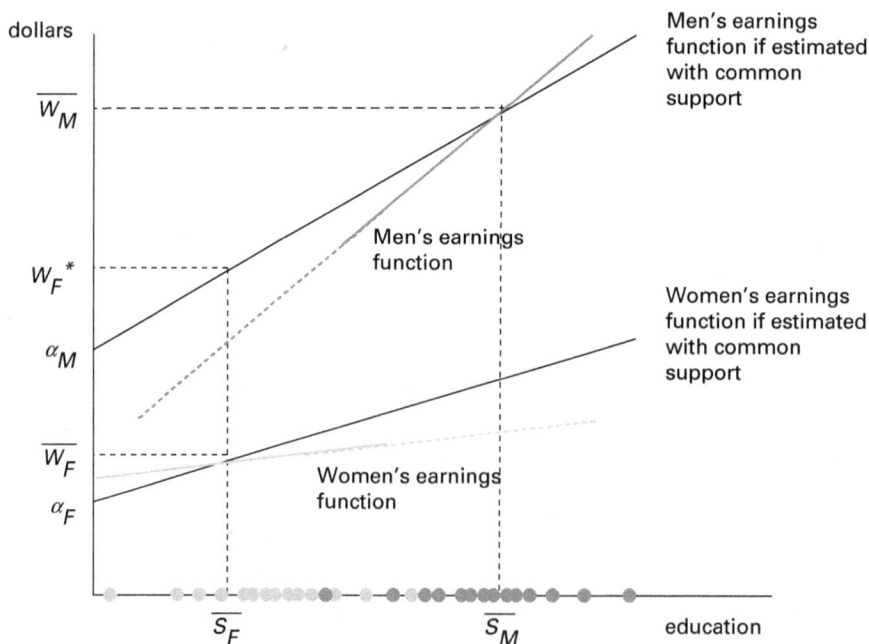

Note: The dashed lines indicate the out-of-support prediction based on a linear regression model. Although in this graph the out-of-support predictions increase the role of returns (that is, out-of-support regression from men is steeper than the support regression and vice versa for women), the results could also go in the opposite direction.

indicated by the dashed light gray line, whereas the opposite is true for men, indicated by the dashed dark gray line.

Ñopo (2008) developed a matching technique from the impact evaluation literature to solve the bias explained above. This technique refines the Oaxaca-Blinder decomposition terms by (a) changing the meaning of the "unexplained" component, which is estimated only using the sample of men and women with characteristics in the common support; and (b) separating the "explained" component into two parts: one due to a different distribution of characteristics *within the common support*, and the other due to the fact that some men have no comparable female counterparts and vice versa, that is, the effect of being *outside the common support*. The methodology does not require one to estimate an earnings equation; hence, there is no need to estimate validity assumptions for the out-of-support levels of skills. The methodology consists of finding an opposite-sex match for each man and woman in the sample. A match is simply a person (or group of persons) with the same observable characteristics. Thus, the sample can be partitioned into four groups: (a) men with a match, (b) women with a match, (c) men without a match, and (d) women without a match. Then, using the wages of each of these groups and using the wages computed for the match, the following decomposition is proposed:

$$\Delta_O = (\Delta_M + \Delta_F + \Delta_X) + \Delta_U, \tag{6.13}$$

where the overall gender wage gap is now decomposed as follows:

- *The difference in wages between men with a match and men without a match*, Δ_M: This component accounts for the part of the gap that would disappear if there were no males with characteristics that remain unmatched by the females in the sample—or if these unmatched males were paid on average the same as the matched ones (basically, characteristics would need to have no effect on wages outside the support).
- *The difference in wages between women with a match and women without a match*, Δ_F: This component is the part of the gap that would disappear if there were no females with characteristics that remain unmatched by the males in the sample, or if unmatched females were paid, on average, the same as matched females.

- *The two components similar to the characteristics, Δ_X, and wage structure effects of the Oaxaca-Blinder decomposition, computed for the men and women in the common support, Δ_U:* The interpretation of these two components is essentially the same as for the Oaxaca-Blinder decomposition, but one needs to keep in mind that they are estimated on a sample that is different from the one Oaxaca-Blinder would use—the sample of men and women that are matched on the basis of observed characteristics. In other words, given that no earnings equation was estimated, the skills and wage structure effects are estimated comparing the counterfactual distributions of each sex over the common support of characteristics.

Δ_M, Δ_F, and Δ_X can all be ascribed to differences in observed characteristics between men and women, so in a sense they all amount to an "explained" component of the wage gap. The term Δ_U is the "unexplained" component, the term attributable to differences in unexplained characteristics of matched individuals, as well as to the existence of discrimination.

Interpreting the Results

Oaxaca-Blinder

Table 6.5 and figure 6.6 show the results of Oaxaca-Blinder decompositions for Nepal using the 2010–11 household survey. These results do not correct for selection. The decomposition figures summarize the main messages of the decomposition results. For example, ADePT figure 13a (figure 6.6) shows that of the 0.47 log point difference between male and female wages, 0.19 log points are explained by observable characteristics using the human capital model (education, age, and residence) and women as the reference group. If men were used as the reference group, the explained component results in 0.13 log points out of the 0.47. The user may find it useful to describe the results in percentages as opposed to log points.

The tables provide a more detailed description of the decomposition results. The first column of ADePT table 13a (table 6.5) shows the estimates of the decomposition for the human capital model using females as the reference group for the counterfactual, and the second column uses men. The first row indicates the raw gender wage gap, that is, the simple difference between the average of the log wage of men and women. The average log

Table 6.5: ADePT Gender Table 13a, Nepal 2010–11

Table 13a: Oaxaca-Blinder Decomposition (Human Capital Model): Wage Earners

	Female	Male	Average
Gap	0.47	0.47	0.47
Explained			
Total	0.19	0.13	0.16
Age	0.07	0.05	0.06
Education	0.15	0.10	0.13
Region and urban residency	−0.03	−0.02	−0.02
Unexplained			
Total	0.28	0.34	0.31
Age	−0.14	−0.12	−0.13
Education	−0.30	−0.25	−0.28
Region and urban residency	−0.14	−0.16	−0.15
Constant	0.86	0.86	0.86
In percentages			
Gap	100.00	100.00	100.00
Explained			
Total	39.71	27.91	33.81
Age	14.46	9.82	12.14
Education	32.31	21.67	26.99
Region and urban residency	−7.06	−3.58	−5.32
Unexplained			
Total	60.29	72.09	66.19
Age	−29.80	−25.15	−27.48
Education	−64.22	−53.58	−58.90
Region and urban residency	−29.76	−33.25	−31.51
Constant	184.08	184.08	184.08

Source: ADePT Gender using Nepal 2012.

earnings of men are higher than those of women by 0.47 log points. The explained component or composition effect is 0.13 log points and the unexplained component or wage structure effect is 0.34 log points, using men as the reference. Each of the components is further decomposed according to the detailed version of the decomposition by highlighting the contribution of each variable or group of variables to explain the gender gap in pay. The explained component of the decomposition is interpreted as the additional amount of money women would earn—on average (and in log points)—if they were to have, as a group, the same average characteristics that prevail among men. This reason is mostly due to education, implying that if women were as educated as men, the gender gap in pay would reduce in 0.1 log points—or by 20 percent (the bottom panel of the table presents the numbers in percentages).

Figure 6.6: Oaxaca-Blinder Decomposition, ADePT Figure 13a, Nepal 2010–11

Figure 13a: Oaxaca-Blinder Decomposition (Human Capital Model): Wage Earners

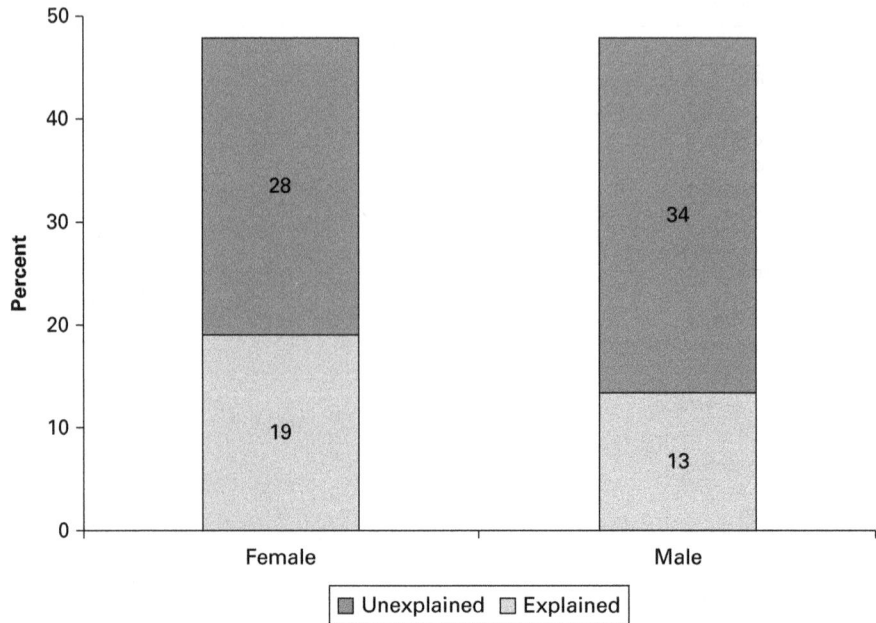

Source: ADePT Gender using Nepal 2012.

Turning to the unexplained component, the difference between men's and women's average log wages is positive and large. That factor indicates that both discrimination and unobservables may play a very important role in the gender gap in pay. Women's estimated returns to experience (proxied by age), education, and place of residence are higher than those of men, but the effect of the constant (which captures the effect of "group membership" and can be seen in this context as a catchall term for unobservables) offsets that effect. The constant captures the pay gap for the base category, which in this case corresponds to the youngest, without any education, and living in rural areas.

Moreover, part of the wage structure or discrimination component can reveal differences in unobserved skills. Men and women have very different employment histories. It should be noted that the magnitude of the unexplained component could also reflect the fact that the parsimonious human capital model may not do a good job of explaining more of the gender gap in pay; important unobserved productivity characteristics could play a relevant role.

Table 6.6: ADePT Gender Table 13b, Nepal 2010–12

Table 13b: Oaxaca-Blinder Decomposition (Human Capital Model with Selection Correction): Wage Earners

	Female	Male	Average
Gap	−0.23	−0.23	−0.23
Explained			
Total	0.11	0.11	0.11
Age	0.06	0.07	0.06
Education	0.10	0.06	0.08
Region and urban residency	−0.04	−0.02	−0.03
Unexplained			
Total	−0.34	−0.34	−0.34
Age	0.13	0.12	0.13
Education	−0.06	−0.02	−0.04
Region and urban residency	−0.21	−0.23	−0.22
Constant	−0.21	−0.21	−0.21
In percentages			
Gap	100.00	100.00	100.00
Explained			
Total	−49.44	−49.06	−49.25
Age	−25.54	−29.54	−27.54
Education	−41.49	−26.88	−34.19
Region and urban residency	17.60	7.35	12.48
Unexplained			
Total	149.44	149.06	149.25
Age	−57.62	−53.63	−55.62
Education	24.99	10.38	17.68
Region and urban residency	89.53	99.77	94.65
Constant	92.54	92.54	92.54

Source: ADePT Gender using Nepal 2012.
Note: Unweighted results. Weights not supported for the two-step model.

ADePT Gender also produces richer versions of this model. ADePT Gender table 13c includes a richer specification that includes occupation and industry controls (full model), and ADePT tables 13b and 13d correct for nonrandom selection of women in the labor market. For the full model, the results are interpreted in the same way as for the simple Oaxaca-Blinder decomposition. The occupation and industry variables capture not only the differences in the payoffs of the different jobs (due to supply and demand equilibrium effects) but also the fact that women self-select–by choice or given constraints—into different jobs. For the selection-corrected decomposition, the effect of the additional variable—the Mills ratio—can combine in different ways into a pure selection effect, or in the wage structure. The user with large and significant selection effects interested in further exploring this aspect of the results can consult Neuman and Oaxaca (2004).

Juhn-Murphy-Pierce

ADePT table 16a (table 6.7) and ADePT figure 16a (figure 6.7) report results from the Juhn-Murphy-Pierce decomposition performed on 2008 data from Panama. The first column reports the difference between the *pth* percentiles of the male and female wage distribution, as it arises in the sample (the observed wages). The first column shows the raw gender wage gap at each percentile—that is, the simple differences in the average log wage between men and women. As expected, the raw gap evaluated at the median is close to that of the mean calculated for the Oaxaca-Blinder decomposition (0.42 versus 0.47 log points, respectively). The gap at the median tends to be lower than the gap at the mean, as some outlier value always raises the mean average. The gap is larger at the bottom of the wage distribution curve, which suggests the existence of "sticky floor" effects—it then narrows at higher percentiles. The term *sticky floor* refers to a situation when women cannot start climbing the job ladder: they are stuck in low-remunerated jobs compared with similar men. In the case of Panama, no "glass ceiling" effect is observed. The term *glass ceiling* refers to the situation when women have the same high skills as men but cannot achieve high-level positions, such as top executives or government officials. The next columns of table 6.7 allow the user to pin down which factors are more relevant for determining these trends.

As with the Oaxaca-Blinder presentation of the results, ADePT figure 16a allows the user to quickly visualize the major patterns by looking at how the different components change along the wage distribution, whereas the table

Table 6.7: ADePT Gender Table 16a, Panama 2008

		Female			Male		
	Gap	Endowments	Price	Unobservables	Endowments	Price	Unobservables
Percentile							
p5	0.319	−0.105	0.345	0.078	−0.100	0.338	0.081
p10	0.277	−0.107	0.323	0.061	−0.094	0.317	0.055
p25	0.105	−0.238	0.336	0.007	−0.189	0.298	−0.004
p50	0.048	−0.230	0.297	−0.020	−0.197	0.251	−0.006
p75	−0.106	−0.325	0.262	−0.043	−0.289	0.204	−0.021
p90	−0.034	−0.214	0.223	−0.043	−0.191	0.186	−0.029
p95	0.078	−0.113	0.201	−0.010	−0.103	0.175	0.006

Source: ADePT Gender using Panama 2008.
Note: p = percentile.

presents the exact magnitude of each component and how the results vary if the group of reference is changed (men versus women). First, the "endowments" component shows the difference between the quintiles of the male distribution of wages and the counterfactual distribution, the one that would arise if characteristics were distributed as in the female group (see appendix D for mathematical derivation). It can be seen that the differences are consistently positive—women's observable characteristics are such that if returns to them and the distribution of unobservables were identical to those prevailing among men, the gender gap would be smaller. The size of this effect varies along the wage distribution, with very large effects at the very bottom (0.281 log points at the 5th percentile). The second column shows the part of the gap that is explained by differences in the returns to labor market skills—the result of women being paid less than men for their observable characteristics. This component of the gap that is attributable to different labor market prices of observable characteristics is sizable and positive across quintiles. The fact that the

Figure 6.7: ADePT Gender Figure 16a, Nepal 2010–11

Figure 16a: Decomposition of Earnings by Percentile (Human Capital Model): Wage Earners

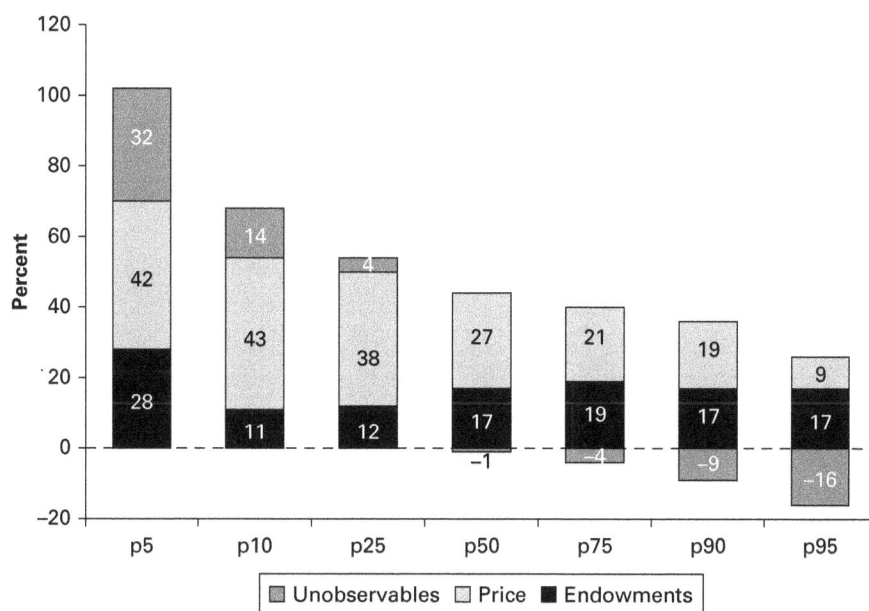

Source: ADePT Gender using Nepal 2012.
Note: p = percentile.

price effect is smaller at higher quintiles indicates that women are more likely to be remunerated for their observable characteristics than men are.

The third column displays what changes when we finally compare the male earnings distribution to the female earnings distribution—a change that is attributable to unobserved characteristics and their prices. This component also decreases from the bottom to the top of the wage distribution, and it even becomes negative for the top half of the distribution. A negative coefficient means that the gender gap in pay would be even larger if women were paid the same as men. This result might seem odd at first, but it can be explained by a nonrandom selection effect. The problem of selection of women does not apply only to participation in the labor market; it can also apply to the occupation or sector in which they work, or how likely they are to reach top positions compared with men. Thus, one possible explanation for this result is that high-skilled women that work are very likely to reach top positions, whereas top positions for men are occupied by high-skilled and low-skilled men. Thus, on average, women at the top would have better unobservable characteristics than men at the top, and that is why they are paid relatively better than men. A story like this would undoubtedly require additional research. The analyst who encounters this type of result should look further into who these women are, how large the group is, and what types of jobs they do.

Ñopo

Finally, this section switches to the most recently developed methodology that ADePT Gender uses. As stated above, this is a nonparametric method that builds on the program evaluation literature. Its main contribution is that it takes into account the fact that not all working women have the same characteristics as working men, and it measures how much of the gap can be attributed to that fact (called the lack of common support).

Table 6.8 corresponds to ADePT table 15a and shows the output of the Ñopo decomposition for Nepal in 2010–11. Each row shows the control that was added in the regression. In each successive row, a variable (or set of variables) is added. This stepwise practice responds to the fact that the methodology is path dependent, as it works with marginal distributions. Thus, by comparing rows, it can be observed how much more is explained by the additional variable (or set of variables). The contribution of each additional variable to explain the gap depends on what was explained before its addition and the correlation between the variables in each consecutive step.

Table 6.8: ADePT Gender Table 15a, Nepal 2010–11

	Male							Female						
	D	DO	DM	DF	DX	% male	% female	D	DO	DM	DF	DX	% male	% female
Age	0.473	0.432			0.041	1.000	1.000	−0.473	−0.462			−0.011	1.000	1.000
Age, urban	0.473	0.456			0.017	1.000	1.000	−0.473	−0.519			0.046	1.000	1.000
Age, urban, region	0.473	0.472	0.001		0.000	0.997	1.000	−0.473	−0.506		−0.001	0.034	1.000	0.997
Age, urban, region, education	0.473	0.344	0.080	0.005	0.044	0.820	0.974	−0.473	−0.285	−0.005	−0.080	−0.103	0.974	0.820
Age, urban, region, education, sector	0.473	0.321	0.027	0.047	0.078	0.488	0.802	−0.473	−0.168	−0.047	−0.027	−0.231	0.802	0.488

Source: ADePT Gender using Nepal 2012.

Note: D = overall or raw gender wage gap; DF = difference in wages between women with a match and women without a match; that is, difference from being out of support from women; DM = difference from being out of support for men; DO = unexplained component; DX = explained component.

199

The change in the coefficient previously included when more variables are added responds to the correlation among the previously and newly included variables.

The first column of data shows the raw gender gap in pay, which should be the same value presented in the first row of the Oaxaca-Blinder table. The second column shows the part that is unexplained (D0) and the fifth column the part that is explained by differences in characteristics (DX). The two columns in the middle indicate the part of the gap that is explained by lack of common support: by having men who do not have women's characteristics (DM) or women who do not have men's characteristics (DF). For example, when looking at the fourth row ("Age, urban, region, education"), it can be seen that 17 percent of the gender wage gap (the result of dividing 0.08 by 0.473) is due to men's average educational attainment that is higher than women's. Only an additional 10 percent (the result of dividing 0.05 by 0.473) comes from having women with levels of education for which there are no comparable men. Overall, then, the part of the raw gender gap that is explained by lack of common support (0.080 + 0.005 = 0.085 log points) is very small. If these effects are large in magnitude, the user should examine them further by identifying those persons and characteristics that are present in only one group of men (or women).

A natural next step, not reported in this version of ADePT Gender but that is straightforward to compute, is to further decompose the common support using Oaxaca-Blinder. The user can do this by recalculating the Oaxaca-Blinder tables combined with an if-condition that excludes those observations for which there are men but no similar women, and vice versa.[14]

Notes

1. Chapter 3 of this book includes the definition of *earnings* and their relationships to such associated concepts as wages and income.
2. The term *wage structure* refers to the relationship of wages and different jobs, either within a firm or more generally in the labor market.
3. Although earnings are computed using wages, and hours of work are usually collected as part of the labor module of a labor force survey for wage workers, earnings for the self-employed are computed using variables on revenues and costs (in some cases, benefits) from household enterprise modules in multitopic surveys.

4. Notice that in the substitutions below, area A equals 1/2.
5. Another advantage of this family of indicators is that it is possible to decompose the measure of inequality into two components: inequality *within* groups and inequality *between* groups.
6. In this case, given that the log function is a monotonic function, the percentiles can be calculated over the distribution of wages or over the distribution of log wages.
7. The only exception is the entropy measure for $c = 2$.
8. Density distribution functions of the log of a variable have the property of being approximate to normal.
9. See figure 10.6 in chapter 10.
10. Biases could be even more complicated. Assume, for example, that the returns to education for men and women are the same, but the returns to education also increase with the number of years of experience. If men have more experience than women, and experience is not included in the wage equation, the estimated education coefficient will pick up the returns to education and part of the experience return. The unaware analyst may misinterpret the results and conclude that a gender gap exists in the returns to education.
11. For more details, consult Jann (2003).
12. The term *Heckit* is the informal way of referring to the Heckman two-step selection model, as the term is the combination of Heckman and probit (which is the model used in the first step of the two-step estimation procedure).
13. The term *Mills ratio* is the coefficient γ that enters in the equation to describe the correction for nonrandom selection. Chapter 7 succinctly shows the derivation of the coefficient.
14. The output of the Ñopo decomposition provided in the econometric software Stata provides this level of detail.

References

Atkinson, Anthony B. 1970. "On the Measurement of Inequality." *Journal of Economic Theory* 2 (3): 244–63.

Autor, David H., Laurence F. Katz, and Melissa S. Kearny. 2008. "Trends in U.S. Wage Inequality: Revising the Revisionists." *Review of Economics and Statistics* 90 (2): 300–323.

Bedard, Kelly. 2001. "Human Capital versus Signaling Models: University Access and High School Dropouts." *Journal of Political Economy* 109 (4): 749–75.

Blau, Francine D., and Lawrence M. Kahn. 1997. "Swimming Upstream: Trends in the Gender Wage Differential in the 1980s." *Journal of Labor Economics* 15 (1): 1–42.

Blinder, Alan S. 1973. "Wage Discrimination: Reduced Form and Structural Estimates. *Journal of Human Resources* 8 (4): 436–55.

Borjas, George. 2005. *Labor Economics*. 3rd ed. New York: McGraw-Hill.

Cowell, Frank A. 2000. "Measurement of Inequality." In *Handbook of Income Distribution*, vol. 1, edited by Anthony B. Atkinson and François Bourguignon, 87–166. Amsterdam and New York: Elsevier.

DiNardo, John, Nicole M. Fortin, and Thomas Lemieux. 1996. "Labor Market Institutions and the Distribution of Wages, 1973–1992: A Semiparametric Approach." *Econometrica* 64 (5): 1001–44.

Fortin, Nicole, Thomas Lemieux, and Sergio Firpo. 2011. "Decomposition Methods in Economics." *Handbook of Labor Economics*, vol. 4, edited by Orley Ashenfelter and David Card, 1–102. Amsterdam: Elsevier.

Foster, James, Suman Seth, Michael Lokshin, and Zurab Sajaia. 2013. *A Unified Approach to Measuring Poverty and Inequality: Theory and Practice.* Washington, DC: World Bank.

Gardeazabal, Javier, and Arantza Ugidos. 2004. "More on Identification in Detailed Wage Decompositions." *Review of Economics and Statistics* 86 (4): 1034–36.

Heckman, James. 1974. "Shadow Prices, Market Wages, and Labor Supply." *Econometrica* 42 (4), 679–94.

Jann, Ben. 2003. "The Blinder-Oaxaca Decomposition for Linear Regression Models." *Stata Journal* 8 (4): 453–79.

Juhn, Chinhui, Kevin M. Murphy, and Brooks Pierce. 1991. "Accounting for the Slowdown in Black–White Wage Convergence." In *Workers and Their Wages: Changing Patterns in the United States*, edited by Marvin H. Kosters, 107–43. Washington, DC: AEI Press.

———. 1993. "Wage Inequality and the Rise in Returns to Skill." *Journal of Political Economy* 101 (3): 410–42.

Katz, Lawrence F., and David H. Autor. 1999. "Changes in the Wage Structure and Earnings Inequality." In *Handbook of Labor Economics*, vol. 3, edited by Orley Ashenfelter and David Card, 1463–555. Amsterdam: Elsevier.

Katz, Lawrence F., and Kevin M. Murphy. 1992. "Changes in Relative Wages, 1962–1987: Supply and Demand Factors." *Quarterly Journal of Economics* 107 (1): 35–78.

Mulligan, Casey B., and Yona Rubinstein. 2008. "Selection, Investment, and Women's Relative Wages over Time." *Quarterly Journal of Economics* 123 (3): 1061–110.

Nepal, Government of. 2012. "Nepal: Living Standards Survey 2010–2011, Third Round." Central Bureau of Statistics, National Planning Commission Secretariat, Kathmandu. http://microdata.worldbank.org/index.php/catalog/1000.

Neuman, Shoshana, and Ronald L. Oaxaca. 2004. "Wage Differentials in the 1990s in Israel: Endowments, Discrimination and Selectivity." CEPR Discussion Paper 4709, Centre for Economic Policy Research, London.

Ñopo, Hugo R. 2008. "An Extension of the Blinder-Oaxaca Decomposition to a Continuum of Comparison Groups." *Economics Letters* 100 (2): 292–96.

Oaxaca, Ronald L. 1973. "Male-Female Wage Differentials in Urban Labor Markets." *International Economic Review* 14 (3): 693–709.

Oaxaca, Ronald L., and Michael R. Ransom. 1994. "On Discrimination and the Decomposition of Wage Differentials." *Journal of Econometrics* 61 (1): 5–21.

Panama, Government of. 2008. "Encuesta de Niveles de Vida 2008" ("Living Standards Survey 2008"). Ministerio de Economia y Finanzas, Panama City. http://microdata.worldbank.org/index.php/catalog/70.

World Bank. 2012. *World Development Report 2012: Gender Equality and Development.* Washington, DC: World Bank. https://openknowledge.worldbank.org/handle/10986/4391.

Yun, Myeong-Su. 2005. "A Simple Solution to the Identification Problem in Detailed Wage Decompositions." *Economic Inquiry* 43 (4): 766–72.

Chapter 7

Technical Notes on Labor Market Analysis

This chapter introduces technical and complementary discussions on topics that contribute to the understanding of the tables and graphs covered in chapter 6. The first part discusses the main theories of discrimination that inspired the use of decomposition methods to measure it.

Discrimination Theories

The bulk of the literature on gender inequality focuses on defining and measuring discrimination. Most of chapter 6 focuses on decomposition methods that were originally developed to measure discrimination. Even if nowadays there is a better sense of what the unexplained component in the decomposition analysis captures—and of what it measures beyond discrimination[1]—it is worthwhile spending some time reviewing the theoretical models that motivated this strand of the literature. Thus, this section provides an overview of the concepts and models on discrimination. The review is not intended to be comprehensive but instead aims to provide a minimum theoretical framework for interpreting the results produced by ADePT Gender. Examples of more comprehensive reviews made by economists are Altonji and Blank (1999); Bertrand (2011); and Blau, Ferber, and Winkler (2006). This section also briefly discusses how these formative theories for economists can be bridges to the theories developed by other social sciences that also focus on women's issues.

Labor market discrimination exists when two equally qualified workers are treated differently solely on the basis of their gender (or any another characteristic that does not affect their productivity). Under this definition, discrimination will result in lower wages for women than for men who are equally productive. However, discrimination can take other forms that result in differences in productivity between men and women. For example, women may end up being less productive if they are discriminated against by receiving inferior on-the-job training. Moreover, discrimination may discourage women from investing in human capital and thus can result in lower productivity. Some authors refer to these effects as indirect or feedback effects.

ADePT Gender produces several decomposition methodologies that should be used with caution. Decomposition methodologies are measurement tools and do not allow the user to identify any of the mechanisms that result in the different forms of discrimination. Next, this section describes the most prominent models used to formalize some of these mechanisms that were developed by economists a few decades ago, when they started measuring the gender wage gap and its sources. Three main theories in labor economics frame gender discrimination in employment and wages. The first is the theory of taste discrimination developed by Gary Becker (1957), with three types of economic agents exerting discrimination: employers, employees, and consumers. Each of these versions results in different labor market equilibrium outcomes. The second theory is based on statistical differences in men's and women's characteristics. The last model—overcrowding—examines the case where too many women chose one specific occupation.

Taste Discrimination Theory

Becker's theory of discrimination is grounded in prejudice and translates this concept to basic labor economics models. Discrimination is introduced into the models by monetizing the cost or disutility of an economic agent who is prejudiced against a certain group. The monetary cost or disutility is usually denominated discrimination effect d, which is introduced in the models as a positive number (Borjas 2005).[2] Taste discrimination models have thus far three different versions, depending on the identity of the agent who holds the prejudice: the employer, the employee, or the customer. Each of the versions of the theory is based on a small number of assumptions, but with powerful results that lead to very different outcomes that explain the observed facts, as described next.

Employer Discrimination

Assume that there are two types of workers: men and women. Employers must decide how many of each type to hire: E_m and E_f. Both types are equally productive and can be perceived as perfect substitutes for the firm. Thus, the firm output will depend on the total number of workers, regardless of the workers' sex. For the firm, hiring an additional worker increases the product in MP_E (that is, the marginal product of labor for the firm). Without discrimination, wages for members of each group should be equal, as they are equally productive. The firm hires workers until the point at which the additional cost of a worker is higher than the additional revenue, usually called the value of the marginal product of labor, VMP_E. The employer's decision rule regarding hiring becomes

- If $w_M < w_F$, then hire only men;
- If $w_M > w_F$, then hire only women; and
- If $w_M = w_F$, then hire either men or women.

In equilibrium and without discrimination, all men and women offering labor should be hired, and all would receive the same wage because it is assumed that they are equally productive.

Assume now that all employers are prejudiced against women. That prejudice is modeled by increasing the cost the employers face when hiring women to $w_F(1 + d)$. As explained above, d is the monetization of the cost or disutility that generates to the employer for hiring female workers. The employer's decision rule now becomes

- If $w_M < w_F(1+d)$, then hire only men;
- If $w_M > w_F(1+d)$, then hire only women; and
- If $w_M = w_F(1+d)$, then hire either men or women.

Then, women will earn less than men (in an amount equal to d), employers have lower profits (they are reduced from an amount represented by the triangle ACw_{M1} to an amount represented by the triangle ABw_{M0}), and overall employment is lower from E_1 to E_0, as shown in figure 7.1, panel a.

If some employers discriminate (for example, male managers) but others do not (for example, female managers), then the result is a fully segregated workforce. Male owners will hire only men, and female owners will hire only women. But female firms will have higher profits (as explained above); thus, we may think they would kick some male employers out of the market. If very few women are business owners because of any other constraints, the result will be more male employers, and some women will need to work for them. In this latter case, the average raw gap in pay will depend on how many women work for male employers. This situation can be visualized in a graph that shows the relative wage of men and women and the labor supply of women. Figure 7.1, panel b, shows two cases: (a) one in which all women are employed in female-managed firms represented by the supply S_{F0} and (b) one in which some female workers need to work for male managers; thus, a positive gender gap in pay occurs. These two cases can also be represented by looking at the firms. In the former case, male-managed firms will hire E_{M0} and pay wages w_{M0} and female-managed firms will hire E_{F0} and pay the same wages (see figure 7.1, panels c and d). However, if some women need to work in male firms, wages will go up for men to $w_{M1} = w_{M0} + d$ (see figure 7.1, panel c).

In sum, as long as prejudice exists among employers—and thus segregated employment—firms will have different profits. Firms that are prejudiced have lower profits, as they have higher costs since they hire the relatively more expensive type of labor. The relationship between profits and the coefficient of discrimination is decreasing: the greater the discrimination, the smaller the profits. This behavior, together with the minority group's labor supply, determines the equilibrium wages in the labor market. If women's wages are too high relative to men's wages, no firm will hire them. If women's wages are too low relative to men's wages, then all firms—even those with high discrimination effects—will hire them. Thus, women's wages must be low enough to induce some firms—those with the lower discrimination effect—to hire women but high enough to still have some firms—those with the higher discrimination effect—hire men. In equilibrium, the female-to-male wage ratio will be less than 1.

This model generates two results that can be contrasted with real data: (a) women are paid less than men, and (b) firms have segregated workforces—that is, they hire only men or only women. This fact is consistent with occupational segregation. Most important, this theory implies that discrimination should not persist over time, since competition will push discriminatory firms out of the market.

Figure 7.1: Graphic Representation of Employer Discrimination

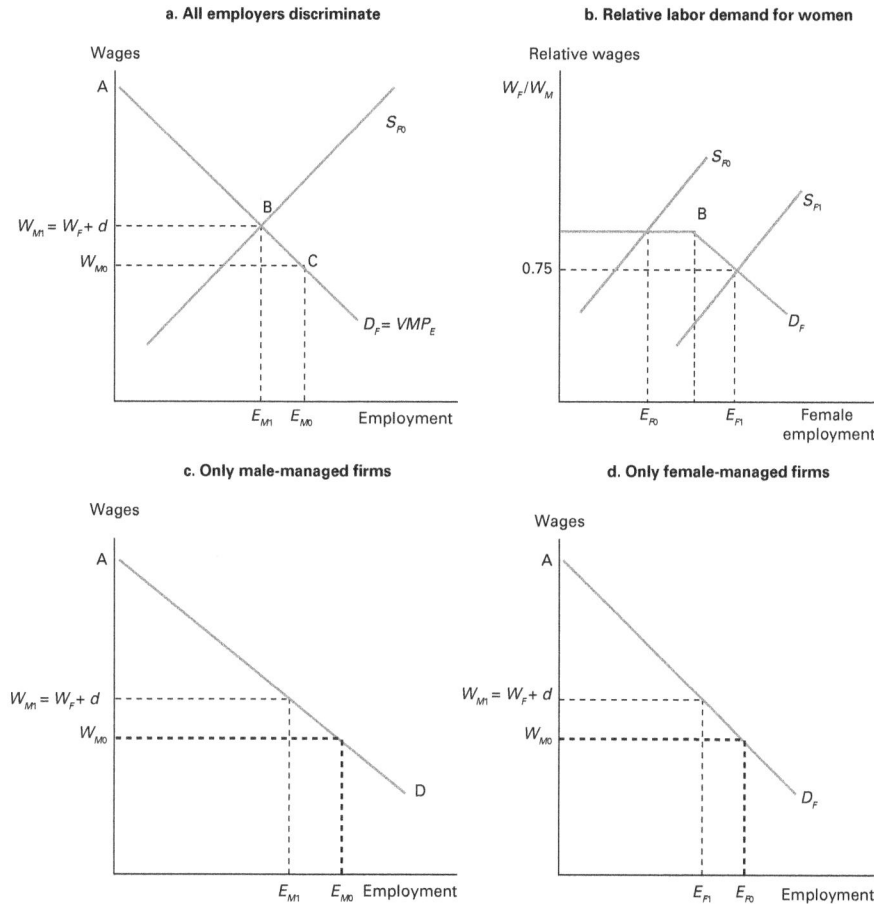

a. All employers discriminate

b. Relative labor demand for women

c. Only male-managed firms

d. Only female-managed firms

Employee Discrimination

Different equilibrium outcomes arise if employees are prejudiced against women, even if the employers are gender neutral. In other words, it can be assumed that male workers have a disutility from working with female workers. As before, this cost or disutility can be monetized by introducing a loss to their wages that becomes $w_M(1-d)$. For simplicity, assume that women do not care about the gender of their coworkers, so the value of their wage remains w_F. Men and women are equally productive and thus perfect substitutes in the production function of the employer. Because workers with prejudice will not be willing to work in firms that hire men and women, the best strategy for employers is to hire only men or only women. If the firm would instead choose to have both genders in its workforce, it will have to pay more to men (who are prejudiced against women) to induce them to work, which will incur higher costs. In equilibrium, and because of the perfect segregation of men and women, all firms have the same profits.

As in the previous model, here firms have segregated workforces, but there is no gap in wages. Thus, with equally productive men and women, employee discrimination is not enough to explain the observed gender wage gap.

Customer Discrimination

Another source of discrimination might be customers, who make purchasing decisions on the basis of a seller's gender and not solely on the product's price. Assume now that all products are homogeneous and produced in a competitive market at cost (equal to its price) p. Male customers prefer to buy from male sellers as opposed to female sellers. When male customers buy from female sellers, they experience a disutility that can be monetized via the price, increasing it to $p(1+d)$ if a male customer buys from a female seller.[3]

Under this scenario, the best strategy for profit-maximizing employers is to hire both men and women and to place men in those occupations or positions that require interaction with customers who discriminate against women. This strategy does not result in any profit loss or workforce segregation, as long as firms manage to sort workers into occupations according to whether they face discrimination. If this is the case, women's wages won't be affected. However, if employers are unable to place women in those occupations where they do not need to interact with discriminatory clients, their wages can be reduced to compensate for the revenue loss.

This model predicts that women are segregated into occupations that do not require client contact, and that firms that have more client interaction would hire fewer women than those that do not.

Other Forms of Discrimination

It is important to note that other forms of interaction occur where women may be subject to discrimination. For example, it is common for men to benefit more than women from mentor–protégé relationships. Women are often excluded from this form of career development, both when the mentor is a man and when the mentor is a woman. Despite the qualitative evidence in this area, there are still very few quantitative studies that could measure these effects. Rothstein (2000) has measured the consequences of having male bosses for male and female employees. Cardoso and Winter-Ebmer (2010) find that women benefit more from higher wages in female-led firms than in male-led firms. More recently, Flabbi and others (2014) and Gagliarducci and Paserman (2014) discuss the effects of managers' gender on gender gaps in pay and other labor market outcomes.

Women are often excluded from informal networks that tend to arise at the workplace, both those that involve supervisors and those that involve peers. Job-related meetings were or are held at men's clubs or in sports bars that males know their female peers are likely to avoid. The lack of inclusion in informal networks may result in differences in productivity as well as differences in career and promotion opportunities. Some of these examples are also discussed by Babcock and Laschever (2003) when presenting evidence of why women do not negotiate salaries and promotions the same way men do.

Statistical Discrimination Model

The models described above show how prejudice can give rise to gender wage gaps and employment segregation—either by occupation or by firm. However, similar results can arise even in the absence of prejudice, when belonging to a particular group suggests information about a worker's productivity.

Statistical discrimination arises when an employer cannot observe all the characteristics of the work in an individual but gathers information about them using statistics from the group to which the individual belongs. Suppose an employer needs to decide whether to hire a man or a woman. Each of the candidates has shown the same observable characteristics: they have the same qualifications, they performed identically in the interview, and they express the same interest and attitude toward the job. For the employer, it is important to hire someone who is reliable and who will be available to work longer hours or on weekends, if needed. During the interview, both candidates state they are able and willing to work extra hours if needed. Thus, on paper and with all the observable individual information, the man and the woman appear equal.

However, the employer knows that women, on average, tend to work fewer hours than men, because they are more prone to having family responsibilities. Therefore, the employer infers that the woman has a higher probability of being unable to work longer hours. As a result, the employer uses information derived from the group and hires the man. Although the employer does not hold any prejudice against women in general, and both candidates might be equally productive and will exert the same effort on the job, the woman ends up being discriminated against because of a characteristic of the group to which she belongs.

Finally, notice that the models of statistical discrimination, as well as the models of taste for discrimination, may have indirect or feedback effects, as they might influence women's behavior toward productive investments.

Other Theories of Discrimination

Bergmann (1971) developed another interesting model that results in discrimination.[4] Her overcrowding model describes the consequences of discrimination in a partial equilibrium approach. If for whatever form of discrimination, women are circumscribed to female occupations for which there is less demand or more supply than in male occupations, women will end up with lower wages, regardless of their productivity and their sector of employment. This results from the fact that no movement of labor occurs between male and female sectors. Figure 7.2 shows the theory in a simple supply-and-demand graph.

Figure 7.2: Overcrowding Model Resulting in Discrimination

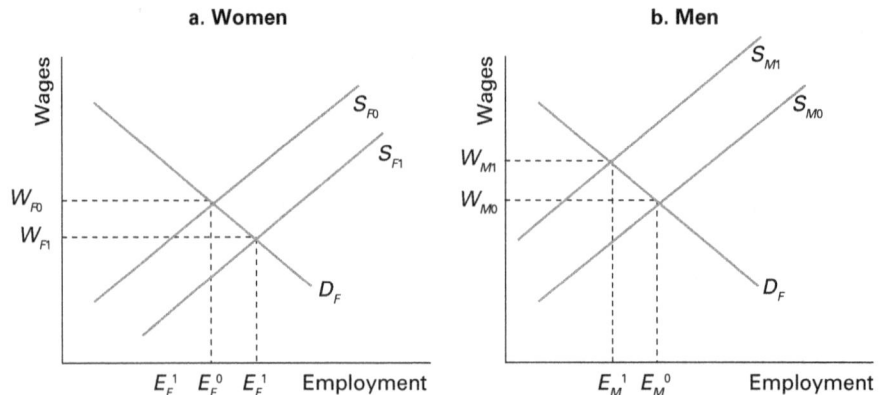

a. Women

b. Men

Models of glass ceilings—and before that, of internal labor markets—are also used to explain women's lower wages. In these models, women are not promoted in the same way as men or are placed into units that do not benefit from career development. One example is the model developed by Doeringer and Piore (1985) that divides jobs into primary and secondary types, and where employers generate separate labor markets within the firm. Each of the units or type of job benefits from different career perspectives within the firm, regardless of the skills needed or the productivity of the tasks. The models described above for taste discrimination or statistical discrimination are also consistent with these models coming from the personnel economics strand of literature. For more details, see Bertrand (2011) or Blau, Ferber, and Winkler (2006).

Earnings Equations

The earnings equation is the workhorse of modern labor economics. Despite being developed more than 50 years ago, it is still a relevant instrument for research and policy making. The main reason is that because of its parsimonious specification, it fits several data sources and country contexts extremely well, and it allows measuring productivity for different groups of workers. It has been widely used mainly to understand returns to education but also to investigate other problems, such as gaps in pay by gender, ethnicity, language, labor turnover, and occupational choice, to name a few. It has been applied to both developed and developing countries, from wage earners to farmworkers. For example, Psacharopoulos compiles and updates Mincerian returns to education with an emphasis on developing countries in a series of papers (1972, 1973, 1985, 1989, 1994; and Patrinos and Psacharopoulos 2011). and 2011 with Patrinos). Banerjee and Duflo (2005) and Montenegro and Patrinos (2014) follow up using the same standard Mincer specification to ensure comparability. The Mincer earnings equation is also used extensively by cross-country studies analyzing the relationship between human capital and education and economic growth, which include developing countries in their samples (for example, Hanushek and Kimko 2000; Krueger and Lindahl 2001).

The earnings equation is mostly attributed to Jacob Mincer (Mincer 1958; Mincer and Polachek 1974), but it is also considered part of the *human capital theory* developed by Gary Becker (1964).[5] The earnings equation is tremendously suitable for studying the gender gap in pay, as it serves to measure differences in wages that could be attributed to education, experience, and more. It has become the cornerstone of measuring gender gaps in pay, and it opens the way to several decomposition techniques described in chapter 6, and that is why it is important to understand them.

The human capital theory is built on a simple model that explains labor productivity. It was initially based on a few key assumptions that led to straightforward testing and interpretation. In a nutshell, the idea is that productivity differences can be influenced (only) by differences in individual productivity, which in turn are determined by investments in education or training by individuals throughout their lives. This idea was supported by a theoretic model of investment in human capital (Becker 1964; Ben-Porath 1967; Mincer 1958; Mincer and Polachek 1974) and by an econometric model based on a log-linear function of wages on education and experience—the *Mincer earnings equation*. Although superseded in some aspects by modern approaches that address causality and heterogeneity concerns, the earnings equation is still the cornerstone of the analysis of many labor issues, including gender gaps in pay (Lemieux 2006).

Initially, the earnings equation was associated with a model for compensating wage differentials (Mincer 1958). To induce workers to undertake the additional schooling necessary for certain occupations, they must be compensated by sufficiently large earnings over the course of their working lives. Two conditions must be satisfied in equilibrium: (a) the present value of future earnings in occupations that require education minus the cost of education should be equal to the present value of future earnings of occupations that do not require occupation, and (b) labor markets are in equilibrium. Thus, the equilibrium determines the rate of return on education investments. Later, Becker (1964) formulated this model by differentiating between general human capital that can be applied to any job and specific human capital that enhances the productivity of only one particular job. Then, Ben-Porath (1967) introduced the dynamic human capital model that incorporates the possibility of continuing training throughout the working life.

Next, the earnings equation began to be interpreted as a hedonic price function that reflects the equilibrium of supply and demand for workers at each level of schooling and experience, or what Heckman, Lochner, and Todd (2006) call *the accounting-identity model* based on Mincer (1962) and the dynamic human capital theory of Ben-Porath (1967).

Both formal schooling (general human capital) and on-the-job training (specific human capital) assumed to be valuable only to a particular firm determine the dynamics of life-cycle earnings.

These models are usually used to explain gender gaps in education and in earnings. Because women (or their parents) anticipate labor force interruptions over the working life because of childbearing, or simply because a society's values may dictate that women should work at home, gaps in education disfavoring women appear. However, gender differences in pay can also result from investing in skills that are associated with low-paid occupations. Figure 7.3 plots different patterns of earnings associated with the working life (that is, evolution of earnings with time or age) and how earnings equations can explain gender gaps in pay. The line marked by the segment o'J in figure 7.3 reflects the maximum earnings capacity associated with the maximum level of education. As expected, earnings rise continuously with each level of (potential) experience. Workers with lower

Figure 7.3: Graphic Visualization of Mincer Equation

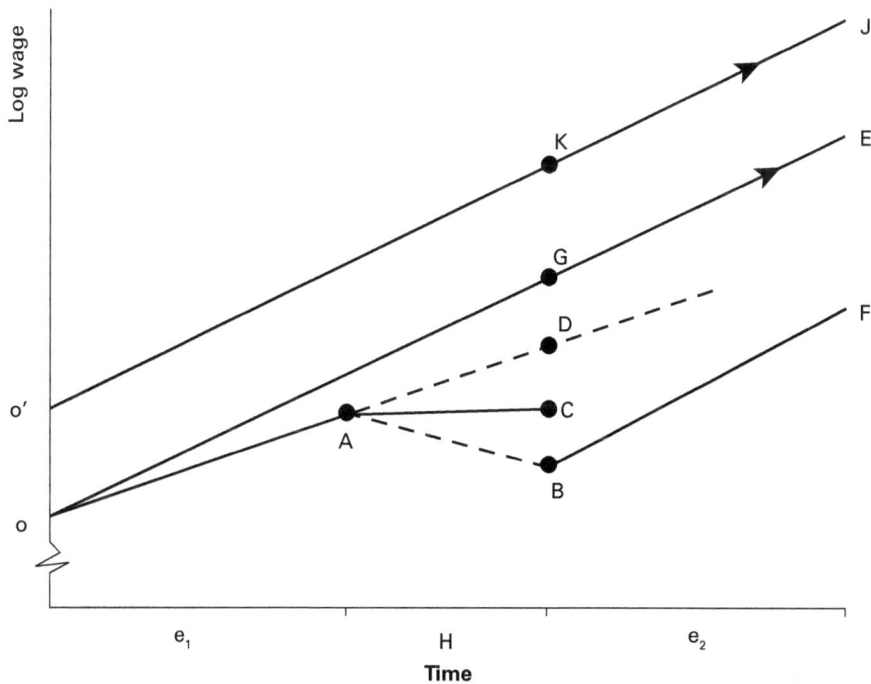

Source: Goldin and Polachek 1987.

levels of education (as is the case of women in many countries) have lower levels of earnings, indicated by the line oE. Moreover, women tend to be intermittent workers, as they usually leave the labor force during the years they rear their children. Intermittent workers usually have a different age-earnings profile. The slope (that is, returns to experience) is smaller, indicated by the segment oA on the line oF. When interrupted, earnings do not increase, as workers do not accumulate experience or continue to invest in skills to avoid depreciation. This outcome is indicated with the flat segment AC. Finally, most intermittent workers take a wage cut in real terms when they return to employment. Thus, the cost of the intermittency can be separated into two components: the depreciation of skills (BC) and the lost wages due to lack of accumulation of experience (CD). DG represents additional earnings lost because of the lack of on-the-job training associated with forecasted interruptions (both from employers and employees).

Now moving on to econometrics, the baseline formula of the earnings equation is

$$\ln w_{gi} = \beta_0^g + \rho^g S_{gi} + \beta_2^g Exp_{gi} + \beta_3^g Exp_{gi}^2 + \varepsilon_{gi}, \qquad (7.1)$$

where i indicates individuals and g is gender: g = male (M), female (F), w_{gi} is the hourly rate of pay of individual i of gender g, S_{gi} is years of schooling, Exp_{gi} is the potential experience of individual i in years as a proxy of experience, and ε_{gi} is an independently and identically distributed (normal) error term. The error term is assumed not to be correlated with the education decision. Potential experience is defined as *age – years of education – age of entrance to elementary school.*[6] The key parameters of interest are ρ^M and ρ^F, which are the rates of return to education for men and women, and β_2^M and β_2^F, which are the returns to experience, also for men and women. It is worth noting a few assumptions embedded in the specification of the earnings equation. First, we discuss those related to the connection between the theoretic model and the econometric model. Then, we tackle the functional form of the equation and how it fits the data.

Regarding the link between the theoretic model and the empirics, it has been noted that the earnings equation fits the accounting-identity model better than the compensating wage differentials model. As explained by Heckman, Lochner, and Todd (2006), in the compensating wage differentials model, individuals invest in education on the basis of its internal rate of return. Instead, ρ^g in equation (7.1) captures the average rate of schooling across all schooling investments and labor market experience levels. Generally, people refer to ρ as the rate of return and not as the internal rate of return or marginal return of education as it comes out of the theory.

Although the theory refers to the stream of earnings over the working life cycle of an individual—male or female—equation (7.1) is usually estimated over a cross-section of observations at a point in time, as opposed to the longitudinal analysis of a birth cohort. Using cross-section data to approximate the working life cycle implicitly assumes that the prices—or rates of return for skills—are in a steady state; that is, constant over time. It is assumed that no productivity growth occurs, and if it does, the supply and demand of skills are perfectly adjusted to maintain the equilibrium prices. However, there are reasons to believe that this is not the case. First, the rate of return of education (or more correctly, the average marginal return of education) has changed over time for different cohorts, as supply and demand do not fully adjust at the same time, thus moving equilibrium prices over time. Second, it has been found that cohorts of new entrants face relatively lower earnings (possibly because of more on-the-job training needed at the start of their careers) compared with older cohorts with the same level of education. This effect results in a steeper age-wage profile.[7] In the same way, notice that the theory model refers to the ex ante stream of earnings, whereas the estimates are done with the ex post stream of earnings.

All of these concerns are relevant regardless of the worker's gender. However, if they have different magnitudes for men and women, they become a concern for the use of the decomposition results described in chapter 6. Take, for example, the last caveat of ex ante versus ex post stream of earnings. If both men and women correctly predict their future labor force participation and stream of earnings, working with the ex post earnings will not necessarily produce any additional bias in the differences in rates of return of education between men and women. However, if women overestimate their future stream of earnings—or underestimate labor market discrimination in the form of lower wages—they can invest more than the optimal amount in education and have lower rates of return to education than men. Alternatively, the equilibrium prices of the returns to skills can be thought to be within occupation, and it can be easily conceived that some occupations have no productivity growth and some occupations have changes in equilibrium prices. If skills' price movements are different for men and women, then the assumptions again can have implications for estimating the gender gap in pay and its determinants.

Functional Form of the Earnings Equation

Moving to the functional form of the earnings equation, the log-linear regression model in education is a key empirical implication of the multiplicative effect of education on identical individuals' earnings.[8] Though most of the testing has been done for developed countries, in general, the log-linear function has been found to fit the data well in developed and developing countries. Most of the studies use a linear form on years of education, though there are theoretical and practical reasons to consider alternative specifications. For example, signaling models of education assume that education does not affect labor productivity but instead regard it as a device used by workers to signal employers and thus sort themselves into high- and low-ability types.[9] This theory in practice is also called "credential" or "sheepskin" effects.

Moving into the returns to experience, the earnings equation (7.1) shows linear effects on the quadratic polynomial in experience. If the relation between log earnings and experience is approximately parallel for different levels of schooling, the relation between log earnings, schooling, and experience becomes the sum of the effects. The relationship between age and log earnings does not have the same shape across different levels of education—the age-earnings profiles get steeper as education increases. This outcome implies that log earnings are not an additively separable function of age and education. Nevertheless, Mincer noted that the relationship between log earnings and potential experience remained approximately constant in shape across levels of education (experience-earnings profiles were parallel). This effect allows for an additive specification of the earnings equation when using potential experience instead of age, which is more parsimonious. The quadratic term captures the concave relationship between experience and log earnings. The picture is similar for developing countries, with the age-earnings profiles somewhat flatter in many cases.

Box 7.1 explains how to interpret the coefficients in the Mincer earnings equation, and box 6.2 in chapter 6 shows the specifications chosen by ADePT Gender to be used in the decomposition analysis. The specifications of the regression models used as a basis for the decomposition analysis follows the models used by Blau and Kahn (1996, 1997, 2004) and many others in the literature (Weichselbaumer and Winter-Ebmer 2005). ADePT Gender does not include marital status or number of children as control variables. These variables could affect productivity, but they can also affect discrimination, choice of tasks within certain occupations, and so on. Thus, their inclusion has raised some controversy. Empirical evidence shows that marital status and children raise men's wages but lower women's wages (Blau and Kahn 1997; Korenman and Neumark 1991; Neumark and Korenman 1994; Waldfogel 1997, 1998a, 1998b).

Box 7.1: Interpreting Coefficients in a Log-Linear Regression

The standard interpretation of a regression coefficient β is that a one-unit change of the regressor in question results in β units of change in the average of the dependent variable, while holding all other regressors constant.

The dependent variable will often enter the regression equation in log form:

$$\ln y = \alpha + \beta x + \varepsilon.$$

In this case, coefficients will represent marginal effects on the average of the log of the dependent variable. However, we are usually interested in quantifying the effects of regressors on the original dependent variable in levels. To do so, we should interpret the coefficients as percentage changes of the original dependent variable.

More specifically, a one-unit change in x will result in $(\exp(\beta) - 1)$ percentage points of change in the geometric mean of y (since taking the arithmetic average of the logarithm of a variable amounts to taking the geometric average of the original variable). This expression is actually very close to β itself when the latter is "small" (between −0.1 and 0.1 as a rule of thumb), so that directly interpreting the regression coefficients as percentage changes of the dependent variable measured in levels is a good approximation of the true marginal effects.

In the case of the regressor of interest, x, which is a binary 0–1 dummy variable, the same expression and approximation apply. However, when the dependent variable is in levels, one must be careful to interpret the discrete change of the dummy in the right way: $(\exp(\beta) - 1)$ represents the percentage points of change in the geometric mean of y when x switches from 0 to 1, which is the effect of switching from the group indicated by a 0 (the excluded category) to the group indicated by a 1.

Econometric Concerns

Model specification and goodness of fit. A key assumption underlying the econometric model of the earnings equation is that schooling accurately represents the opportunity set by a typical individual. The main problem stems from the failure to observe ability—which is a factor in the education decision—or other skills (see more below). In this case, the estimated earnings equation will produce a biased estimation of the returns to education. This problem is a clear example of omitted variable bias. The literature has overcome this problem in two ways: (a) by using natural experiments (Card 1999) and (b) by using quantile regressions (Fortin, Lemieux, and Firpo 2011). The other key assumption underlying the econometric model of equation (7.1) is that there are no heterogeneous effects. It was explained above that the return to experience β might be different for different levels of education. And then without saturating the regression, effects working at the (sub)group level can be counterbalanced and can be missed in the average estimate.[10]

Adding variables that capture a richer set of skills to the Mincer equation can be important for improving the measure of productivity by gender, reducing potential biases arising from potentially different correlations between ability and education by gender and increasing the percentage of the gender gap in pay that is explained by observed characteristics. The term *skills* refers to the capacity to perform different tasks. The Skills Toward Employment and Productivity (STEP) surveys conducted by the World Bank classify skills into three groups: (a) cognitive skills, (b) socioemotional skills, and (c) job-relevant skills. Box 7.2 presents the definitions of each type of skill, as well as the main variables that the STEP initiative collects around the world.

These measures of skills have quickly gained acceptance. Economists have applied more sophisticated quantitative methods to theories that have a long tradition among psychologists and sociologists. However, achievement tests, grades, and credited education do not explain everything about life earnings,[11] implying something important was still missing in the Mincer equation. Moreover, quantifiable and reliable cross-country comparable measures are now being collected, including the Organisation for Economic Co-operation and Development's (OECD) Programme for the International Assessment of Adult Competencies and the World Bank's STEP program. However, these studies still suffer from identification problems, as recently described by Heckman and Kautz (2012). Fortin (2008) adds measures of several noncognitive factors to the basic Mincerian specification before decomposing the gender wage gap for young workers in the United States. He finds that these noncognitive factors—in particular, a composite measure of the extent to which workers find money and career success valuable in life—account for a small but nontrivial part of the gender gap in pay. Meanwhile, Mueller and Plug (2006) use the "Big Five," an established taxonomy of personality traits.[12]

Besides adding variables that are associated with productivity such as skills, authors have added other variables that are indirectly related to skills. On the one hand, analysts add variables related to competing responsibilities in the household. In particular, they add dummies for marriage and number and age of children. One of the main researchers of marriage penalty is Waldfogel, who has shown in various papers (Berger and Waldfogel 2004; Blau, Kahn, and Waldfogel 2000; Han and others 2008; Joshi, Paci, and Waldfogel 1999; Sigle-Rushton and Waldfogel 2007; Waldfogel 1997, 1998a, 1998b, 1999) that marriage constitutes a penalty for women, whereas it increases men's wages. However, many have argued that there is no reason to predict that married women with children should be expected to earn less than men per hour. If that is the case, it is because women do not have certain skills or are being discriminated against, and thus the variables should be left out the regression.

Authors sometimes include other variables that aim to capture other wage-enhancing theories. For example, workers earn more when they are in a better job match, and job matches are improved by searching for the best opportunity. It has been proved that changing jobs helps a worker find the right match and increases wages (Light and Ureta 1990, 1992, 1995; Posadas 2009; Royalty 1998). Thus, variables that capture previous job-switching behavior can help explain current wages.

Heterocedasticity. The Mincer earnings equations are estimated using a linear regression model corrected by heterocedasticity. The linear regression model gives the best linear unbiased estimates, under certain assumptions. The first is that the error terms are homocedastic; that is, the standard deviation of the error term is not correlated with any of the included explanatory variables. The transformation to log of earnings in practice ensures that the errors are approximately homocedastic, but it is still best to obtain homocedastic consistent standard errors (Cameron and Trivedi 2005). ADePT Gender corrects the estimate for heterocedasticity using robust standard error correction. Neglecting the correction for heterocedasticity when the errors are heterocedastic—as is often the case for cross-sectional data—can lead to deflation or inflation of the true standard errors, with implications for the statistical significance of gender differences. If errors are indeed homocedastic, White's estimated standard errors are less efficient than standard errors estimated with ordinary least squares. One way to deal with heterocedasticity is to estimate quantile regressions while simultaneously being informative about distributional issues.

Omitted variable bias. Schooling is not randomly assigned; rather, it is an outcome that depends on choices made by individuals and their parents. The human capital theory treats schooling as an investment by individuals in themselves, and ρ is interpreted as a measure of the return to education. Thus, education becomes an endogenous variable. Under these circumstances, unless we can argue that schooling depends on a set of variables that is independent of the error term, the estimates of ρ should not be taken as causal—that is, interpreted as the effects of an additional year of education on earnings. However, even if the econometrician cannot make the latest assumption but can assume that education depends in the same way on the same set of variables for men and women, then it is like assuming that the bias is equal for both men and women. In addition, although ρ would not be causal, the gender difference in the returns can be consistently estimated. As long as the bias is the same for men and women, omitted variables should not bias the decomposition results that follow, which require only caution in their interpretation.

Partial equilibrium. The earnings equations are derived from a *partial equilibrium* approach, and thus the interpretation of the results is limited. For example, under partial equilibrium, it is not possible to capture an increase in the returns to education that incentivize women to acquire more education and enter the labor force, causing in turn a change in the price. This chain of effects is more likely to be measured using structural models, which are based on several assumptions and are computationally more demanding.

Nonrandom Selection into the Labor Force

Estimates of the Mincer earnings equation can be biased if they are based on a nonrandom sample of the working-age population. The key technical terms used in this subsection are introduced in box 7.2. The understanding

Box 7.2: Technical Terms Related to Nonrandom Selection of Women into the Labor Force

Selection bias exists in many problems in economics. It is present in most cases where the analyst can observe only the outcome of a previous maximization choice. For example, when looking at the returns of occupations, it might be tempting to say that certain occupations have larger returns than others. However, the counterfactual—that is, an individual's earnings had he or she chosen a different occupation—cannot be observed.

More generally, this is a problem of *nonrandom sample selection*, where respondents fail to provide answers to certain questions, which leads to missing data (either for dependent or independent variables). Since the analyst cannot observe the complete distribution, the estimates will be biased unless the missing data are random—that is, not correlated with the included variables.

Incidental truncation occurs when the analyst does not observe the complete distribution of the outcome variable y because of the outcome of another variable. The leading example is estimating the so-called wage offer function in labor economics. When estimating a Mincer equation, the analyst observes the wage offer only for those individuals who work. But for those currently out of the labor force, we do not observe the wage offer. Because working may be systematically correlated with unobservables that affect the wage offer and the working decision, the estimates of the Mincer equation will be biased.

of the correction of selection is important for the interpretation of the results discussed in chapter 6, so the analyst can assess whether to work with the simple Oaxaca-Blinder decomposition with selection correction of women into the labor force or with more sophisticated decompositions that do not control for it (Juhn-Murphy-Pierce or Ñopo). This section also helps explain the interpretation of the Mincer equation using the Heckit methodology that corrects the problem. But before delving into the details of the econometric formulation, a simple example illustrating the origin and magnitude of the nature of the problem is presented.

Suppose you are interested in estimating the returns to education for women in a country where female labor force participation is low, around 50 percent. If women are randomly selected from the working-age population, the estimates will be unbiased.[13] Now, let's assume the opposite: women are not randomly selected and that less educated women are less likely to work than more educated women. One reason is that women with less education are more likely to earn lower wages, which in turn might not be enough to buy household goods, such as food and childcare. To further simplify the case, assume that the women have two levels of education: poorly educated and highly educated. In our simple example, only a fraction (less than 100 percent) of poorly educated women end up working, whereas all highly educated women work.

Let's assume wages are observed for the subsample of women who work—the nature of the phenomenon we are observing forces us to limit our analysis to a selected sample. However, this sample is not random, in the sense that it might be very different from the overall population of women. Thus, educated women will be overrepresented in the selected sample, with respect to the general female population. On its own, however, this fact does not bias the estimation of the earnings equation (Achen 1986). If the only variable that influences selection (education itself) is exogenous, then we have what is called *deterministic selection*,[14] and it is solved by including education variables in the regression.

Now, let's make the assumptions more realistic. Assume that participation does not depend on the level of education (or skills) but on an unobservable variable called *effort* or *motivation*. High-effort women are more likely to be more productive, to receive higher (potential) wages, and thus to work. Very likely, high-effort women will also be better educated as part of their type. Thus, the selected sample, made up mostly of educated women, will still include some uneducated women; however, they will not be representative of uneducated women in general, because their high level of motivation will "compensate" for their lack of education. The uneducated women in our sample will be (selectively) the ones with higher potential wages. Education and unmeasured motivation will be correlated in the selected sample whether or not they are in the overall population, which will lead us to confound their effects on wages. In practice, it will underestimate the effect of education on wages, because in the selected sample, women with little education are unusually motivated and still earn high wages. In fact, if women were to enter the labor force randomly, their level of education would pay off more.

This type of pattern is usually denominated *positive selection* (Blundell and others 2007; Olivetti and Petrongolo 2008). Finally, returns to education are such that highly educated women's wages are on average higher than those of poorly educated women.

Figure 7.4 illustrates the selection problem graphically for the two instances. The *x*-axis represents the two levels of education, poorly educated and highly educated, and the y-axis reflects wages. If we could observe the wages for all women, conditional on their education level, the sample would be the one depicted by the dark gray circles. The implied effect of education on earnings as estimated by linear regression would be the slope of the dark gray line. However, we observe the wages for only those women who choose to participate in the labor market—the light gray dots. We see selection at work for the poorly educated group—only some women here choose to work. Panel a represents deterministic selection; not all women with little education enter the sample, but their participation is random *conditional on education*. The fact that they are missing does not affect the estimated slope of the regression line. In panel b, we see endogenous selection. What changes is that the women we do observe are not representative of the whole distribution of wages conditional on having a low level of education (that is, are not randomly selected, even after controlling for their level of education). The reason is that an unobserved variable—motivation—mediates participation, so that the sample of women for which the wage is observable (the orange dots) gives us a biased estimate of the education coefficient—the slope of the orange line is flatter. We are underestimating the effect of education on wages, because we are confounding it with the effect of motivation on wages via selection.

Figure 7.4: Graphic Representation of Selection Bias

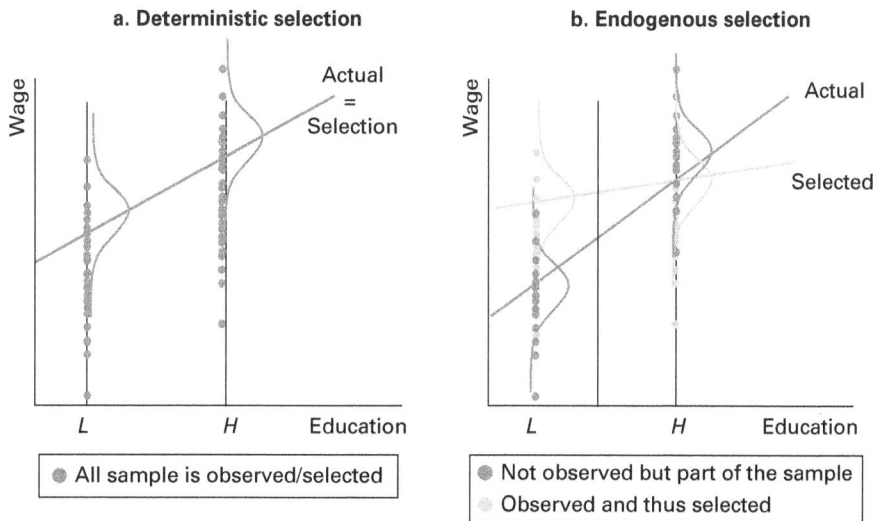

a. Deterministic selection

b. Endogenous selection

All sample is observed/selected

Not observed but part of the sample
Observed and thus selected

Note: L = poorly educated; H = highly educated.

It is clear from this simple illustration that the selection bias is exacerbated (a) the lower the participation of low-skill or low-effort females in the labor market and (b) the stronger the correlation between the (endogenous) participation decision and the variable of interest—wages. No concerns about selection bias exist for men, because usually all of them work. However, in countries with low male labor force participation (postconflict or high levels of disabilities), the user should explore whether the probability of being disabled is correlated with education and thus potentially affects the estimated returns to education for men as well.

Two commonly used methods address selection bias in econometrics. The first is the two-step Heckman correction, also known as *Heckit*. The second is simply the (one-step) maximum likelihood that might yield more efficient estimates. ADePT Gender shows that the Heckit estimates as the interpretation of the coefficient is more intuitive—the user can simply think that another variable is added to the earnings equation to capture the decision to work or not to work, and correct the bias. This variable is the Mills inverse ratio, and its omission can be thought as causing the bias.

Heckman Two-Step Selection Correction Model

The Heckit model is computed in two steps. First, a participation equation is estimated, which estimates the probability that a woman is working on the basis of variables that are related to her productivity in the labor market and to other factors that influence her decision to work but that do not affect wages. These are usually called *exclusion variables*, as they are needed to identify the model. In the original work of Heckman, the probability of working is estimated using a probit model like the following:

$$\Pr[Working] = \varphi_1^F + \varphi_2^F S_F + \varphi_3^F X_F + \varphi_4^F X_F^2 + Z + \varepsilon, \qquad (7.2)$$

where all the variables of the Mincer equation (7.1) are included, ε is a white noise error, and the vector Z is a set of exclusion variables, such as number of children, dependent elderly, and marital status, that are determinants of labor force participation but not of wages. In a way, it assumes that women with care responsibilities are less likely to work than women without them. Some academics have noticed that these variables are not actually exogenous to the potential wage (Kunze 2008). It can be hypothesized that women with lower potential wages are more likely to become housewives and have more children than women who pursue a career. In other words, both the marital status and the number of children are endogenous variables to the labor market participation decision and to wages.

Thus, some authors have argued in favor of adding nonearned income (such as a husband's labor income) as the exclusion variable in vector Z. Women whose husbands earn higher wages have less need to work than women who live in households that struggle to make ends meet. However, some authors have also argued that this variable can be endogenous to women's wages if there is assortative matching—that is, women with higher potential earnings marrying high-earning husbands (Burdett and Coles 1999; Chiappori, Iyigun, and Weiss 2009).

Despite these criticisms, these variables are still the most common choice, even in recent academic publications. For example, Christofides, Polycarpou, and Vrachimis (2013) use as exogenous variables the number of children under 16, childcare provisions, and income from property rents and financial assets. Mulligan and Rubinstein (2008) use the number of children ages 0–6 interacted with marital status, and Beblo and others (2003) use marital status, number of children, and nonearned income.

In the second stage, the earnings equation is estimated adding the Mills inverse ratio, λ, as an explanatory variable to correct for selection issues.[15] The earnings equation for the human capital model is

$$\ln w_F = \alpha_0^F + \rho^F S_F + \beta_1^F X_F + \beta_2^F X_F^2 + \gamma \lambda (Z_j \phi) + \epsilon_i. \qquad (7.3)$$

The regression (7.3) is the basis of the Oaxaca-Blinder decomposition with selection correction. Most of the time, the bias correction is introduced for women only, since it is assumed that all men work. The coefficient accompanying the inverse Mills ratio, γ, indicates the type of selection effect—positive or negative. When γ is positive, skilled women are more likely to work than unskilled women. This situation is typical of most developed countries.[16] When γ is negative, skilled women are less likely to work than unskilled women. Although higher-skilled women would earn more and thus have a larger opportunity cost for staying out of the labor force, they are usually married to husbands who also have high earnings and thus can afford to stay out of the labor market. This was the case of the United States in the 1940s, 1950s, and 1960s, when the rates of participation for black women were high and rates for white women were lower (Cunningham and Zalokar 1992; Mulligan and Rubinstein 2008).

Notes

1. That is, the unexplained component in the decomposition captures the effects of unobservable skills and the underlying sorting of women because of preferences or any other decision.
2. If a positive preference for a certain group is present—for example, female employers prefer to work with female workers—then the coefficient d will be positive.
3. Assume that women face no disutility by buying from men or women.
4. For more details on these theories, see Borjas (2005).
5. Although Becker and Mincer did not coauthor any scientific papers, they mutually benefited from their interactions, mostly in the years they led the Labor Lab at Columbia University (Grossbard 2006).
6. The most common age of entrance to elementary school is six.
7. See, for example, Beaudry and Green (2000) for Canada.
8. For more details, see Lemieux (2006, 130–32).
9. See Cahuc and Zylberberg (2004) for a brief explanation of the Spencer model applied to education, and Bedard (2001).
10. See Angrist and Pischke (2008) for a description of fully saturated models.
11. For example, adolescent achievement test scores explain only about 15 percent of the variance in later-life earnings (Heckman and Kautz 2012).
12. The "Big Five" personality traits are (a) extraversion, (b) agreeableness, (c) conscientiousness, (d) neuroticism, and (e) openness to experience (Mueller and Plug 2006).
13. If female labor force participation is very low, the precision of the estimates could be affected in small household surveys.
14. Notice, however, that if the true value of β varies across observations, then what we estimate on the selected sample is the parameter for the specific selected population.
15. See appendix E for the steps that explain how the inverse Mills ratio is computed.

16. See Blundell and others (2007) for the United Kingdom and Olivetti and Petrongolo (2008) for a sample of 26 countries in the Organisation for Economic Co-operation and Development.

References

Achen, Christopher H. 1986. *Statistical Analysis of Quasi-Experiments*. Berkeley: University of California Press.

Altonji, Joseph G., and Rebecca M. Blank. 1999. "Race and Gender in the Labor Market." In *Handbook of Labor Economics*, vol. 3, edited by Orley Ashenfelter and David Card, 3143–259. Amsterdam: Elsevier.

Angrist, Joshua D., and Jörn-Steffen Pischke. 2008. *Mostly Harmless Econometrics: An Empiricist's Companion*. Princeton, NJ: Princeton University Press.

Babcock, Linda, and Sara Laschever. 2003. *Women Don't Ask*. Princeton, NJ: Princeton University Press.

Banerjee, Abhijit V., and Esther Duflo. 2005. "Growth Theory through the Lens of Development Economics." In *Handbook of Economic Growth*, vol. 1, edited by Philippe Aghion and Steven N. Durlauf, 473–552. Amsterdam: Elsevier.

Beaudry, Paul, and David Green. 2000. "Cohort Patterns in Earnings and the Skill-Biased Technical Change Hypothesis." *Canadian Journal of Economics* 33 (4): 907–36.

Beblo, Miriam, Denis Beninger, Anja Heinze, and François Laisney. 2003. "Measuring Selectivity-Corrected Gender Wage Gaps in the EU." Discussion Paper 03-74, Centre for European Economic Research, Mannheim, Germany.

Becker, Gary. 1957. *The Economics of Discrimination*. Chicago: Chicago University Press.

———. 1964. "Investment in Human Capital: A Theoretical Analysis." *Journal of Political Economy* 70 (5, part 2): 9–49.

Bedard, Kelly. 2001. "Human Capital versus Signaling Models: University Access and High School Dropouts." *Journal of Political Economy* 109 (4): 749–75.

Ben-Porath, Yoram. 1967. "The Production of Human Capital and the Life Cycle of Earnings." *Journal of Political Economy* 75 (4): 352–65.

Berger, Lawrence, and Jane Waldfogel. 2004. "Maternity Leave and the Employment of New Mothers in the United States." *Journal of Population Economics* 17 (2): 331–49.

Bergmann, Barbara R. 1971. "The Effect on White Incomes of Discrimination in Employment." *Journal of Political Economy* 79 (2): 294–313.

Bertrand, Marianne. 2011. "New Perspectives on Gender." In *Handbook of Labor Economics*, vol. 4, edited by Orley Ashenfelter and David Card, 1543–90. Amsterdam: Elsevier.

Blau, Francine D., Marianne A. Ferber, and Anne E. Winkler. 2006. *The Economics of Women, Men, and Work*. 5th ed. Upper Saddle River, NJ: Pearson/Prentice Hall.

Blau, Francine D., and Lawrence M. Kahn. 1996. "International Differences in Male Wage Inequality: Institutions versus Market Forces." *Journal of Political Economy* 104 (4): 791–837.

———. 1997. "Swimming Upstream: Trends in the Gender Wage Differential in the 1980s." *Journal of Labor Economics* 15 (1): 1–42.

———. 2004. "The US Gender Pay Gap in the 1990s: Slowing Convergence." NBER Working Paper 10853, National Bureau of Economic Research, Cambridge, MA.

Blau, Francine D., Lawrence M. Kahn, and Jane Waldfogel. 2000. "Understanding Young Women's Marriage Decisions: The Role of Labor and Marriage Market Conditions." *Industrial and Labor Relations Review* 53 (4): 624–47.

Blundell, Richard, Amanda Gosling, Hidehiko Ichimura, and Costas Meghir. 2007. "Changes in the Distribution of Male and Female Wages Accounting for Employment Composition Using Bounds." *Econometrica* 75 (2): 323–63.

Borjas, George J. 2005. *Labor Economics*. New York: McGraw-Hill.

Burdett, Kenneth, and Melvyn G. Coles. 1999. "Long-Term Partnership Formation: Marriage and Employment." *Economic Journal* 109 (456): 307–34.

Cahuc, Pierre, and André Zylberberg. 2004. *Labor Economics*. Cambridge, MA: MIT University Press.

Cameron, A. Colin, and Pravin K. Trivedi. 2005. *Microeconomics: Methods and Applications*. 1st edition. Cambridge, UK: Cambridge University Press.

Card, David. 1999. "The Causal Effect of Education on Earnings." In *Handbook of Labor Economics*, vol. 3, ed. Orley Ashenfelter and David Card, 1802–59. Amsterdam: Elsevier.

Cardoso, Ana Rute, and Rudolf Winter-Ebmer. 2010. "Female-Led Firms and Gender Wage Policies." *Industrial and Labor Relations Review* 64 (1): 143–63.

Chiappori, Pierre-André, Murat Iyigun, and Yoram Weiss. 2009. "Investment in Schooling and the Marriage Market." *American Economic Review* 99 (5): 1689–713.

Christofides, Louis N., Alexandros Polycarpou, and Konstantinos Vrachimis. 2013. "Gender Wage Gaps, 'Sticky Floors' and 'Glass Ceilings' in Europe." *Labour Economics* 21 (C): 86–102.

Cunningham, James S., and Nadja Zalokar. 1992. "Economic Progress of Black Women, 1940–1980: Occupational Distribution and Relative Wages." *Industrial and Labor Relations Review* 45 (3): 540–55.

Doeringer, Peter B., and Michael J. Piore. 1985. *Internal Labor Markets and Manpower Analysis.* Armonk, NY: M. E. Sharpe.

Flabbi, Luca, Mario Macis, Andrea Moro, and Fabiano Schivardi. 2014. "Do Female Executives Make a Difference? The Impact of Female Leadership on Gender Gaps and Firm Performance." CEPR Discussion Paper 10228, Centre for Economic Policy Research, London.

Fortin, Nicole M. 2008. "The Gender Wage Gap among Young Adults in the United States: The Importance of Money versus People." *Journal of Human Resources* 43 (4): 884–918.

Fortin, Nicole, Thomas Lemieux, and Sergio Firpo. 2011. "Decomposition Methods in Economics." In *Handbook of Labor Economics*, vol. 4, edited by Orley Ashenfelter and David Card, 1–102. Amsterdam: Elsevier.

Gagliarducci, Stefano, and M. Daniele Paserman. 2014. "Gender Interactions in Firm Hierarchies: Evidence from Linked Employer-Employee Data." Unpublished manuscript. Institute for the Study of Labor, Bonn.

Goldin, Claudia, and Solomon Polachek. 1987. "Residual Differences by Sex: Perspectives on the Gender Gap in Earnings." *American Economic Review* 77 (2): 143–51.

Grossbard, Shoshana. 2006. "Jacob Mincer 1922–2006." *Review of Economics of the Household* 4 (4): 441–42.

Han, Wen-Jui, Christopher Ruhm, Jane Waldfogel, and Elizabeth Washbrook. 2008. "The Timing of Mothers' Employment after Childbirth." *Monthly Labor Review* 131 (6): 15–27.

Hanushek, Eric A., and Dennis D Kimko. 2000. "Schooling, Labor-Force Quality, and the Growth of Nations." *American Economic Review* 9 (5): 1184–208.

Heckman, James J., and Tim Kautz. 2012. "Hard Evidence on Soft Skills." *Labour Economics* 19 (4): 451–64.

Heckman, James J., Lance J. Lochner, and Petra E. Todd. 2006. "Earnings Functions, Rates of Return and Treatment Effects: The Mincer Equation and Beyond." In *Handbook of the Economics of Education*, vol. 1, edited by Eric A. Hanushek and Finis Welch, 307–458. London and Amsterdam: Elsevier, North-Holland.

Joshi, Heather, Pierella Paci, and Jane Waldfogel. 1999. "The Wages of Motherhood: Better or Worse?" *Cambridge Journal of Economics* 23 (5): 543–64.

Korenman, Sanders, and David Neumark. 1991. "Does Marriage Really Make Men More Productive?" *Journal of Human Resources* 26 (2): 282–307.

Krueger, Alan B., and Mikael Lindahl. 2001. "Education for Growth: Why and for Whom?" *Journal of Economic Literature* 39 (4): 1101–36.

Kunze, Astrid. 2008. "Gender Wage Gap Studies: Consistency and Decomposition." *Empirical Economics* 35 (1): 63–76.

Lemieux, Thomas. 2006. "The 'Mincer Equation' Thirty Years after Schooling, Experience, and Earnings." In *Jacob Mincer: A Pioneer of Modern Labor Economics*, edited by Shoshana Grossbard, 127–45. New York: Springer Science.

Light, Audrey, and Manuelita Ureta. 1990. "Gender Differences in Wages and Job Turnover among Continuously Employed Workers." *American Economic Review* 80 (2): 293–97.

———. 1992. "Panel Estimates of Male and Female Job Turnover Behavior: Can Female Nonquitters Be Identified?" *Journal of Labor Economics* 10 (2): 156–81.

———. 1995. "Early-Career Work Experience and Gender Wage Differentials." *Journal of Labor Economics* 13 (1): 121–54.

Mincer, Jacob. 1958. "Investment in Human Capital and Personal Income Distribution." *Journal of Political Economy* 66 (4): 281–302.

———. 1962. "Labor Force Participation of Married Women: A Study of Labor Supply." In *Aspects of Labor Economics*, edited by H. Gregg Lewis, 63–105. Princeton, NJ: Princeton University Press.

Mincer, Jacob, and Solomon Polachek. 1974. "Family Investments in Human Capital: Earnings of Women." *Journal of Political Economy* 82 (Supplement): S76–S108.

Montenegro, Claudio E., and Harry Anthony Patrinos. 2014. "Comparable Estimates of Returns to Schooling around the World." Policy Research Working Paper 7020, World Bank, Washington, DC.

Mueller, Gerrit, and Erik J. S. Plug. 2006. "Estimating the Effect of Personality on Male and Female Earnings." *Industrial and Labor Relations Review* 60 (1): 3–22.

Mulligan, Casey B., and Yona Rubinstein. 2008. "Selection, Investment, and Women's Relative Wages over Time." *Quarterly Journal of Economics* 123 (3): 1061–110.

Neumark, David, and Sanders Korenman. 1994. "Sources of Bias in Women's Wage Equations: Results Using Sibling Data." *Journal of Human Resources* 29 (2): 379–405.

Olivetti, Claudia, and Barbara Petrongolo. 2008. "Unequal Pay or Unequal Employment? A Cross-Country Analysis of Gender Gaps." *Journal of Labor Economics* 26 (4): 621–54.

Patrinos, Harry A., and George Psacharopoulos. 2011. "Education: Past, Present and Future Global Challenges." Policy Research Working Paper 5616, World Bank, Washington, DC.

Posadas, Josefina. 2009. "An Investigation of Gender Differentials in the Labor Market." PhD dissertation, Boston University.

Psacharopoulos, George. 1972. "Rates of Return on Investment in Education around the World." *Comparative Education* 16 (1): 54–67.

———. 1973. *Returns to Education: An International Comparison.* Amsterdam: Elsevier; San Francisco: Jossey-Bass.

———. 1985. "Returns to Education: A Further International Update and Implications." *Journal of Human Resources* 20 (4): 583–604.

———. 1989. "Time Trends of the Returns to Education: Cross-National Evidence." *Economics of Education Review* 8 (3): 225–31.

———. 1994. "Returns to Education: A Global Update." *World Development* 22 (9): 1325–43.

Psacharopoulos, George, and Harry A. Patrinos. 2004. "Returns to Investment in Education: A Further Update." *Education Economics* 12 (2): 111–34.

Rothstein, Donna S. 2000. "Early Career Supervisor Gender and the Labor Market Outcomes of Young Workers." In *Gender and Family Issues in the Workplace,* edited by Francine D. Blau and Ronald G. Ehrenberg, 210–55. New York: Russell Sage Foundation.

Royalty, Anne Beeson. 1998. "Job-to-Job and Job-to-Nonemployment Turnover by Gender and Education Level." *Journal of Labor Economics* 16 (2): 392–443.

Sigle-Rushton, Wendy, and Jane Waldfogel. 2007. "Motherhood and Women's Earnings in Anglo-American, Continental European, and Nordic Countries." *Feminist Economics* 13 (2): 55–91. Reprinted in *Feminist Economics*, edited by Lourdes Benaria, Ann Marie May, and Diane Strassman. Cheltenham, UK: Edward Elgar, 2009.

Waldfogel, Jane. 1997. "The Effect of Children on Women's Wages." *American Sociological Review* 62 (2): 209–17.

———. 1998a. "The Family Gap for Young Women in the United States and Britain: Can Maternity Leave Make a Difference?" *Journal of Labor Economics* 16 (3): 505–45.

———. 1998b. "Understanding the 'Family Gap' in Pay for Women with Children." *Journal of Economic Perspectives* 12 (1): 137–56.

———. 1999. "Family Leave Coverage in the 1990s." *Monthly Labor Review* 122 (10): 13–21.

Weichselbaumer, Doris, and Rudolf Winter-Ebmer. 2005. "A Meta-Analysis of the International Gender Wage Gap." *Journal of Economic Surveys* 19 (3): 479–511.

PART IV

Conclusions

Chapter 8

Reflections on What ADePT Gender Does and What It Does Not Do

Despite considerable advances in recent decades, gender inequality remains pervasive worldwide and in many dimensions of life. The nature and extent of gender-related differences vary considerably across countries and regions, but the evidence is striking. In no region of the world are women equal to men in legal, social, and economic rights, nor do they achieve equal outcomes. According to the *World Development Report 2012: Gender Equality and Development* (World Bank 2012), gender gaps are significant and widespread in endowments, economic opportunities, and agency, and they are particularly large for the poor, for ethnic minorities, and for other disadvantaged groups. Women and girls bear the largest and most direct costs of these inequalities, but the costs cut more broadly across society, as gender inequality impedes a country's ability to grow, to reduce poverty, and to build effective institutions. For that reason, gender equality is an important development issue. Similarly, strengthening the capacity to quantify the size of the prevailing gender differentials, to understand their nature and causes, and to monitor progress in reducing existing gaps is a priority for policy makers and development practitioners more broadly.

ADePT Gender is an important tool for building this capacity. It is designed to facilitate the standardized analysis of gender inequalities—and their determinants—by allowing users to easily derive a detailed profile of existing gender gaps in outcomes in the three dimensions identified by the *World Development Report*—endowments, economic opportunities, and agency. If several years of the same survey are available, users can also assess progress in reducing inequalities by comparing results over time. Moreover, the easiness with which profiles can be derived facilitates cross-countries comparison.

Above all, the software's strength lies in its ability to produce very quickly—with relatively limited resources—a large volume of quantitative information. Users can also focus on specific groups of interest—such as the young, the poor, and so on—by disaggregating the analysis results on the basis of existing variables. Additional pluses are: (a) the information is systematically organized in standardized tables and preformatted graphs, so that they can represent the skeleton of a country gender profile; and (b) the use of standardized commands and elaborate error messages significantly reduces the likelihood of errors. In addition to profiling gender gaps across a number of indicators, users can also carry out simple analyses of the factors that lead to gender inequality and that perpetuate it over time. The speed at which ADePT carries out the analysis and its high degree of accuracy also foster the opportunity to use international comparisons to assess the effects of different policy and social environments and to enrich the policy dialogue. The software can also be used for simple simulations of the potential effect on gender equality of both gender-sensitive and gender-blind policy reforms.

Particular attention is given to the analysis of gender inequality in the labor market, as differential access to economic opportunities is a major source of disadvantages in other areas for women and girls. In this area, ADePT Gender can do a simple analysis of the gender gaps in earnings and perform a number of decompositions. The technical chapters in this manual provide interested readers with useful theoretical background to the more sophisticated analysis carried out by ADePT.

Gender equality is an important development issue that has attracted a wealth of research and that continues to receive a great deal of attention in the academic community and in the policy debate. It covers a broad range of issues and has used a variety of methodologies and approaches, with different degrees of complexity. ADePT is a software package designed simply to generate standardized tables and charts summarizing the results of simple diagnostics based on household data (Lokshin and others 2013). It allows users to profile gender differences in a variety of core indicators of welfare and empowerment and to identify some of the major driving forces. However, ADePT software is not intended to be used for sophisticated econometrics. In addition, although it is important to obtaining a comprehensive profile of gender inequalities, a number of key issues cannot be addressed using only standard household data. As ADePT is designed for use with household data, these issues are better analyzed with other instruments. Thus, the gender profile that emerges is comprehensive but not exhaustive, and the analysis allowed in the program has only a limited degree of sophistication. The user interested in broader and deeper analysis of gender equality is well advised to look at the wide range of alternative tools available.

References

Lokshin, Michael, Sergiy Radyakin, Zurab Sajaia, and William Creitz. 2013. *ADePT User Guide*. Version 5. Washington, DC: World Bank.

World Bank. 2012. *World Development Report 2012: Gender Equality and Development*. Washington, DC: World Bank. https://openknowledge.worldbank.org/handle/10986/4391.

APPENDIXES

Fields, Variable Definitions, and Variable Requirements

Field	Variable definition	Variable requirement	Internal check
Main			
Household ID	Household identifier.	One variable or set of variables, numeric or alphanumeric (numeric variables have to be integers)	If household ID is one variable or a set of numeric variables, ADePT Gender checks whether it or they are integers
Household weights	Survey sample weights. Household surveys assign a specific household weight to each household. The weight is used to give each sample household a level of representation in the total household population. Household weights adjust for the differences in the probability of selecting a household in the household population. Weights need to be applied when tabulations have to produce a proper representation. In a database of individuals, the household weights should not vary among individuals within the household.	Continuous variable	
Urban	Rural or urban household residence (urban = 1).	Binary variable	Binary variable and one of the values is 1
Region	Variable indicating the geographical region.	Categorical variable	Integer variable
Poverty line	(a) The threshold level of per capita consumption, expenditure, or household income, above which a person is no longer considered poor or (b) an indicator of poverty status of household (poor = 1) (binary variable). It should be measured for the same frequency (annual, monthly, and so on) and currency (local currency or U.S. dollars, real or nominal) as the welfare aggregate.	Constant value variable	Single value, no larger than mean/median/p60 value of the welfare aggregate

(continued)

Appendixes

Field	Variable definition	Variable requirement	Internal check
Welfare aggregate	The variable that captures well-being; typically, total per capita consumption, but it can also be total per capita household expenditure or total per capita household income. Alternatively, the measures can be corrected for adult equivalent. If the welfare aggregate is a categorical variable for quintiles or deciles, the value 1 corresponds to the bottom quintile or decile of consumption, expenditure, or income. The quintile (decile) is a categorical variable that divides the population, sorted according to the welfare aggregate, in 5 (10) equal parts.	Continuous variable	Continuous variable
Gender	Sex of individual (male = 1).	Binary variable	Binary variable with one of the values equal to 1
Age	Age of individual (in years).	Integer variable	Integer variable between 0 and 99
Household head	Head of household (head = 1).	Binary variable or expression	Binary variable with one of the values equal to 1, only one household member per household is head, and head is at least age 15
Marital status	Marital status.	Categorical variable	

Human capital

Current school year

Primary	Attended primary school in current year (attended = 1).	Binary variable or expression	Binary variable with one of the values equal to 1
Secondary	Attended secondary school in current year (attended = 1).	Binary variable or expression	Binary variable with one of the values equal to 1
Postsecondary	Attended postsecondary school in current year (attended = 1).	Binary variable or expression	Binary variable with one of the values equal to 1
Grade	Grade of attendance within specified education level.	Categorical variable	

Completed education

Primary	Completed primary school (completed = 1).	Binary variable or expression	Binary variable with one of the values equal to 1
Secondary	Completed secondary school (completed = 1).	Binary variable or expression	Binary variable with one of the values equal to 1
Postsecondary	Completed postsecondary school (completed = 1).	Binary variable or expression	Binary variable with one of the values equal to 1
Education (years)	Grade completed at the highest level.	Categorical variable	Categorical variable
Literate	Reads and writes (yes = 1).	Binary variable or expression	Binary variable with one of the values equal to 1

(continued)

Field	Variable definition	Variable requirement	Internal check
Health and nutrition			
Health and nutrition	Variable or set of variables that represents health or nutrition outcomes with nonmissing values for men and women, boys and girls. Examples of nutrition indicators are prevalence of underweight for children under five years of age, such as weight for age (underweight), height for age (stunting), weight for height (wasting), the *Z*-scores coming from the latter; or consumption below the minimum level of dietary energy consumption.	Binary variable(s) or continuous variable(s)	Available for men and women in the same age range
Maternal health	Variable or set of variables that represents maternal health outcomes. These variables are only for women of reproductive age (15–49). Examples are prenatal and postnatal care variables: attended prenatal control visits at health facility, birth attended at a health facility, postnatal control visits at health facility, unmet need for family planning, and so on.	Binary variable(s) or continuous variable(s)	Missing values for men and women outside the reproductive age (15–49)
Economic opportunities			
Economic status and work characteristics			
Employed	Employment status. An individual (of legal employment age) is considered employed if during the survey reference period (usually the past week or past month) the individual (a) worked for a wage or salary, (b) worked for profit or family gain, (c) was either employed by a third party or was self-employed for at least one hour, or (d) had a wage job, self-employment, or enterprise but was temporarily absent from work (because of vacation, maternity leave, sick leave, or other type of leave) (employed = 1).	Binary variable or expression	Binary variable with one of the values equal to 1
Unemployed	Unemployment status. Working-age individuals are considered unemployed if, during the survey reference period (usually the past week), they were (a) without work in either paid employment or self-employment, (b) available for work, and (c) actively looking for work (unemployed = 1).	Binary variable or expression	Binary variable with one of the values equal to 1
Work category	Wage worker, self-employed, and so on. The work category variable indicates the type of worker's employment. For example, wage and salaried workers, self-employed workers, unpaid family workers. Sometimes, wage workers are divided into private sector and public sector.	Categorical variable	Categorical variable (that can take a maximum of XX values)
Agriculture	Works in agriculture (yes = 1).	Binary variable or expression	Binary variable with one of the values equal to 1; with nonmissing values for employed individuals
Broad sector	Categorical variable indicating the sector of employment: agriculture, manufacturing, or services.	Categorical variable	Categorical variable that can take a maximum of three values; with nonmissing values for employed individuals

(continued)

Field	Variable definition	Variable requirement	Internal check
Sector	Categorical variable indicating a finer sector of employment classification, such as one-digit ISIC.	Categorical variable	Categorical variable that can take a maximum of 10 values; with nonmissing values for employed individuals
Detailed sector	Categorical variable indicating an even finer sector of employment classification, such as four-digit ISIC.	Categorical variable	Categorical variable; with nonmissing values for employed individuals
Occupation	Job occupation (such as professional) for example, one-digit ISCO.	Categorical variable	Categorical variable; with nonmissing values for employed individuals
Formal status	Employed in the formal sector (yes = 1). The definition of formal work varies. The term *informality* means different things to different people. It refers here to owners (self-employed) and workers (informal salaried). Informal workers are usually those who do not have social security or medical benefits and are therefore unprotected. Formal salaried workers are defined as those who enjoy labor protections.	Binary variable or expression	Binary variable with one of the values equal to 1; with nonmissing values for employed individuals
Full time	Works full time (yes = 1). Whether a worker is employed full time or part time depends on the standard hours worked in the week of reference (or the usual week in the past calendar year), as defined by the country's labor code. Most countries define full time as working at least 35 hours per week, but in some countries, this number increases to 40 or even 48 hours per week. If a full-time variable is not specified but the variable number of hours worked is, ADePT Gender assumes 40 hours is the full-time threshold.	Binary variable or expression	Binary variable with one of the values equal to 1; with nonmissing values for employed individuals
Earnings	Monthly, weekly, daily, or hourly earnings (consistent with hours of work if specified).	Continuous variable	
Hours	Hours worked per day, week, or month (consistent with earnings).	Continuous variable, nonnegative	
Access to productive resources			
Resources	For example, savings account, land. Categorical variable that indicates ownership/control/management/use arrangements, with mutually exclusive categories: (a) only man, (b) only woman, or (c) both man and woman.	Categorical variable	
Voice, agency, and participation			
Marriage and fertility			
Age at first marriage	Woman's age at first marriage (in years).	Continuous integer variable	
Age at first birth	Woman's age at first birth (in years).	Continuous integer variable	

(continued)

Appendix A: Fields, Variable Definitions, and Variable Requirements

Field	Variable definition	Variable requirement	Internal check
Birth date	Date of mother's birth, in CMC format.	Continuous variable	
Interview date	Date of the interview, in CMC format.	Continuous variable	
Children's birth date	Date of birth of each child, in CMC format.	Continuous variable	
Agency			
Agency outcomes	For example, decision making (female respondent), involvement in decisions about food expenditure (wife only, husband only, or both).	Dummy variable (0 or 1 value) or continuous variable	

Note: CMC = century-month code; ISIC = International Standard Industrial Classification; ISCO = International Standard Classification of Occupations; p = percentile.

Demographic and Health Survey Agency Variables

This appendix describes five tables and two graphs that explore voice and agency outcomes.

	DHS module			
	Women		Men	
	V	VI	V	VI
Expression/question				
Control over resources				
Who usually makes decisions about major household purchases?	x	x	x	x
Who usually decides how your (husband's/partner's) earnings will be used: you, your (husband/partner), or you and your (husband/partner) jointly?	x	x	x	
Who usually decides how the money you earn will be used: you, your (husband/partner), or you and your (husband/partner) jointly?	x	x	x	x
Would you say that the money that you earn is more than what your (husband/partner) earns, less than what he earns, or about the same?		x		x
Who usually makes decisions about health care for yourself: you, your (husband/partner), you and your (husband/partner) jointly, or someone else?	x	x		x
Do you own this or any other house, either alone or jointly with someone else?		x		x
Do you own any land, either alone or jointly with someone else?		x		x
Household owns TV or radio:	x	x	x	x
Do you listen to the radio at least once a week, less than once a week, or not at all?				
Do you watch television at least once a week, less than once a week, or not at all?				

(continued)

	DHS module			
	Women		Men	
	V	VI	V	VI
Does this household own any livestock, herds, other farm animals, or poultry?	x	x	x	x
Does any member of this household have a bank account?	x	x	x	x
Ability to move freely				
In the past 12 months, how many times have you been away from home for one or more nights?	x	x	x	x
Who usually makes decisions about visits to your family or relatives?	x	x	x	
Decision making over family formation				
Age at first marriage?	x	x	x	x
How old were you when you first started living with your (husband/partner)?	x	x	x	x
How old were you when you had sexual intercourse for the very first time?	x	x	x	x
Can you say no to your (husband/partner) if you do not want to have sexual intercourse?	x	x		
If a wife knows her husband has a disease that she can get during sexual intercourse, is she justified in asking that they use a condom when they have sex?	x	x	x	x
Could you ask your (husband/partner) to use a condom if you wanted him to?	x	x		
Would you say that using contraception is mainly your decision, mainly your (husband's/partner's) decision, or did you decide together?	x	x		
Have you ever heard of (contraception method)?	x	x	x	x
Which method are you using?	x	x	x	x
Reason for not using		x		x
Do you know of a place where a person can get female/male condoms?		x		x
If you wanted to, could you yourself get a condom?	x	x	x	x
If you could go back to the time when you did not have any children and could choose exactly the number of children to have in your whole life, how many would that be?	x	x	x	x
If you could choose exactly the number of children to have in your whole life, how many would that be?				
How many of these children would you like to be boys, how many would you like to be girls, and for how many would the sex not matter?	x	x	x	x
Have you ever used anything or tried in any way to delay or avoid getting pregnant?	x	x		
Do you agree with the following statement? "Contraception is women's business and a man should not have to worry about it."			x	x
Do you agree with the following statement? "Women who use contraception may become promiscuous."			x	x

(continued)

	DHS module			
	Women		Men	
	V	VI	V	VI
Freedom from the risk of violence				
In your opinion, is a husband justified in hitting or beating his wife in the following situations: if she goes out without telling him, if she neglects the children, if she argues with him, if she refuses to have sex with him, if she burns the food?	x	x	x	x
Knowledge				
Have you ever heard of a sexually transmitted infection?	x	x	x	x
Have you ever heard of an illness called AIDS?	x	x	x	x
Knowledge of transmission methods: Can people reduce their chance of getting the AIDS virus by having just one uninfected sex partner who has no other sex partners? Can people get the AIDS virus from mosquito bites? Can people reduce their chances of getting the AIDS virus by using a condom every time they have sex? Can people get the AIDS virus by sharing food with a person who has AIDS? Can people get the AIDS virus because of witchcraft or other supernatural means? Is it possible for a healthy-looking person to have the AIDS virus?	x	x	x	x
Do you know of a place where people can go to get tested for the AIDS virus?	x	x	x	x
Have you ever been tested to see whether you have the AIDS virus?	x	x	x	x
When you are sick and want to get medical advice or treatment, is it a problem to get permission to go to the doctor?		x		
Do you read a newspaper or magazine at least once a week, less than once a week, or not at all?	x	x	x	x

Note: AIDS = acquired immune deficiency syndrome; DHS = Demographic and Health Surveys.

Tests of Statistical Significance

Users might be interested in knowing whether the differences between men's and women's indicators are statistically significant. Whether differences are significant depends on the distribution of values of the indicators or variables and the number of observations, not simply on the absolute value of the difference itself. Differences that are relatively small in magnitude might be statistically significant, whereas differences that are large in magnitude might not be. This appendix explains the basic tests for establishing whether observed differences for men and women are statistically significant. We first discuss tests to compare means and then consider tests to compare distributions. All the inputs for these calculations are produced by ADePT, as the formulas require means, standard deviations, and frequencies.

Means Tests

The student's t-test is a widely used statistical method to compare group means. It was developed by the statistician William Gossett, who called himself *Student*. To perform a t-test, the mean of the variable to be compared should be interpretable and random—that is, a variable whose values change randomly, not a constant.

The t-test is based on the following assumptions: (a) samples are randomly drawn (b) from normally distributed populations with (c) unknown population variances. Assumption (a) guarantees the absence of selection bias, such that the two groups to compare have a systematic difference due to a nonrandom sampling to select individuals with properties that the researcher prefers or that follow a pattern known but not observable to the analyst. If this were the case, the comparison of means between the nonrandom samples with another one is neither reliable nor generalized. Assumption (b) is the key assumption underlying the t-test. If this assumption is not fulfilled, the sample mean is not an unbiased estimator of central tendency, and the t-test will not be valid. The violation of normality is more problematic in the one-tailed test than in the two-tailed test, since in the former this violation could more easily influence statistical inferences. Nevertheless, thanks to the central limit theorem, the normality assumption is not that problematic. The theorem states that the distribution of a sample mean is approximately normal when its sample size is sufficiently large ($n_1 + n_2 \geq 30$).[1] Hence, the t-test can be safely used if the sample size is moderate, except when there are severe outliers.

Three types of t-tests can be performed: one-sample t-tests, paired t-tests, and independent sample t-tests. Independent sample t-tests are the ones relevant for the users of ADePT Gender, since the objective is to assess whether the observed mean differences between men and women are statistically significant. Instead, the one-sample t-test[2] is used to assess whether the population mean is different from a hypothesized value—usually zero—and the paired t-test[3] is used to compare two means on the basis of samples that are matched in some way; in other words, to examine whether the mean of the differences between the pairs is discernible from zero. Hence, the underlying methods of these two types of t-tests are identical and are not accurate for studying gender differences in most cases.

Independent Sample t-Test

When assessing gender differences, the researcher usually wants to know whether the observed differences in the mean of the variables of interest of the two samples are statistically significant—that is, whether the mean difference of the two groups is discernible from zero in a statistical way, which means that the two-sample means are sufficiently different from each other to be declared different, and the difference observed is not because of chance or a data peculiarity. To prove this, an independent sample t-test must be performed, since the two groups of interest (women and men) contain individuals who are not paired or matched in any way and who were selected for the same population and thus exposed to identical conditions.

In statistics, the hypothesis to reject (or not) in order to answer the research question is called a *null hypothesis* (H_0). It is contrasted with an *alternate hypothesis* (H_a). The null hypothesis in an independent two-sample t-test is

$$H_0: \mu_F = \mu_M.$$

In other words, the population means of the male and female samples are the same, which is exactly the same to postulate

$$H_0: \mu_F - \mu_M = 0.$$

In other words, the mean difference between the male and female samples is zero. The researcher may or may not have expectations about the direction of the findings based on previous theoretical or empirical work. Depending on the design of the study, the researcher should decide the type of alternate hypothesis to formulate: a one-sided hypothesis or a two-sided hypothesis. The former corresponds to a two-tailed test and the latter to a one-tailed test.

The *two-tailed t-test* should be performed if the researcher is interested only in testing whether the population means are equal and does not have an a priori expectation about the direction in which the alternate hypothesis should move regarding the null hypothesis. In this case, the alternate hypothesis is

$$H_a: \mu_F \neq \mu_M.$$

In other words, the population means of the male and female samples are different. Reorganizing the terms,

$$H_a: \mu_F - \mu_M \neq 0.$$

The mean difference between the male and female samples is different from zero.

The *one-tailed t-test* is appropriate if the researcher is interested in whether one mean is larger than the other. The alternate hypothesis could be

$$H_a: \mu_F > \mu_M.$$

In other words, the population mean of the female group is larger than the population mean of the male group. Again, this is exactly the same as

$$H_a: \mu_F - \mu_M > 0.$$

The mean difference between the female and male samples is greater than zero.

The null hypothesis is the same for both the two-tailed and one-tailed t-tests.

The t-statistic is used to evaluate whether a statistic (for example, a mean) is significantly different from a certain value. Algebraically, it is defined as

$$t_{\hat\mu} = \frac{\hat\mu - \mu_0}{\sigma},$$

where $\hat\mu$ is an estimator of the parameter μ, μ_0 is the value that the parameter takes under the null hypothesis, and σ is the standard error of the estimator $\hat\mu$. The t-test statistic applied to compare the means of two populations is

$$t_{\hat\mu} = \frac{\widehat{\mu_F} - \widehat{\mu_M} - 0}{\hat\sigma},$$

where $\hat\sigma$ is the standard deviation of the sampling distributions. Under the normality assumption, the null hypothesis, and equal population variances, the t-statistic follows a student's t-distribution with $n-2$ degrees of freedom.[4]

The t-statistic is calculated as follows:

1. Calculate the mean value for each distribution, that is, men and women.
2. Estimate the variance to obtain the standard deviation. This can be done in two ways. If the variances of the populations from which the samples are drawn are assumed to be equal, then compute the test as

$$t_{\hat{\mu}} = \frac{\widehat{\mu_F} - \widehat{\mu_M} - 0}{\hat{\sigma}_{pool}\sqrt{\dfrac{1}{n_F} + \dfrac{1}{n_M}}} \sim t\left(n_F + n_M - 2\right)$$

where

$$\hat{\sigma}^2_{pool} = \frac{(n_F - 1)\widehat{\sigma_F}^2 + (n_M - 1)\widehat{\sigma_M}^2}{n_F + n_M - 2}.$$

Alternatively, the variances can be assumed to come from populations with different variances. Some authors recommend always using the t-statistic that assumes the population variances are unequal, since in most cases both versions of this test lead to the same result. Some studies argue that the tests used to determine variance equality are unreliable. This decision is up to the researcher. Under this assumption, the t-test is computed as

$$t_{\hat{\mu}}^{ap} = \frac{\widehat{\mu_F} - \widehat{\mu_M} - 0}{\sqrt{\dfrac{\hat{\sigma}^2_F}{n_F} + \dfrac{\hat{\sigma}^2_M}{n_M}}} \sim t\left(estimated\ degrees\ of\ freedom\right).$$

The user can actually test which assumption is correct, as described in box C.1.

Box C.1: Test of Variance Equality for Two Populations

The folded form F-test is commonly used to test variance equality. It is also a hypothesis test, in which the null hypothesis is that the two populations have the same variance $\left(H_0\colon \sigma^2_F = \sigma^2_M\right)$. The test statistic for the F-test is an F-statistic that is the ratio between the larger sample variance $\left(\widehat{\sigma_l}^2\right)$ and the smaller one $\left(\widehat{\sigma_s}^2\right)$. It has an F-distribution with $n_l - 1$ and $n_s - 1$ degrees of freedom:

$$\frac{\widehat{\sigma_l}^2}{\widehat{\sigma_s}^2} \sim F\left(n_l - 1,\, n_S - 1\right).$$

If the null hypothesis of equal variances is not rejected—the value of the F-statistic is inside the confidence interval with a given level of significance—the pooled variance can be used to obtain the denominator of the t-statistic by taking its square root. The pooled variance is a weighted average of the two sample variances.

Several methods are used to approximate the degrees of freedom, but the most common is the Satterthwaite method. It is important to keep in mind that the approximation is a real number, not necessarily an integer.

Once the test statistic is calculated, it should be determined whether this value is contained in the interval in which the true value of the statistic is within the probability chosen by the researcher—$(1-\alpha)100\%$. If it is, the null hypothesis is not rejected; remember that to calculate the t-statistic, the null hypothesis was assumed to be true. Otherwise, it is rejected, and the differences observed in the mean of men and women samples are statistically significant with a confidence level of $(1-\alpha)100\%$.

The confidence level $(1-\alpha)100\%$ is the percentage of all possible samples that can be expected to include the true population parameter; α is the level of significance, which is the probability that the true value of the statistic is not contained in the confidence interval, and therefore the null hypothesis is rejected although it should not be—this mistake is called a type 1 error. Usually, α is set at 1 percent, 5 percent, or 10 percent.

The confidence interval for the t-statistic calculated with a given level of significance α and for a two-tailed test is

$$\Pr\left[-t_{\alpha/2,df} \leq t_{\hat{\mu}} \leq t_{\alpha/2,df}\right] = 1 - \alpha,$$

where $t_{\alpha/2}$ and $-t_{\alpha/2}$ are the critical values of $t_{\hat{\mu}}$ (limits of the confident interval) that could be drawn from the statistic t table for a $\alpha/2$ level of significance and the corresponding degrees of freedom. The region between the critical values in the distribution is called the acceptance region, whereas the rest is called the rejection or critical region (see figure C.1).

The confidence interval for the t-statistic calculated with a given level of significance α and for a one-tailed test is

$$\Pr\left[t_{\hat{\mu}} < t_{\alpha,df}\right] = 1 - \alpha$$

or

$$\Pr\left[t_{\hat{\mu}} > -t_{\alpha,df}\right] = 1 - \alpha,$$

depending on the alternative hypothesis formulated. The equation in panel a of figure C.1 corresponds to the example used in the one-tailed t-test section

Figure C.1: Rejection and Acceptance Regions

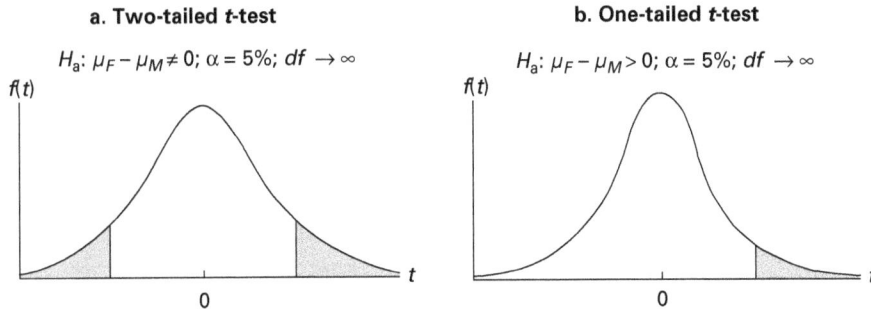

a. Two-tailed t-test

$H_a: \mu_F - \mu_M \neq 0; \alpha = 5\%; df \to \infty$

b. One-tailed t-test

$H_a: \mu_F - \mu_M > 0; \alpha = 5\%; df \to \infty$

($H_a: \mu_F - \mu_M > 0$), since the rejection area is always associated with the alternative hypothesis (see figure C.1).

Again, if the t-statistic calculated is not contained in the confidence interval, there is evidence to reject the null hypothesis. Therefore, the mean differences between men and women in the variable of interest are statistically different from zero and thus statistically significant. If a one-tailed test was also evaluated, the differences observed are different from zero, and there is evidence to conclude that one mean is greater than the other—for the example, this would be the mean of the female population.

It is worth mentioning that the same inference can be made using the p-value of the statistic, which is the exact level of significance—that is, the lowest level of significance at which a null hypothesis can be rejected. For example, if the researcher knows that the exact probability of the t-statistic is outside the confidence interval, he or she can decide whether to reject the null hypothesis at this level instead of deciding a priori the α. Evidently, if $p < \alpha$, then the null hypothesis is rejected with a $1-p$ confidence level and therefore with a $1-\alpha$ confidence level too.

Statistically Different Distributions

When a user is interested in knowing whether the differences observed between women and men in a certain *categorical* variable are statistically different from zero, a chi-square goodness-of-fit test should be performed to compare the two distributions. Given that the comparison is between distributions as opposed to a single measure—such as the mean—all the categories into which the data have been divided are used.

Follow these steps to perform a chi-square goodness-of-fit test:

1. Form a hypothesis about the way in which the distribution of the variable of interest behaves. For example, the observed distribution of women's educational attainment behaves as the observed distribution of men's education attainment, as in ADePT table 2a (described in chapter 4). The null and alternative hypotheses of a chi-square test is

$$H_0: O_i = E_i.$$

The observed number of cases in each category is equal to the expected number of cases in each category,

$$H_a: O_i \neq E_i,$$

where O_i is the frequency of occurrence for each category i in which the women's sample has been grouped, and E_i is the expected frequency of occurrence for each category i that corresponds to the men's sample, following the example taken from ADePT table 1a. If the observed number and expected number of cases are different for the two populations, the null hypothesis should be rejected.

2. Calculate the test statistic. Suppose that the data have been grouped in m categories, $i = 1, 2, 3, ..., m$. Our example of ADePT table 1a has four categories ($m = 4$): (a) no education, (b) primary complete, (c) secondary complete, and (d) postsecondary complete. The statistic is

$$\chi^2 = \sum_i^m \frac{(O_i - E_i)^2}{E_i}$$

and has a chi-square distribution with $m-1$ degrees of freedom if the data are obtained from a random sample, and the expected frequency of each category is at least five. Large values of the statistic lead to a rejection of the null hypothesis, since they indicate that the difference between the observed and expected values is large as well.

3. Reject (or accept) the null hypothesis by comparing the value obtained in the second with the critical value of the chi-squared distribution with $m-1$ degrees of freedom and the chosen level of significance α (concepts explained in the previous section on means tests). If the value of the statistic is greater than the critical value, the null hypothesis should be rejected; otherwise, it should be accepted with a confidence level of $(1-\alpha)100\%$.

The chi-square goodness-of-fit test is always a right-tail test.

Notes

1. n_i is the number of observations in the group i.
2. The one-sample t-test is adequate for those problems that look for evidence to conclude that the mean of the population from which the sample is taken is different from a specified value of interest that could be a standard drawn from the literature.
3. The paired t-test is appropriate for those studies that assess the mean differences between two paired groups: before and after data on a single group of individuals, two variables on the same individual, or a group matched one-to-one to a second group.
4. Numbers of values that are not estimated are free to vary.

Juhn-Murphy-Pierce Decomposition

This appendix describes the mathematical steps for progressing from equation (6.10) to equation (6.11) in chapter 6 for the Juhn-Murphy-Pierce decomposition. The earnings equation (6.10) can be rewritten to extract this information from the error term. It can be rewritten as $\varepsilon_{gi} = F_g^{-1}(p_{gi} | X_{gi})$, where p_{gi} is the percentile of individual i of gender g in the distribution of residuals computed using all workers of gender g; $F_g(\cdot)$ is the cumulative distribution function of residuals for gender g, conditional on observed characteristics; and $F_g^{-1}(\cdot)$ is its inverse (or quantile function). This yields equation (D.1):

$$\ln W_{gi} = \beta^g X_{gi} + F_g^{-1}\left(p_{gi} | X_{gi}\right). \tag{D.1}$$

Next, define a benchmark coefficient, β^* (including both constant and education coefficients), and a benchmark distribution of residuals, $F^{*-1}(\cdot)$. In practice, these benchmarks can be chosen in several ways. They can coincide with one of the gender-specific coefficients and distributions, either the male or female one; or, in the same spirit as the pooled Oaxaca-Blinder decomposition, with some "summary" of coefficients and residual distributions—either from a pooled model using all workers (men and women) or from a simple average of gender-specific coefficients and distributions.

ADePT Gender defines the benchmark as the coefficients and residual distribution from the pooled regression as in equation (6.5) in chapter 6. The intuition behind the Juhn-Murphy-Pierce decomposition is that by using equation (D.1), one can create different counterfactuals based on the returns to observed and unobserved skills. In particular, one can simulate three types of counterfactuals, each with an expression for males and one for females:

Outcomes if only observed characteristics vary between groups:

$$Y_F^X = \beta^* X_{Fi} + F^{*-1}(p_{Fi} \mid X_{Fi}) w_M^X = \beta^* X_{Mi} + F^{*-1}(p_{Mi} \mid X_{Mi}). \quad \text{(D.2)}$$

Outcomes if only observed characteristics and returns to observed characteristics vary between groups:

$$\begin{aligned}
w_M^{obs} &= \beta_M X_{Mi} + F^{*-1}\left(p_{Mi} \mid X_{Mi}\right), \\
w_F^{obs} &= \beta_F X_{Fi} + F^{*-1}\left(p_{Fi} \mid X_{Fi}\right).
\end{aligned} \quad \text{(D.3)}$$

Outcomes if observed characteristics, returns to observed characteristics, and unobservable characteristics and their returns (that is, the distribution of residuals) all vary between groups:

$$\begin{aligned}
w_M^{unobs} &= \beta_M X_{Mi} + F^{-1}\left(p_{Mi} \mid X_{Mi}\right), \\
w_F^{unobs} &= \beta_F X_{Fi} + F^{-1}\left(p_{Fi} \mid X_{Fi}\right).
\end{aligned} \quad \text{(D.4)}$$

Naturally, w_g^{unobs} coincides with the original gender-specific wage equation.

From this last step, the derivation of equation (6.11) is straightforward.

Mathematical Derivation of the Mills Ratio Variable Included in the Mincer Equation

This appendix shows the mathematical derivation of the reservation wage that is used for the conceptual development of the selection procedure developed by Heckman and discussed in chapter 7. The contribution of Gronau's model and its use by Heckman to move to the econometric Heckit model can be explained using the household time allocation model introduced in chapter 5. Figure E.1 plots the maximization problem that results in the hours of work supplied. The figure plots three different wages, which are indicated by the slope of the different dashed lines. At the lowest wage (the slope of the small dashed line), the woman prefers not to work, as she can obtain a level of utility Y that is higher than any other utility obtained by working a positive number of hours. At the highest wage (the slope of the dotted line), the woman prefers to work a positive number of hours and to reach utility level Z. The reservation wage is that which makes a woman indifferent to working or not working. In the figure, this is indicated by the slope of the large dashed line, for which any small increase in the wage (the slope of the budget restriction pivoting upward) will induce her to work, and any smaller wage will make her prefer not to work.

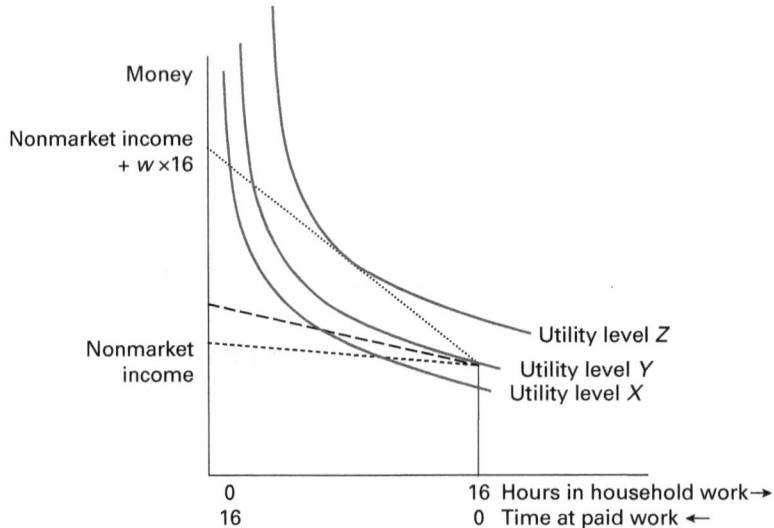

Figure E.1: Graphic Representation of the Reservation Wage

Mathematically, the market wage is determined by an equation for a subsample of the working-age population:

$$\ln w_i = X_i\beta + \epsilon_i,$$

and the reservation wage can be assumed to depend on productivity variables and variables that affect the utility of staying at home,

$$\ln w_{Fi}^R = X_{Fi}\beta^R + Z_{Fi}\psi^R + \xi_{Fi},$$

where w_F^R is the reservation wage of woman i, X_i is a vector of variables capturing productivity (or the potential wage), and Z_i is a vector of variables capturing the utility of staying home. Here, for simplicity in the notation, the vector $X_F\beta^R = \alpha_0^R + \rho^R S_F + \beta_1^R X_F + \beta_1^R X_F^2$ of equation (6.1). The subindex F is also dropped for simplicity.

A woman would work if and only if the utility of (at least) one hour of work is greater than the utility of not working at all. The wage that makes a woman indifferent to working or staying home is called the *reservation wage*. Women work if their potential wage, w_i, is higher than the reservation wage

$$\Pr[working_i] > 0 \Leftrightarrow \ln w_i - \ln w_i^R > 0,$$

after replacement by respective equations, this is equivalent to

$$\Pr\left[working_i\right] = \Pr\left[y_i^* = 1\right] \equiv \left(X_i\beta + \epsilon_i\right) - \left(X_i\beta^R + Z_i\psi^R + \xi_i\right)$$

$$\equiv X_i\beta - X_i\beta^R - Z_i\psi^R + \epsilon_i - \xi_i$$

$$\equiv X_i\varphi + Z_i\alpha + \varepsilon_i > 0,$$

but it can see only employed or selected workers, where $y^* = 1$ indicates that the worker is employed and otherwise is 0. The regression conditional expectation function for y over the selected sample is

$$E\left(w_i \mid X, y_i^* = 1\right) = X\beta + E\left(\epsilon_i \mid X, y_i^* = 1\right).$$

It is clear that for β to be consistent, we need the usual ordinary least squares' assumption that ϵ_i be mean independent of X; ϵ_i also needs to be mean independent of the selection rule. The Heckman selection model tackles this problem by obtaining a consistent estimate of the term $E(\epsilon_i \mid X, s = 1)$ and including it in the regression.

The model is defined by an outcome equation (which contains the parameters of interest to the researcher) and a selection equation:

$$\ln w_i = X_i\beta + \epsilon_i,$$

$$\Pr[y_i^* = 1] = X_i\varphi + Z_i\delta + \varepsilon_i.$$

Here, the notation of equations (7.2) and (7.3) is used. The model is estimated under the following assumptions:

- y_i^* and Z_i are observed in the full sample.
- y_i is observed only over the selected sample, or when $y_i^* = 1$[1].
- Both the outcome and the selection equations are "good" models, in that the regressors are exogenous: $E(\epsilon_i \mid X, Z) = E(\varepsilon_i \mid X, Z) = 0$.
- The error term of the selection equation is distributed as a standard normal, $\varepsilon \sim N(0,1)$.
- $E(\epsilon_i \mid \varepsilon_i) = \gamma\varepsilon$ (u is not mean independent from ε, and the relationship between the two random errors is linear; this in turn implies $\epsilon_i = \gamma\varepsilon_i + \xi$, where ξ is a random disturbance).

In this setup, the conditional expectation function becomes

$$E\left(w|X, y_i^* = 1\right) = X\beta + E\left(\varepsilon_i|X, \varepsilon > -Z\delta\right),$$

$$= X\beta + E\left(\gamma\varepsilon + \xi|X, \varepsilon > -Z\delta\right),$$

$$= X\beta + \gamma E\left(\varepsilon|\varepsilon > -Z\delta\right).$$

Having assumed a functional form for ε allows one to use the properties of the truncated normal distribution and obtain

$$E\left(w|X, y_i^* = 1\right) = X\beta + \gamma \frac{\phi(-Z\delta)}{1 - \Phi(-Z\delta)} = X\beta + \gamma \frac{\phi(Z\delta)}{\Phi(Z\delta)} = X\beta + \gamma\lambda(Z\delta),$$

where $\lambda(.)$ is the inverse Mills ratio, a nonlinear monotone decreasing function of the probability that an observation is selected. It provides a functional form for the term that was omitted from the naive regression of y on X in the selected sample.

It might be useful to mention that the case in which $\gamma = 0$ (there is no correlation between the error terms of the outcome and selection equations) amounts to a scenario where the selection is random, or the selection process is ignorable; whereas in the case of $\gamma \neq 0$, if X and Z are completely independently distributed, omitting the last term will not result in the endogeneity of X, and will not impede identification of β (exogenous or deterministic selection).[2]

Heckman proposed a way to estimate the missing term of the regression using a two-step method. First, obtain consistent estimates of δ by running a probit model of s on Z, $Pr(y_i^* = 1|Z) = \Phi(Z\delta)$; then, plug $\hat{\delta}$ into λ and obtain consistent estimates of β and γ by running ordinary least squares on the selected sample. It must be noted that the usual ordinary least squares variance–covariance matrix is no longer adequate in this case, given that (a) the error term of the outcome equation is intrinsically heterocedastic because of selection, and (b) one of the regressors, $\lambda(Z\hat{\delta})$, is an estimate itself. Heckman provides a consistent estimator of the covariance matrix in this case, but asymptotic efficiency is lost.

Notes

1. X_i can be observed either in the full sample or for only the selected observations; the crucial part is that the outcome equation can be estimated only over the restricted sample, for which $y_i^* = 1$.
2. In practice, it is common for X and Z to be partly or even completely overlapping. The higher the correlation among X and Z, the greater the multicollinearity between X and the regressor containing Z. At the estimation stage, this will cause problems with identifying the coefficients. In the extreme case in which X and Z are indeed identical, identification relies solely on the nonlinearity of the Mills ratio.

Index

Boxes, figures, maps, notes, and tables are indicated by *b*, *f*, *m*, *n*, and *t* following the page number.

www.ingramcontent.com/pod-product-compliance
Lightning Source LLC
Chambersburg PA
CBHW080414270326
41929CB00018B/3021